DJ
A Sporting Legend

with
Martin Breheny

BLACKWATER PRESS

Design and Layout: Design Spec
Cover photo: Don Harper
Cover Design: Artwerk

ISBN 978-0-9576170-9-4

BWP Ltd., 1-5 North Frederick Street, Dublin 1
Printed in the Republic of Ireland.
jloconnor@eircom.net

The author and publisher would like to thank Sportsfile and John Knox for the use of their photographs.

Contents

FOREWORD

Is cúis onóra agus bhróid domsa, mar chathaoirleach CLG Cill Chainnigh, fáiltiú roimh beathaisnéis DJ Carey, laoch iomaná and fíor mhac Cill Chainnigh. Guím rath ar an obair and tá súil agam go mbainfidh na léitheorí taitneamh as.

In sport, the term 'legend' is used so freely as to have almost lost its currency. For that reason, I am immensely honoured to greet this book, and welcome the biography of a man who truly deserves the epithet. For DJ Carey was, and is, a hurling legend, a peerless exponent of all that is best in the game. His skill, artistry, elegance and sportsmanship set him apart as one of the greatest ever hurlers.

We in Kilkenny, who have watched and wondered at his prowess, from his earliest days as the little 'Dodger' of the primary hurling leagues, through his under-age and college days to his progression to the black and amber at minor, under 21 and senior level, are privileged to have seen and known him.

On the national stage he won (and broke) the hearts of countless thousands with his wizardry. We all have favourite memories of his magical moments – the high fetches, the marvellous passes, the feints, the blinding runs, the glorious scores he created and executed. It is no wonder that, at the height of his powers, great numbers from outside Kilkenny came to see him perform in our local championships for his beloved Young Irelands. They were not disappointed.

It is probably no accident that DJ's grand-uncle, Paddy Phelan, was regarded by those who saw him as the most stylish and elegant hurler in Ireland. While sadly, no film record survives of his illustrious ancestor, we are blessed that DJ's exploits are fully recorded and documented for posterity to be enjoyed by future generations.

It is worth stating that even as I write, DJ, at 42, continues to play with, and manage, his Young Irelands special junior team, a testament to his love of his club and the game.

As Chairman of Kilkenny County Board, I must also compliment DJ on his selfless readiness to visit clubs all over the country for medal presentations and other functions. We are extremely grateful for the gentlemanly and sporting manner in which he has always represented his club, his county and the game he graced so well.

Ned Quinn
Chairman Kilkenny County Board
October 2013

DJ - A PERSONAL REFLECTION

Life offers up endless opportunities to grow. The trick is to make the best of NOW.

Stop thinking about what might have been and look to what can be.

Along the way, there have been many sweet surprises. An inspiring friend taught me to see that disappointments and struggles keep you humble, successes and achievements keep you growing but only determination, faith and ownership of yourself keep you going.

Stay focused and realise that nothing limits you except your fears.

Another great lesson I have learned is in realising life isn't perfect. We are all programmed for high expectations and losses. Sometimes you just have to let go rather than hold on.

Be flexible. Allow life to run its course with the ups and downs and then it will be easier to find your inner space and place of peace.

We need to live and enjoy each day. Celebrate your efforts and not just the outcomes. And always remember, light trumps darkness every time.

DJ Carey
October 2013

CHAPTER 1

HOME IS WHERE THE HURLEY IS

Your ball DJ – go, go, go.

Instinctively, my left hand shoots into the air to grab the sliotar as it drops down in an inviting arc. I've done it thousands of times over the years but this one is special. I'm back hurling again, back in the red and white of my beloved club, Young Irelands of Gowran, back with my neighbours, friends and colleagues.

This is what I love best. A hurley in my hand, a game to be played, a challenge to be taken on. It's an exhilarating feeling. Everything else can be put on hold. I have had my share of health, personal and business issues over recent years but I can put them all to one side this evening.

In April 2013, Gowran were playing Fenians in a special junior hurling game and if I hadn't come on as a sub we would have been playing with fourteen men. We weren't over-loaded with subs to start with and when we picked up a few injuries, I had a choice to make. I could watch as fourteen lads battled on against fifteen or whip off the tracksuit, grab a hurley and have a go.

I'm managing the Gowran intermediate and special junior teams along with Dick O'Neill, one of the men who taught me so much of what I know about hurling, Eoin Farrell and Alan Roche. I'm enjoying it thoroughly and it also gives me a chance to put something back into the club that helped make me the player I was. When I took the job, I hadn't really thought about playing, but needs must, and on this unseasonably cold spring evening in Johnstown, the manager had to become a player again.

Now, it's time to make my first catch. Unfortunately, I get the timing slightly wrong and the ball lands on the top of my index finger. The pain is instant, jolting through the finger like an electric shock. Ah well, what's another break? I spent so much time in St. Luke's hospital in Kilkenny over the years getting fingers mended that I was nearly as knowledgeable as the doctors on what was required.

The latest repair will have to wait. We're losing to the Fenians so there's work to be done. I score a goal later on but we still lose by two points. Still, as I leave the field, I feel as if I'm wrapped in a lovely warm glow. I'm back hurling and while I won't be wearing the black-and-amber of Kilkenny any time soon, there's still a lot of satisfaction to be had from tipping around with Gowran.

I have played a reasonable amount since coming back last April, either starting games or coming on as a sub, and while the legs aren't as nifty as they used to be, the sense of enjoyment is the same as it always was. That's the great thing about sport. Once you can play at some level, there's fun to be had.

I enjoy the sense of involvement, that special feeling which comes from being part of a team, striving to achieve something as a group. And since hurling has been my passion ever since I was a kid learning the game under the watchful eye of my uncle Martin, it's unlikely to fade at this stage.

I suppose hurling was in my genes. My grand-uncle Paddy Phelan was a Kilkenny great in the 1930s-40s. His reputation lives on as he was chosen at left half-back on both the Teams of the Century and Millennium. My aunt Peggy won four All-Ireland senior camogie medals, including one in 1974 which was the first year Kilkenny took the title.

I consider myself lucky to have had a wonderful career in hurling and I'm delighted to now be able to put something back into the game as a mentor with my club. As for the playing bug, it's still there and I'll indulge it for as long as I can.

One of the really enjoyable aspects of playing this year was that I got a chance to play on the same team as my eldest son, Seán, who is sixteen. I didn't think it would happen – especially when I had health problems last year – so I'm savouring every opportunity I get to play with him. It's an unusual – but lovely – feeling to be playing on the same team as your son and while we are doing things at a very different pace, we work well off each other. Like I did in the 1980s, Seán is attending St. Kieran's College and enjoying his hurling.

My younger son, Mikey, who is fourteen, loves hurling too (both of the lads love golf as well) and is now wondering if I can hang around for a few more seasons so that he can play with me on a Gowran team. Who knows? One day at a time and all that. Maybe the three of us will don the red-and-white in a few years' time.

I'm at my most content on the hurling field. I always have been. I feel at home there – happy, comfortable, secure. I suppose that, in a way, it defines who I am. Life has thrown me plenty of ups and downs but the important thing is to take the positives from wherever you can find them. You can lose money in business – which I know all about – but nobody can ever take away my achievements on the hurling field with Kilkenny or Gowran. They remain permanent, an expression of who I am and irrespective of what anyone does or says, they will always be there.

I have, over the years, been the victim of all sorts of rumours but it passes over my head now. I always believe that when a person is pointing the finger at someone else, there are three fingers pointing in the other direction – right back in the face of the individual who is doing the pointing in the first place. Quite possibly, it's their own story they're telling but it's easier to point at someone else.

It's the same on a pitch. The player who is moaning to his colleagues about what they are doing wrong is very often the guy who isn't performing himself. The loudest talker is not always making the most sense.

To me, everything is about being positive now. I've had tough times, personally, professionally, emotionally, but I'm getting through them. I would consider myself a strong person who can deal with whatever is thrown at him, however hard it might be.

I have good friends, people who I trust and who I know are there because they are genuine. I regard friends as people who are always there for you and who don't judge you. They understand what you're about and accept you for what you are. They tell you if they have heard rumours about you because they care. Otherwise, you wouldn't hear what's being said and lies can go unchecked. It's the same with me. I would go to a friend and tell them if rumours were flying around about them. I would ask them did they need anything and what I could do to help.

Good friendships are really important and I have some really great ones, the best of which is with my former wife, Christine. That might seem unusual but it happens to be true. Christine is happily married again, but we remain close friends as well as parents to our two lads. We were married for nine years before being divorced in 2004.

Everyone gets married with the intention that it will be for life but sometimes it's not. It's a fact of life and there is nothing anyone can do about it. Things happen, circumstances arise, relationships change. It's a common story all over the world. Our separation was as clean as it's possible to have. We arranged our financial affairs without solicitors because we were able to sit down and work through it. We got it legally formalised when we were finished but it was our agreement, not one drawn up by someone else.

Obviously, divorce is a very raw experience emotionally but we coped. We put the two lads first all the time and worked from there. The run-up to our divorce was tough, not just because it's the nature of these things, but because I was being hounded by sections of the media. I was living in Mount Juliet at the time and got regular visits and phone calls from journalists, asking if I would talk about my situation.

It was a private matter between Christine and me, yet some newspapers seemed to think it was okay to pry into our affairs in the hope of getting a story. I certainly wasn't going to facilitate them and neither was she. Still, it was there in the background all the time. Some of the papers eventually ran with the news of our separation on the morning of the 2003 All-Ireland final.

It was presented under the guise of sympathy, along the lines of: "isn't it tough on DJ having this in the background as he prepared for an All-Ireland final" but, in reality, it was done for maximum impact on the day. There was nothing I could have done about it even if I did think it unfair. Being hounded by the media in the run-up to the final wasn't exactly helping my preparation but it was outside my control so all I could do that was ignore it as best I could. I was captain that year and utterly determined to ensure that nothing would distract me but all the time the media intrusions were going on in the background before coming to the fore on the day of the final. It wasn't right but I had to take in anyway.

I was an amateur sportsman, playing hurling for his county, not a publicity-seeking celebrity who wanted to be in the papers all the time. It was even more unfair on Christine who was being dragged into the public eye because I happened to be a well-known hurler.

We got through it as best we could but it was a difficult time. I'm happy to say that ten years on, we are now the best of friends. Indeed, I'll go as far as to say that I don't know where I would have been without her when I was sick last year. She did all she possibly could for me in what was a very tough time, while also looking after the lads. But then that's her nature.

Whatever my personal health or business difficulties were at any time, she was the one person who was always there to help me. She didn't need to but she chose to. I will always be grateful for that.

After our separation, I got into a relationship with Sarah Newman which lasted for nine years. I met Sarah through Barbara Galavan, who had produced a DVD on my life and times. Sarah was a well-known business woman and because I had a high profile in sport, we were regularly invited to support various charity events, which we readily did.

This led to us being photographed regularly at events and before you know it you're classed as some sort of socialite, even when you were only there to support a good cause in the first place. Unfortunately, that's what happens in a small county like Ireland, where unfair motives can be attached to the most innocent of events. If I could help a charity in some way I would.

Courting publicity was never my thing. I was always co-operative with sports journalists because I felt I had a responsibility to promote hurling. If I could do that by giving interviews, I would do it all the time. Beyond that, I was a private person. At no stage did I ever want to be classed as a socialite or someone who liked being seen in trendy places about town.

The whole celebrity thing made me uncomfortable. You meet so many genuine people in sport that it would be easy to think everyone is the same elsewhere but that's not the case. In business situations, you will find people who tell you how great you are but you know full well that they aren't remotely sincere.

They are what I would call the networking set. They talk to you for a while but then invite you to meet someone else. It's part of the networking system and is something I have no time for whatsoever. Over the years, I attended fewer and fewer events not just because of that, but because I didn't want people to think I wanted to be seen everywhere.

I was never the socialite type. I'm a hurler, a sportsperson, a confident guy on the field. I can do media and talk easily to people but I'm also essentially a private person. Being seen out and about is not what I do.

My relationship with Sarah ended last year. It broke down for various reasons, all of which are personal to us. It's part of life, tough and painful, but both of us had to get on with it.

My business problems have got plenty of public airing in recent years and all I can say is that I'm working through them. I made a lot of mistakes, as did many others, but I'm trying to correct them as best I can.

It's not easy and there's no point denying that the last few years have been very stressful but it's the hand I have been dealt and I'll play it to the best of my ability. I have done nothing wrong, can look everyone in the eye and, most of all, I'm content in myself.

I'm busy with a new business project, GO2 Communication, Ireland and will be involved in a hurling coaching and ambassadorial role with Carlow Institute of Technology. I am also working with famous energy healer, Michael O'Doherty, developing a programme on stress, burn-out and various other issues that impact on so many people nowadays. Michael is an expert in that area and I'd like to think that my personal experiences can give a practical expression to the programme we are planning to roll out for people of all ages.

I certainly know plenty about coping with stress whether it's caused by business, personal or health issues but I've come through it and I think my experience can be helpful to others who are going through a difficult time.

I'm 42, I'm healthy again, I have two lovely sons and some great friends. Nowadays, I count my blessings and look forward to the future in a very positive way. Sport had helped me to do that and I have no doubt that it will continue to do so for the rest of my days.

CHAPTER 2

FACE TO FACE WITH HARSH REALITIES

In early August this year, I got the best news imaginable. I was given the medical all-clear. The various health problems I experienced over the previous sixteen months have been sorted out and I'm in fine fettle again.

It's a great feeling after going through a very difficult period. Let me start at the beginning. In April 2012, I was in Kilkenny Garda Station having a form signed to get a car back on the road when I collapsed. I had been getting very bad headaches for a while but put them down to stress, related to personal and business matters. I had also been experiencing chest pains but attributed them to the same thing.

I reckoned it couldn't be anything else. Nothing serious anyway. I had always kept myself in good shape, never smoked or taken alcohol so what could go wrong? Quite a lot, it seems, as it can for anybody. After I collapsed in the Garda Station, I was taken to St. Luke's Hospital in Kilkenny where I was diagnosed with a condition called pericarditis, a virus that attacks tissue around the heart wall.

I spent a week in hospital and when I was being discharged I was told I would need a brain scan to check why I had collapsed. It seems the pericarditis wouldn't cause that to happen on its own. The scans delivered some chilling results. Seven clots and two aneurisms showed up.

Whatever about the clots, the aneurisms could have been very dangerous. I underwent an operation straightaway and, thank God, all went to plan. I'm fine now. The doctors are quite happy that all is well and that I should have no more problems in that direction.

I'm no medical expert but my understanding of an aneurism is a bleed that can lead to a brain haemorrhage. It sounds serious and it is.

The whole experience was very frightening, but not nearly as worrying as when you consider what might have happened. It's scary having an operation that has anything to do with your brain but it's a lot better than putting up with splitting headaches, especially when you don't know what's causing them.

Naturally, I was curious to find out what caused the pericarditis, the blood clots and the aneurisms. It seems the pericarditis was straightforward enough. I had been hit by a virus which could have targeted anyone. But the other problems were more frightening and potentially, more dangerous.

Before I deal with an issue which I think all hurlers should address, I want to go back to the day I collapsed in Kilkenny Garda Station and was taken to hospital. Word spread very quickly – so quickly, in fact, that it reached my son Mikey, before anyone had a chance to tell him exactly what happened.

A lad in school told him that I had committed suicide. Apparently, he got it from some social media site. Now imagine a 13-year-old being told that his father had committed suicide when, in fact, all that had happened was that I had collapsed due to a something brought on by a virus. Luckily, Christine (my ex-wife) was on the scene very quickly to re-assure Mikey that everything would be fine, but it was a horrible experience for him.

There was also a rumour that one of the lads from the Gowran hurling team had cut me down off a tree. I don't get angry easily but it makes my blood boil to think that irresponsible people will use social media in such a disgusting way.

You will probably always have people like that in the world but they should not be allowed to get away with it. Much tighter controls should apply to social media sites and far greater responsibility should be placed on those who own and run them at a considerable profit.

I also believe that far stricter regulations should apply to mobile phones. They can be used as very hurtful and damaging instruments, yet can be bought on a pay-as-you-go unregistered basis. Not only that, but it's possible to block the number on the phone so that the receiver has no idea who is texting or calling.

In my view, there should be two requirements. One, all mobile phones should be registered but only after the purchaser has provided proven details of name and address. Two, it should not be possible for the holder to withhold the number when dialling or texting. Put the two together and you cut out the vast majority of the misery which the sinister use of mobile phones can cause.

As for Twitter, Facebook and other social media sites, they should be held much more to account for what passes through them. Hiding behind the argument that they are the medium, not the message, is not good enough. If nasty, hurtful stuff and lies are being put out there, then those behind the means by which is it carried must be held responsible.

At the very least, they should be made to facilitate any investigation into the source of the nasty stuff. That should happen as a matter of course and not after some long drawn-out process where the person making the complaint can be made to feel as if he or she is in the wrong. Social media is great but not when used in the irresponsible manner which resulted in my then 13-year old son hearing that his father had committed suicide. Then, it's a malicious weapon which has to be counteracted.

Anyway, back to my health scare in April 2012. Strange as it might seem, I was lucky to contract the heart virus as it set off a chain of events, leading to the discovery of the clots and aneurisms which, thankfully, were dealt with by the medical experts.

In fact, the reason I'm even writing about them is because I think every hurler – both at club and county level – should have a brain scan. You've taken the hits – now go and make sure they have done no damage. And if they have, you need to know.

I always wore a helmet during games and training ever since I was a kid, so people might think it's a bit alarmist to blame hurling for what happened to me. I'm not blaming the game, but I am pointing out that it probably was responsible for leaving me with no option but to have an operation connected with the brain, which is the last thing anybody wants.

The medical view was that, most likely, my condition had been caused by taking knocks to the head. Once you wear a helmet, which is compulsory now but which wasn't in my playing days, you think you're safe but it's not that simple. Just because you are wearing a helmet doesn't mean your head is fully protected.

I read recently that in boxing, where headguards were made mandatory in the amateur game many years ago, there's a doubt over whether they do more harm than good. The argument put forward is that the impact of a punch on a boxer wearing a headguard is more damaging to the brain than if he wasn't wearing one. It has something to do with the transfer of force and the jolting impact of the head inside the helmet.

I have no idea whether it's true or whether the same applies to the hurling helmet but it makes you think, doesn't it? The standard of the hurling helmet is much better nowadays than when I started out, but you still don't know what impact on the head a blow on the metal really has. From what I was told, it can be quite serious.

As I've said, I always wore a helmet but as to how good it was, well that's another matter. I got it as a present at Christmas when I was four years old and it turned out to be the only one I ever had. Now, it was either too big for me back then or too small for me when I became an adult but, either way, it was my constant companion all through my career.

I'm not sure what health and safety experts would have made of it but I have my suspicions that they would not have regarded it as the ultimate in protective gear. Still, once it stopped me from getting belts to the head, I was happy, but there's more to protection than that. Besides, it was taped, riveted and mended in various ways so often that I'm sure it had some sort of identity crisis, but I had grown so attached to it that I wouldn't get another one. Anyway, I assumed it was doing its job in terms of minimising the impact of knocks to the head.

The thing about all sportspeople is that they will try to hide injuries, concussion or anything else that might stop them from playing. You see it all the time in rugby nowadays where players will do anything they can to make sure they are not assessed as suffering from concussion so that they can play again the following week. Also, there have been lots of examples in American Football of players who were left with permanent problems because of blows they took to the head. That's scientifically documented and leaves no arguments.

For all that, every sportsperson will cheat when it comes to letting on they are not as badly injured as it might look. I did it myself over the years. Take a blow to the head but ignore it, unless there's blood involved. Never mind that something dangerous might be going on without any visible signs.

That's how players are. It's all about the next game, the next challenge. What player is going to miss a game because he's suffering from headaches? And who would listen to him? You're not playing because you have a headache! Are you a man or a mouse? Headaches, how are you? Go out there and give the opposition headaches.

When I look back on my club and county career, I reckon I was knocked out six or seven times. By knocked out, I mean taking a blow to the head that left me concussed, even if I tried to ignore it most of the time. I remember playing a game with Gowran at one stage, when I took a blow to the head but carried on anyway, as you do.

Nobody took much notice until we got a close-in free pretty much in front of goal and I aimed for the corner flag. Kevin Fennelly was in charge of Gowran at the time and at that stage he realised there was something seriously wrong and took me off. Up to then, I had been playing away as if nothing had happened, presumably being guided only by instinct. I have no recollection whatsoever of the game or the day, which shows just how badly dazed I was.

God knows what damage that or indeed any of the other blows I took over the years did to me. My type of game left me open to heavy knocks. When I got the ball, I would put the head down and charge for goal. Now, if you're doing that all through your playing career, it's inevitable that you'll get hit quite a lot. Some may be intentional, most won't, but the impact is the same either way. The head doesn't differentiate between the intentions of the opponent – it just takes the knocks.

The funny thing is that overall I was fairly lucky with injuries. Obviously, I took a lot of blows to the hand – one finger was fractured seven times – and had some hamstring, shoulder and collar bone injuries too, but nothing major with knees or ankles. I was fortunate in that way, unlike Henry Shefflin, for instance, who has suffered some very bad knee injuries and then had an ankle problem which took a long time to heal this year.

Mind you, I did have a serious eye scare once after taking a nasty blow to the face during a club game. An opponent was trying to lift the ball and as I came up behind him, the top of his hurley jabbed back and caught me just below the right eye, pushing the bone up in my face. I had no sight in the eye for nearly three weeks which, as you can imagine, was a very worrying time. Thankfully, all was well in the end and perfect vision returned.

Up to then, there was no faceguard on my battered old helmet but I had one fitted immediately. I was all in favour of the rule which was brought in a few years ago, making it mandatory for players to wear helmets with faceguards because of the protection they offer for eyes, nose and mouth but there's only a certain amount they can do to save hurlers from the impact of blows to the top of the head.

I don't want to be alarmist about the risks of playing hurling when it comes to head injuries, but I do think players should be aware that when they take a blow it can be dangerous. The scary thing for me was that unless I had the heart issue, caused by a virus which had nothing to do with hurling, I would probably never have had the brain scan which led to the discovery of the blood clots and aneurisms. I would have thought the headaches were just something that happened from time to time. In the long term, it could have been fatal if I hadn't had the operation. That's the stark reality, one that all hurlers should reflect on, not in a panicked sort of way but as a measured health consideration. A scan will either find the problem or show that all is well. Either way, it's worth doing.

What with heart and head issues, I was glad to see the back of 2012 but it obviously decided to pass on some of its nasty ways to 2013. I got pneumonia in January and spent four days in hospital. It seems the operation and other treatments knocked my immune system out of line, leaving me susceptible to infection. Pneumonia took its chance and gave me a lousy start to the year.

Thankfully, it all cleared up and I'm in good shape now. I'm even back hurling with Gowran this year. The speed is gone but I still have an eye for the ball, which helps me out of tight situations. In any event, I still find getting back out on the pitch very enjoyable.

But then, as I've always said, there isn't a more satisfying feeling in the world for me than playing hurling. It was like that from the day I was old enough to take a hurley in my hand and belt the ball off the gable end of our house.

I did it for hours at a time, left and right, low and high. I used to challenge myself by trying to hit the chimney as many times in a row as I could. I have no doubt that it helped make me strike the ball more accurately later in life. If I missed the chimney, the ball would fly 60 or 70 yards away and I'd have to go and collect it, assuming of course that it hadn't got lost over roofs and sheds. The fear of losing the ball would certainly concentrate the mind.

The more often I hit the chimney, the happier I was as I played out my own version of All-Ireland finals. I didn't know at the time that my grand-uncle, Paddy Phelan, who won four All-Ireland medals with Kilkenny in the 1930s, was one of the best hurlers of all time. He was chosen at wing-back on the Teams of the Century and the Millennium but it wasn't until I started to make a name for myself that the connection between us became general public knowledge.

I would have loved to see footage of him but then the same goes for Christy Ring, Mick Mackey, Lory Meagher an all the other great players from the past. I have always considered myself lucky to have been from Kilkenny because it gave me a chance to develop my skills and play at the highest level. I often think of lads born in so-called weaker counties who, however good they might be, never get a chance to win All-Ireland titles or even be part of the big occasions.

I was lucky too that I had natural speed and fortunate as well that there were so many other good players around me in Gowran. Put the whole package together and I'd be the first to admit that good fortune played a large part in making my career. After that, it was up to me to put in the effort which I was happy to do.

I was born in November 1970, two months before two lads by the names of Charlie Carter and Pat O'Neill were added to the Gowran population. Being born in January is a big advantage in the underage GAA world since the start of the year is the cut-off point for various grades. It meant that although there was only a matter of weeks between Charlie, Pat and myself, I was a year older than them in hurling terms.

So when they were still playing U-12, I was too old and so on all the way up to U-21 level, after which age is no longer an issue. When I was a kid, birthday parties around Gowran were very simple. There were around 20 lads in the school and the birthday party circuit consisted of hurling, coke or orange and crisps. The hurling was the best part! We had some smashing games that usually had no time limit. In fact, they would only end when someone got split, accidentally of course. Being a year older (for hurling purposes) than most of my friends was frustrating, especially when they got to the Feile na nGael finals in Wexford which they won. I was delighted for them but disappointed for myself that I couldn't be part of it. Luckily, the age limit for colleges hurling changed in my last year in St. Kieran's which meant I could play on the senior team for a third successive season.

John Knox and Dick O'Neill were the teachers in the local national school and from the first day I went there in 1974, I was in good hands. Two marvellous hurling men, John and Dick were brilliant with kids. They certainly helped me to grow into the game and I'm sure everyone else who came under their encouraging wings would say the same. Dick was a selector with me in Gowran this year, still going strong and as passionate and as knowledgeable about hurling as ever.

There are hundreds of people like Dick and John around the country who put so much into hurling – and indeed others sports – without ever getting the credit they deserve. They might be the quiet men and women of sport but they are also very much the engine that drives it in so many communities.

As I hurled my way through national school, the next big decision was where I would go to secondary school. Well, maybe not that big, but a choice still had to be made between St. Kieran's and Kilkenny CBS. The late Tommy O'Brien was the first lay principal in the CBS and, as well as being a devoted hurling man, he was also big into handball. In fact, he went on to become President of the Handball Association, which was a fitting honour for a man who put so much into the sport.

Anyway, he booked me into the CBS and I would have happily gone along with the flow but for the intervention of Fr. Tommy Maher, the legendary St. Kieran's man. He called out to our house one day to talk about going to St. Kieran's and, shrewd character that he was, he brought a little bribe. He handed me a brand new hurley and sliotar, talked about how I would love St. Kieran's and all the hurling I'd be doing.

Now, one school seemed the same as the next to me but after being handed a hurley and sliotar, plus details of the hurling heaven that awaited me, I wanted to go St. Kieran's. Tommy had to scratch my name from the CBS enrolment list! I still came across him a lot through the handball, which carried fringe benefits. Since Tommy was one of the leading lights nationally on the handball scene, he always got tickets for the All-Ireland finals. They were good ones too, in the Ard Chomhairle section, right in the middle of the lower Hogan Stand.

Tommy would bring me along, lift me over the turnstile and I'd sit on his lap for the game. You wouldn't get away with that nowadays but back then it happened all the time. The funny thing is that despite playing hurling, I was more interested in football. Kilkenny only won one All-Ireland senior hurling title between 1975 and 1982 so I didn't have an immediate sense that the county was among the traditional powerhouses.

I did, however, know that Kerry were real masters in football. I idolised that great Kerry team, in particular, Mikey Sheehy. I loved watching him, the way he made everything look so simple. His footwork was something else. He could wriggle out of the tightest corner without moving especially fast but then his balance was superb so he was able to find escape routes. I also loved the way he took frees. He'd put the ball down, almost casually, take a few steps back and stroke it over the bar. It all looked so effortless, almost like a good golf shot. The famous goal against Dublin in the 1978 All-Ireland final, when he chipped the ball over the retreating Paddy Cullen, typified everything about the true genius Mikey brought to his game.

Mikey was my Kerry hero but I loved the whole team and everything about them. The fielding skills of Jack O'Shea and Seanie Walsh, Pat Spillane's running, 'Bomber' Liston causing havoc on the edge of the opposition square, Mick O'Dwyer patrolling the sideline with the match programme in his hand – I was enthralled by it all. Still, Mikey was the main man for me. I thought he could never make a mistake and have no recollection of him ever missing a free. Mind you, I saw some of those All-Ireland finals on TG4 over the last few years and he did miss the odd one! It shows how the mind can play tricks when you're a child looking at your hero.

If I'd been from Kerry I could not have been any more upset after they lost the 1982 All-Ireland final. I bawled my eyes out when Seamus Darby's late goal for Offaly ended Kerry's five-in-a-row bid. I thought it such a shame that they didn't get to complete their bid to set a record. I never thought back then that Kilkenny would be going for the five-in-a-row in hurling 28 years later and that, like Kerry, they would lose. Still, the big difference was that Kilkenny were well beaten by Tipperary in 2010 whereas Kerry were caught on the line by Offaly in 1982, which made it all the more heart-breaking for Mikey and the lads. I didn't have anything against Offaly, other than the fact that they beat my favourite team which, I suppose, was enough to make them look like demons in my eyes.

Essentially, I was drawn to Mikey Sheehy's game because of his incredible skill. It's the most precious attribute in any sport. It can be worked on but much of it has to be there naturally in the first place. In particular, I love watching the sidestep. One of the drawbacks of Gaelic football and hurling, compared to rugby, is that you can't use the skill in your feet as much as you would like.

Let me explain. In rugby, the skilful player who is good on his feet can beat a few men in a small space and because he doesn't have to play the ball, his movement is everything. In hurling or football, you have to play the ball after sidestepping or else you will be penalised for over-carrying. It reduces the chance to execute the sidestep which, in my view, is a phenomenal skill.

I love watching Brian O'Driscoll and the way he uses his feet. Mind you, I would not fancy playing rugby because I'd be afraid of my life! I'm sure rugby players think the same about hurling so it's a question of what you're used to. Still, I'd prefer to take my chances on a hurling field than in rugby where the power of the modern-day player is awesome.

Brian O'Driscoll stands at around the same height as me but is three stone heavier so you can imagine the power he packs in a tackle. We didn't see much rugby when I was growing up because apart from the Five-Nations championships, there was very little oval ball action on TV. Still, we had a special interest in Kilkenny because our own man, Willie Duggan, was going so well with Ireland and Leinster. As you would expect, I was more taken with the back play than the forward power, generated by Willie and his friends.

Ollie Campbell was brilliant at evading tackles and although I only saw him a few times a year on TV, I used to practise sidestepping, based on how I thought he was doing it. My great soccer hero was Bryan Robson. I just loved watching how he drove himself and his team on. He was also a great man for timing his runs from midfield to perfection, a talent that brought a lot of goals for Manchester United and England. Subconsciously, maybe I was learning from watching Robson making those runs because it was something I loved to do myself when my hurling career took off. Maybe not with the same amount of power as Robson but with a bit more speed!

Pace was always going to be one of my main assets but then it had to be because I sure as hell wasn't built for power, not as a youngster anyway. They obviously noticed that in St. Kieran's and decided to do something about it. I was a day pupil but received a special concession to join the boarders for lunch every day. I'd traipse down to the refectory with them, fill myself up and return for the rest of the day. Mind you, I was still small, even after the special treatment.

Hurling was hugely important in St. Kieran's but I fancied myself a handy footballer too. In fact, we won a Leinster U-14 football title one year. Before that, I got a chance to play football in Croke Park which was a huge thrill.

Back then, there was an inter-city primary schools competition run off every year. Mr. Knox – as we used to call him – asked me did I want to play hurling or football for Kilkenny and, believe it or not, I opted for football. We had a game up in Dundalk and another one against Dublin in Croke Park. We were beaten out the gate by Dublin but it was still a huge thrill to play on the hallowed turf. I never took much notice at the time at how far Kilkenny were behind most other counties in football – it was just one of those things that happened and little heed was paid to it.

St. Kieran's always had great hurling men, such as Fr. Paddy Bollard, Fr. Fergal Farrell, Nicky Cashin, Seamus Knox, Denis Philpott, Tommy Lanigan and, of course, Fr. Maher

The importance of hurling in the college was brought home to me when I got sick before an U-14 final one year. I suffered badly from tonsillitis at the time and was out of school for a week. Still, I got a call the day before the final, inquiring if there was any way I might be able to play. Now, while attending classes and doing all the work that goes with it wasn't in my plans while my throat was so sore, hurling in a final was an altogether different matter.

I played the match, went straight back into the sick bay and was out of school for another week. Not to worry, I'd done my duty to the school by playing the hurling game. I was happy and so were they. While I was handy enough as a player in my early years in St.Kieran's, I was very ordinary by comparison with Adrian Ronan and Pat O'Neill. Adrian was the main man from midfield up while Pat, who was big and strong even then, was a pillar of reliability in defence. I'd sneak in for the odd goal and was a good team player but that was about it.

Still, I was lucky enough to have one great asset – pace. Any player with real pace has a huge advantage and it certainly stood to me all through my career. I played in my first All-Ireland senior colleges' final at the age of sixteen in May 1987 but it wasn't a happy experience as we lost heavily to St. Flannan's of Ennis in Birr.

A crowd of nearly 7,000 turned up but unfortunately for them – and us – the game did not live up to expectations. We started well enough but as the day progressed, St. Flannan's proved much too strong and ran out easy winners, 4-11 to 1-7. A certain Anthony Daly played for St.Flannan's but we weren't on each other as he was on the other corner.

A year later, we had an altogether better day out when we won the title in Walsh Park, beating Midleton CBS in the final. We had nine of the 1987 team and would have been expected to beat Midleton, who were in the final for the first time. However, they made it very hard on us and we didn't help our own cause by shooting no fewer than fifteen wides. We won by six points but the final scoreline flattered us as we a point down with five minutes remaining before goals from Paul Brennan and Eddie Teehan swung the balance our way as we ran out 3-10 to 2-7 winners.

It was a huge win for St. Kieran's who, rather surprisingly, hadn't won the title previously since 1975. We made it a double in 1989 and also gained revenge on St. Flannan's in Nenagh. It was a particularly good day for me as I scored 3-3 of our 3-5 total in a two point win. We trailed at half-time but I got in for two goals early in the second half, which turned the game in our favour. Once again, we made it harder on ourselves than we should have, shooting eighteen wides.

In between the two colleges' wins, I won an All-Ireland minor medal when Kilkenny beat Cork in the 1988 minor final. The record books show that we won by ten points (3-13 to 0-12) but it was nowhere near as easy as it looks. In fact, Cork led by a point after 40 minutes but Paul Treacy and myself scored goals and we kicked on from there.

Afterwards we sat and watched as Galway beat Tipperary in the senior final and, naturally, I was wondering if I would ever get a chance to play in game like that. Three years later, I got to play in my first senior final and would experience it another seven times, five times as a winner. The All-Ireland final wins were high points in a career that took me on an eventful journey which, for the most part, I enjoyed immensely.

I made friends all over the country and abroad, saw parts of the world I might never otherwise have seen and, most of all, was part of something special with Kilkenny and Young Irelands of Gowran. Winning All-Ireland titles was nothing new to Kilkenny but winning county titles certainly was new and exciting territory for Gowran.

I was on the team that won the senior county title for the first time in 1996 and we won a second title in 2002. Those successes are right up there with anything I achieved with Kilkenny in the sixteen years I was lucky enough to wear the famous black-and-amber jersey.

Combined with my love of handball, which I indulged for as long as I could before I found it all but impossible to combine it with the demands of the inter-county scene, hurling provided me with enough wonderful times and experiences to last a lifetime.

However, it wasn't all about highs and glory. There was another side too, one which left me feeling so flat and disillusioned that I felt I had no option but to walk away from the game I loved at the age of 27.

All of which goes to prove that you never know what's going on in somebody else's head. The roar of the crowd is all very fine but when the game is over, players go back to their own world as private individuals who have their personal cares, worries and stresses. The public may not see it that way but, trust me, it's very much the case.

CHAPTER 3

SMALL FISH, BIG POND

"Howya, I'm Christy Heffernan." A massive hand stretched out, its owner smiling warmly.

"I'm DJ Carey," I replied, grinning nervously, not knowing what to say next. After all, this was Christy Heffernan, the massive man from Glenmore, who had been on the Kilkenny team since I was ten or eleven years old, and now I'm meeting him face-to-face for the first time. He seemed to sense my unease.

"Welcome aboard, DJ."

If Christy looked like a giant to me, I must have looked like a little elf to him. At the time, I probably looked like an elf to a lot of people. I was very small and slight but then I was a month short of my 18th birthday and still had an awful lot of growing to do. I was regarded as too small for the Kilkenny minor squad in 1987, even though my hurling might have been good enough. I suppose I was being protected for my own good. Some lads grow very quickly in their early teens; I didn't, but I would catch up later on.

My first meeting with Christy came in October 1988 and I had just come off the Kilkenny minor team that won the All-Ireland the month before, beating Cork quite easily in the final.

Dermot Healy, Eddie Keher and Ollie Harrington were in charge of the seniors and, despite my size, they obviously thought I was ready to be brought into the panel. Adrian Ronan, who had also been on the minor team, was included too. Adrian was stronger than me at the time so it wasn't as much of a risk. In fact, it was no risk at all – Adrian was picked on the team straight away.

Most teams didn't train collectively for the pre-Christmas League games back then so new lads who were brought into the panel just turned up on match day. I got the call from Dermot Healy, who came into St. Kieran's one day to invite me on to the panel for an up-coming League game in Nowlan Park.

Come Sunday, I decided to get there in good time. In fact, I arrived in Nowlan Park at least an hour ahead of schedule. There was no one else around that early but I didn't mind, I just wanted to make sure I was there in good time. This was a new world and I needed to savour it from the start. My mind was racing with the sheer wonder of it all. Me? DJ Carey from Gowran on the Kilkenny senior hurling panel.

Getting called into a senior county squad is still one of the great thrills in Irish sport. You have moved beyond the club scene into something new and exciting, a world every young hurler and footballer thinks about from the minute they are old enough to understand how the game works. I was no different.

The hours, the days, the weeks, the months that I spent belting the ball off the gable end of the house back home in Gowran were all done with the dream in my head that one day I would get to wear the black-and-amber as a senior Kilkenny hurler. It was an ambition that never faded. When I was offered a chance to go to America on a handball scholarship, I had no interest in checking out exactly what was involved. I didn't see it as an opportunity that might actually have changed my life for the better but as a hindrance that would wreck my ambition to hurl with Kilkenny.

I loved handball but not nearly enough to go to America and rule myself out of hurling. No, America was great but it wasn't for me. So on that autumn Sunday in 1988, when I finally took a place in the Kilkenny dressing-room as part of the senior squad, I felt so proud that I could have burst. At the back of my mind, I suppose, I was wondering how I would cope. Colleges and minor hurling were one thing but senior was different altogether. Ready or not, I was heading for a man's world, maybe not straight away but over a period of time, provided of course that I proved myself up to it. That could wait, I thought to myself, as I sat in the Nowlan Park dressing-room on that Sunday afternoon.

Then the lads started arriving, first Big Christy, then the rest. Dermot Healy was new to the set-up, having taken charge after a championship season where Kilkenny had lost the Leinster semi-final to Wexford so there was probably a bit of apprehension among the more senior players who didn't know what direction he was planning to take.

I was far too young to worry – or even think – about that. Being on the panel was more than enough for me. Everything else could wait. I had no idea how I would cope at this level anyway so there wasn't much point thinking about the future. For all I knew, my days on the senior panel might be a short-lived thing.

Ger Henderson had always been my big hero and now here I was in the same dressing-room. As a kid growing up, I just loved watching Ger. His determination, his drive and his sheer will to win were inspiring. Under a high ball, Ger was a sight to behold. Irrespective of how many were around him – be they friend or foe - he was brilliant at making room for himself and clearing the way for the ball to drop into his great big paw. Once he had it, no one would stop him as he drove out before getting in his clearance. To me, he epitomised everything that was good about hurling, the spirit, the manliness and the unyielding belief that no challenge was too big to take on. As a Kilkenny icon, he topped my bill. In the 1987 All-Ireland final against Galway, he took a terrible blow to the hand, sending blood splashing everywhere but however serious the injury was, Ger played on.

There was an All-Ireland final to be played and nothing could interfere with that. Kilkenny lost but it sure as hell wasn't Ger's fault. Kilkenny only conceded 1-12 that day, a score that would not have been enough to win any of the previous All-Irelands since 1954 when Cork beat Wexford by 1-9 to 1-6. That final was, of course played over 60 minutes unlike 1987 which was over 70 minutes.

When a defence restricts the opposition to 1-12, they would normally expect to be on the winning side but not in 1987, much, no doubt, to the disappointment of the Kilkenny backline of Joe Hennessy, Paddy Prendergast, John Henderson, Liam Walsh, Ger Henderson and Seán Fennelly, backed by goalkeeper, Kevin Fennelly.

The trouble was that Kilkenny scored only 0-9, the sort of return you would regard as the minimum for a first-half.

As it happened, the 1987 final turned out to be the last for quite a few of the Kilkenny team, including Ger Henderson. Maybe it was watching Ger perform so many heroics at centre-back over my formative years as an impressionable kid that gave me a hankering to try my luck at centre-back. I'd be a much different type of centre-back to Ger (a much less effective one for a start!) but I liked the idea of playing there to see what it was like to be facing the ball all the time rather than taking it and turning as you have to do in the forwards. It took me a long time to get my chance to try out the No. 6 jersey but it finally came in what was, ironically, my last year with Kilkenny.

In the spring of 2005, Brian Cody said to me one night: "you always fancied yourself as a centre-back, didn't you. Have a go so."

We played James Stephens in a practise game and I did well enough. I was always fairly good under the high ball and could read the play well so I enjoyed the experience. After that, Brian picked me for a League game against Laois with Michael Kavanagh one side of me and JJ Delaney on the other so I was well-minded by two of the best defenders that hurling ever produced.

We won reasonably comfortably and I did okay. Well enough, it seems, to have another go as Brian left me there for the next game against Clare in Nowlan Park. Now, critical Kilkenny eyes would be carefully studying how the new centre-back was going. Early on, I won a ball from a Clare puck-out and sent it straight over the bar. Maybe, playing centre-back is going to be easier than I thought it would. No, it's not. Just as I was about to start enjoying life in my new surroundings, everything changed. Clare took over all over the field and by half-time they were thirteen points ahead.

The No. 6 wasn't the only Kilkenny man who hadn't gone well, but he was the only one playing a long way from his natural home. The experiment was about to end. Brian nodded to me at half-time.

"You go to full-forward," he said. And thus ended my brief career as a wannabe Ger Henderson! We made a bit of a comeback against Clare but still lost by eight points. Ger – the legend was safe! So too was Pat O'Neill's reputation as the best centre half-back Gowran ever produced.

I have to say that all the Kilkenny squad were very welcoming to me when I came into the panel in late 1988. If fact, after a short time I felt like one of the lads. That's the thing about inter-county panels. A dressing-room never remains stagnant, simply because it can't. New faces come in all the time, momentum builds and the enduring process goes on.

A dressing-room is never the property of any group, however long they may be there or how successful they are. Besides, everyone remembers when they joined the panel and how awkward they felt on that first day, so any player who doesn't welcome a newcomer is missing the whole point of teamwork and the ever-evolving nature of team sport.

I was always very conscious of that during my career. The new recruit, sitting quietly in the corner could be the man to win the next All-Ireland for the team while the experienced player, who has been through it all and is now very comfortable in himself within the group, could be the man to lose it. Mind you, the new lad could also be the one to take your place but, hey, that's sport. It's up to you to see the challenge as something to be taken on. If you're up to it, that's fine; if not, then it's time you were gone anyway.

That's how every team sport works. It's always evolving, challenging old habits and introducing new dynamics. No one is ever too young to be a winner just as no one – irrespective of how long they have been aboard or how well they might have done – is too important as to be indispensable.

You don't think of anything like that when you join a panel and I certainly didn't when I slipped shyly into the Kilkenny dressing-room all those years ago. I just kept the head down and got on with the training, while all the time watching, learning and figuring out in my own head how I was coping. I had been at corner-forward on the St. Kieran's and Kilkenny minor teams that won All-Irelands in 1988 but, probably because I was so small, Dermot had me down as goalkeeper in the early days. He was doing that just to get me used to the panel and because I was too small to play outfield.

Kevin Fennelly was first choice goalkeeper – and a good one too – so I was never going to displace him. Not that I wanted to because I never really fancied playing in goal. I always preferred being a poacher to a gamekeeper for the simple reason that I preferred putting something in the bag than trying to prevent it from being raided. I was a sub for a few League games in late 1988 but my first big chance came in early 1989 when Kevin was unavailable for a few games.

I was picked in goal for a League game against Offaly in Birr in mid-February. Adrian Ronan was selected in the full-forward line and since we were both Leaving Cert students in St. Kieran's, it generated big interest among the national media.

Next thing, there's a photographer down from the *Sunday Independent* taking our pictures sitting side by side in the classroom. Their GAA correspondent, Tom O'Riordan was on the phone for an interview and while I hadn't even made my senior Kilkenny debut, I was quite happy to offer my little piece. To be honest, all I could say was that it was a huge honour to be picked for the Kilkenny team which was true. Anyway, I talked for a while and Tom seemed happy enough.

If a Leaving Cert student was selected on a county team nowadays, there's no way the manager would allow any access to him by the media but is that right? Did a picture in the *Sunday Independent* impact negatively in any way on Adrian and me? No it didn't. Did answering questions to such a decent journalist as Tom O'Riordan, cause a problem? No it didn't. In fact, it was a good experience, part of learning the trade as a county player.

My debut day started out wet, cold and miserable. Icy rain fell from skies I could almost touch with my hurley and when we arrived in Birr, we were told that St. Brendan's Park was unplayable. I thought my big day was over before it started and if Kevin was back for the re-fixture, I might not get a look in at all.

Then we were told that O'Connor Park in Tullamore was okay so the motorcade dashed over there. I travelled a lot with John Power, Pat Dwyer and Richie Power in my early days in a car driven by Paddy Treacy. He drove to Tullamore but there was still a doubt about whether the game would go ahead as the rain was bucketing down.

Technically, O'Connor Park might have been playable but everything about the day was so miserable that no one (except probably me) would have complained if the referee, Tipperary man, Gerry Long had called the whole thing off.

Instead, it went ahead in a mud bath, being filled with freezing cold rain which belted down for the entire afternoon. For all that, it was quite a good game which we won by two points (0-13 to 1-8). I did okay, even if I knew right well that if I was to have a future as an inter-county hurler, it wouldn't be as goalkeeper. I had a few shots to save in the first half but it went quiet after that.

As for my hero, Ger Henderson, he was at the heart of the action, at full-back as I recall, but he ended the game on the bench, having been sent off late on with Offaly sub, James Rigney. I let in one goal which I don't think I could have done a whole lot about. It was a great day for Adrian Ronan at the other end. Despite the awful conditions, he scored nine of our thirteen points, mostly from frees but no less noteworthy for that. Taking frees on a wet day can be tricky enough but when your hands are cold and wet it makes it twice as hard but Adrian certainly had his eye in that day.

I played another game or two but then Kevin returned and my days as Kilkenny goalkeeper were over for good. Kevin came back for what was a big game against Tipperary and Dermot felt it was time for a change. Modern-day players will find it hard to believe but back then, you usually found out whether or not you were on the team through the newspapers or radio.

The team was released to the media at night so your fate rested on what you read in your morning newspapers. There were no mobile phones back then – in fact, a lot of people had no house phones either – and since teams didn't train for pre-Christmas League games, the papers played a big role in spreading information.

Even when teams were training together for the championship, they still weren't told the team ahead of the media. It's hard to imagine that happening nowadays but that's the way it was in the 1990s. Mind you, Dermot Healy made an exception when he decided to leave me off for that League clash with Tipperary.

I was walking into St. Kieran's after getting off the school bus one morning when Dermot pulled up alongside me in his car and told me that Kevin was coming back in and I would be dropping to the subs' bench. I was expecting it so it came as no surprise. Anyway, I reckoned that if I was to make it as a Kilkenny player it would be as a forward. I dropped back down to the bench and stayed there for the rest of the season.

We reached the Leinster final in July but lost to Offaly by three points, which didn't do much for the mood in Kilkenny. Up to 1980, Offaly had never won a Leinster title but now they had taken six of ten. As a youngster on the panel, I didn't take much notice of that. History was for others to worry about and all that concerned me was how well I was playing and how much progress I was making.

Older people in Kilkenny were looking at it differently. How had Offaly become such a super-power? Why weren't Kilkenny able to stop them? Dermot Healy had done an awful lot to raise Offaly's boat in the 1980s and now Kilkenny were looking to him to make sure that the 1990s started on a high for Kilkenny.

After all, he was one of our own. He knew what Kilkenny expected and he also had the inside track on the Offaly psyche. Offaly had won the Leinster title in 1989 but surely, in his second season, Dermot would mastermind a Kilkenny response.

If only it were that simple.

My introduction to life as a Kilkenny forward came in October 1989. We played Antrim in the League up in Casement Park in front of a very big crowd. Antrim were on a high at the time, having played Tipperary in the All-Ireland final the month before. They had beaten Offaly in a remarkable semi-final so everyone knew exactly how good they were. Okay, so they lost quite heavily to Tipperary in the final but the win over Offaly was still one of the highlights of the year.

Naturally, Antrim had most of the All-Ireland team on duty for their first League game at home and with a big following behind them, it was always going to be a very hard game for us.

Still, we managed to win it by six points (0-20 to 2-8) after trailing by two points in the third quarter. We scored eight unanswered points in the last eleven minutes, which was impressive stuff in the circumstances. I played at right half-forward (I think Gary O'Kane was marking me) and had a good day, scoring ten points, seven from frees. I checked the papers the following day to see what they thought of it all and was delighted to see that the *Irish Independent* gave me special mention, mostly for good free-taking.

"The amazingly accurate free-taking of former colleges All-Ireland star, DJ Carey contributed greatly to the Kilkenny comeback and it was the Young Ireland teenager who finished top scorer with ten points – all but three from placed balls," noted the report.

I read it a few times just to make sure it was actually me they were writing about.

Over the years, I grew to ignore what was written about me – whether good or bad – but it was nice to get encouraging mentions when I was starting out.

I was more pleased with the three points I scored from play than the seven I got from frees against Antrim but, that apart, the important thing was that my Kilkenny career as a forward had begun. It would last for the next sixteen years.

Being handed a county jersey is a huge thing in any player's life. When I was growing up, I knew of the great Kilkenny legends, even if I hadn't seen them playing. For instance, I always regarded Eddie Keher as a God, even if I saw him playing only once and that was long after his inter-county days were over. He would have been in his forties at the time, but was still playing special junior hurling for the Rower-Inistioge.

Eddie's inter-county career ended when I was around five years old so anything I know about him as a hurler is from hearing all the stories about the talent that made him one of the game's big legends. Mind you. I've heard enough to know that he was indeed something special.

Of course, a lot of things were different in Eddie's time, including far less TV coverage of hurling and football than nowadays. It's hard for the modern generation to understand that years ago the very best players were seen 'live' on TV only in All-Ireland semi-finals and finals as well as the Railway Cup finals on St. Patrick's Day.

In fact, when it came to hurling, only the finals were shown for a long time. It meant that a lot of outstanding hurlers got little or no TV exposure throughout their entire careers. That helped to make the Railway Cup the big events they once were as people knew that if they went to Croke Park on St. Patrick's Day, they would see the best players in action. It was usually Leinster v Munster because that's where the strong power bases were before Galway made a breakthrough in the 1970s.

Despite not seeing players very much on TV, my generation – and those before me – had our own sense of connection with the star names. Just because people didn't see players nearly as often as they do nowadays, they still felt they knew them. You will hear people proclaim that Christy Ring was the best hurler ever, despite never having seen him play. That may well be the case but unfortunately, there's no way of properly analysing it because there's so little footage of him. It's certainly tiny compared to even the most modest talent in the modern game who is guaranteed regular TV exposure because of the vastly-increased coverage.

I was lucky, I suppose, in that 'live' coverage was expanding when I came on the scene. And when Guinness took over as All-Ireland sponsors in 1995, the game's profile soared to a higher level still.

All of which seemed a long way off when I finally secured a starting place on the Kilkenny team in late 1989. The League went well for us and after beating Dublin in the semi-final we lined up against Wexford in the 'home' final. It was my first taste of the big time as a Kilkenny senior and I found myself up against Liam Dunne. Not that all that many balls came in our direction, certainly not from Kilkenny puck-outs as Dermot Healy had instructed Kevin Fennelly to belt them all down the other wing.

Big John McDonald was playing at No. 12 and was a ferocious competitor under the high ball, so Dermot reckoned there was more to be had from going down that side rather than whipping it down my wing. It had worked well in earlier games and it paid off again as we beat Wexford by 3-12 to 1-10.

I got a lucky break off a 45-metre free from out on the wing which somehow crept into the Wexford net. It set us up for a fairly easy win. Two weeks later, we were in Gaelic Park for the League final outright against New York. Played in 40 degrees of heat, we found it hard going and while we won by nine points, we didn't get in for any goal which was most unusual.

I had been to the US quite a few times before for handball, but this was a whole new experience as part of a county team and I thoroughly enjoyed it. Things really were moving on nicely. In the space of fifteen months, I had made my senior inter-county as a goalie, moved on to becoming a forward and won my first national title.

Surely there was more to come in 1990. There was, but not in the form that I – or the rest of the Kilkenny squad – had envisaged. A great black cloud was getting ready to rain on our parade.

CHAPTER 4

LEARNING ON THE JOB

It wasn't exactly straight out of the expert's guide on how to calm a 19 year-old facing up to his first senior championship game but it was said to me anyway.

"If you don't get stuck in, you'll be off after twenty minutes. Remember that now."

The speaker was one of the Kilkenny selectors in the run-up to my senior championship debut against Offaly in June 1990. I thought I had done okay in the League, certainly well enough to earn my place for the start of the championship but I was getting a warning anyway. In fairness, maybe he was trying to tell me in his own sweet way that the championship was different and that whatever I thought I knew about county hurling would count for nothing once the ash started flying in a summer showdown in Croke Park.

He was right. The only miscalculation he made was that I lasted twenty-seven, rather than twenty minutes! Whether that was down to me not getting 'stuck in' or not, I don't know. I did what I could but nothing went my way.

To be honest, the whole day passed me by in a bit of a blur. In fact, it passed us all by, as Offaly hurled us off the field. We never saw it coming. Granted, Offaly had won the two previous Leinster finals and still had most of the 1985 All-Ireland winning team but we had gone very well in the League, particularly in the 'home' final two months earlier against Wexford which we won by eight points.

It was all so very different in the championship. Offaly smashed us from the start and led by 3-6 to 0-0 after 24 minutes. Danny Owens, Joachim Kelly and Pat Cleary had hit the net for Offaly, who were rampant all over the field. We were struggling everywhere. Imagine going that long in any game without getting even a single point. In fact, it took us 25 minutes to score, which must be sort of a record for a Kilkenny team.

I eventually pointed a free – my very first score in championship hurling – but was taken off shortly afterwards, replaced by Lester Ryan. One-up to Brian Whelahan. He was making his first championship start for Offaly and got into the swing of it very quickly. He was marking me and, I'd have to admit, was winning the battle by the time I was taken off.

No one on the Kilkenny team could be remotely happy with their performance that day. How could they after losing by 4-15 to 1-8? The tactic of walloping puck-outs down John McDonald's side, which had worked so well in the League, made no impression on the Offaly half-backs. They mopped up everything, including me!

It was a nightmare from start to finish. It was also a freak. Offaly were very good at the time but they weren't a 16-point better team than Kilkenny. The early goals flattened us and once a game starts running away from you at that sort of speed, it's very hard to retrieve anything. The only saving grace for us – if you could call it that – was that the game was on at the same time as Ireland were playing Egypt in a World Cup soccer clash in Italy and all the media focus was on that.

We weren't on live TV or anything like that so while Offaly's runaway win made the GAA headlines the following day, the reaction to our failure was low key by comparison with what it would be nowadays when hurling is getting a lot more coverage.

It was all-or-nothing back then with no second chance in All-Ireland qualifiers so when we woke up on the morning of June 18, our championship season was over.

Offaly went on to win the Leinster title but were well beaten in the All-Ireland semi-final by Galway, who, in turn, lost to Cork in the final. On a line through that form, it left us fairly well down the pecking order but actually I don't believe that was the case. Offaly had hit one of those days they were well capable of producing around then and we felt the full force of their awesome power.

As for me, I had made my senior championship debut at the age of 19 years and 7 months. It was an important milestone and I will always remember it for that, if not the actual performance.

It was a dismal occasion for all of us – newcomers and experienced – but at least the year still held something for the younger lads on the panel. We had a very good U-21 team and with the seniors out of the championship it meant that more attention could be given to our team. It was my first experience of Nickey Brennan as a manager and I really enjoyed working under him. He ran a great show that year.

We got an early chance for some measure of revenge on Offaly for the senior defeat when the U-21s met them in the Leinster semi-final a few days later. Offaly had won the 1987 All-Ireland minor title, beating Kilkenny fairly handily in the Leinster final, so that team formed the bulk of the 1990 U-21s. It included Brian Whelahan, Declan and Johnny Pilkington, Johnny and Billy Dooley, Joe Errity and John Troy, lads who went on to become household names as seniors over the next few years.

Most of our team were drawn from the 1988 squad that had won the All-Ireland minor title so, in purely age terms, we were a year behind Offaly who had most of the 1987 minors. Between that and the seniors' easy win over Kilkenny, Offaly were hot favourites to beat us but they got a right shock.

Nickey had us really fired up and we more or less did to Offaly what they had done to the Kilkenny seniors, including myself, of course. I was a man on a mission that evening and played really well as we ran out eleven point winners. It was an important win for Kilkenny. There was an awful lot of gloom around after the seniors' defeat and the idea that Offaly would beat us at U-21 as well would not have gone down well.

Laois made us struggle in the final but we got through to an All-Ireland semi-final clash with Galway. We trailed by six points early in the second half but then turned in a massive performance and ran out three point winners. Charlie Carter was brilliant that day as was team captain, Jamesie Brennan.

Tipperary awaited us in the final in a game that drew attention right across the country. Tipperary were going well on all fronts around then, including U-21, where they were the reigning All-Ireland champions. Conal Bonnar and John Leahy played at midfield and among their forwards was a certain Liam Sheedy who would come back to haunt Kilkenny as Tipp's senior manager twenty years later.

It was our day in 1990. A huge crowd turned out in Portlaoise for the final which we won by 2-11 to 1-11. I scored one of the goals in what was an excellent game. Winning that final helped wipe out the sour taste of my senior experience three months earlier and on a wider, and more important scale, pumped renewed optimism into Kilkenny hurling.

Just as Offaly U-21s were well-fancied to beat us in 1990, we were favourites to beat them a year later as we had most of the same team that won the All-Ireland the year before. It didn't work out that way – Offaly beat us in the Leinster final. That often happens at U-21 level where a minor team of two years previously goes better than in the third year when, in theory, they should be stronger.

Winning the 1990 U-21 title was very satisfying. Apart from making up for the awful day against Offaly in the senior championship, it meant that I now had All-Ireland medals in colleges, minor and U-21. There's a strict time limit on winning in those grades and, as events transpired, if we hadn't won in 1990, I wouldn't have a U-21 medal. It's nice to have the full set.

By the time we-assembled for the 1990 National League, Dermot Healy was gone as manager, replaced by Ollie Walsh who had done very well with the junior team. In fact, they won the 1990 All-Ireland so he was the obvious choice to move on to the seniors.

Ollie would go on to lead Kilkenny to three Leinster and two All-Ireland titles over the next three seasons in what was a very happy period in the camp. I was still new to it but could sense from the start of Ollie's reign that it would be most enjoyable.

Still, as with most things in life, you need a bit of luck along the way. Dermot Healy had none, especially in 1990 when we met Offaly on one of their irrepressible days. Nothing went right for us, whereas a year later we got a huge break in our first championship game – the Leinster semi-final against Wexford.

So how many steps did I take without playing the ball that day? It's anything from seven to thirty-seven, according to Wexford supporters! My view is that it was a perfectly legal goal. As it happened, it was also one of the most important goals I ever scored.

Remember the game? We were in the closing minute and Wexford were leading by a point (0-13 to 1-9). We should not have been anything like so close. Wexford had played much better overall but missed a lot of easy chances. We had started without the injured Christy Heffernan and lost goalkeeper, Michael Walsh and right half-back, Liam Walsh to injury in the first half so it really did look like one of those days when nothing would go our way.

Wexford led by three points around the hour mark but we brought it level before Seamus Fitzhenry scored what appeared like the winning point for Wexford. Then, in the final minute, the ball broke kindly in front of me and I set off towards the Wexford goal. Three or four Wexford backs were chasing me down, hurleys thrashing in my direction and suddenly I was faced with a split second decision. We needed a point to draw level, which would have been a great result for us, but I reckoned that if I tried to wind up and swing the hurley, I would have been hooked by one of the chasing posse. Instead, I ran on and booted the ball towards goal. Luckily, it flew past Wexford goalkeeper, Ted Morrissey.

The Wexford backs were screaming at referee, Pat Delaney that I had over-carried but he was having none of it. The goal stood, Kilkenny won and we were on our way. Wexford were doubly annoyed with the referee for not penalising me because they had a goal disallowed in the first half when the referee decided that Eamonn Sinnott was in the square before the ball arrived. Such are the tight margins that can not only decide a game but change the course of history. If we had lost to Wexford that day, who knows what the next few seasons would have brought? Maybe Wexford, not us, would have become the dominant force.

I was delighted with myself after the Wexford win. I scored 1-5 and was also involved in our first goal just before half-time, which was finished by John Power after my shot was saved. It was all so different to the miserable day against Offaly a year before, not just for Kilkenny but also for me personally. I'd made a mark this time so at least I knew I could handle the pressure of playing in the senior championship. A year is a long time to have to wait to get a second chance, but players had no choice back then. That's why the second chance system which applies nowadays is a much better way of doing business. The overall format may be open to question, but nobody can dispute that it makes sense to ensure that every player is guaranteed a minimum of two championship games.

Having beaten Wexford in 1991, we felt we could make a lot more progress but we got an early shock against Dublin who pushed us all the way to the finish line in the final. We looked to be on our way to a fairly easy win when an early goal by Adrian Ronan helped us into a five point lead but Dublin dug in and were back level early in the second half. We went four points clear on the hour mark but Dublin kept coming back at us and while we eventually won by two points, it took a great save from Michael Walsh right at the death to keep us in front. A shot spun through several backs and forwards so Michael didn't see it until very late, but somehow he got a touch to it and pulled off a match-winning save.

No doubt about it, we had enjoyed a fair share of luck against both Wexford and Dublin and there was more to come in the All-Ireland semi-final against Antrim. It's easy to forget nowadays when, unfortunately, Antrim aren't going all that well, just how good they were in the late eighties/early nineties. They reached the 1989 All-Ireland final and could well have beaten us in the 1991 semi-final. It was level later on, after a really good contest when we got a sideline ball and Ollie Walsh waved me over to take it.

He probably thought there was a chance I'd score but, instead, I scuffed it. That's where our good luck kicked in. It could easily have gone to an Antrim man but instead it landed with Eamonn Morrissey, who swivelled and fired the ball over his shoulder. It was pure instinct by Eamonn but he found the target to put us back in the lead. Right man, right place. Eamonn played a blinder that day, scoring 2-4 from open play and generally looking like a man who could do no wrong. From the puck-out, I got the ball and drove it over the bar to put us two points clear. Game over – we were in the All-Ireland final.

We had beaten Wexford, Dublin and Antrim by two points each so I suppose it was to be expected that our luck would run out sometime. It did – in the All-Ireland final! We would have to admit that Tipperary were the better team overall, but a few things happened that day that suggested the gods had taken a turn against us. We lost John Power with a bad injury, conceded a fluke goal, and I was desperately unlucky not to score a goal which might have made a big difference.

In fairness, Tipperary had their problems too. Nicky English and Cormac Bonnar were carrying injuries and had to be replaced in the course of the game but the other member of that deadly full-forward trio chose the biggest day of all to cut loose. Pat Fox hit every sweet spot, scoring 0-5 from play on one of those days when the ball seemed to break his way all the time and every decision he made turned out to be the right one.

Every player has a day like that sometime but when it comes in an All-Ireland final, it's extra special. The reverse can also be true, of course. Indeed, very often the difference between a great performance and an average one is so small as to be almost unnoticeable but, boy, can it change an awful lot. A good example came in the 1991 final. At one stage, Liam Fennelly had a shot blocked and as it came off Ken Hogan, I was charging in. Normally, it would be the simplest of tap-ins but I skidded at the wrong moment and couldn't make contact.

Given that it was touch-and-go all the way through, a goal was always going to be a huge plus for whoever got it first. Had I netted off that half-chance, it might have made all the difference, just as Tipperary's goal did when it eventually came in the second half. Referee, Willie Horgan adjudged that Bill Hennessy had fouled Nicky English about twenty-three metres out and to the left side of the Tipperary attack.

Michael Cleary went for a point but didn't make the cleanest of connections. The ball clipped off Liam Walsh's hurley on its way towards goal and dipped into the net. A total fluke, but it counted every bit as much as if it were the end result of a sweeping move. Michael Cleary was one of the most reliable free-takers in the business at the time and nineteen times out of twenty, would have tapped the ball over the bar, but on the one occasion that he didn't make a proper connection, he was rewarded with what proved to be a match-changing goal.

Now the fact is that the free should never have been awarded in the first place. Liam did absolutely nothing wrong but was still whistled up. I would say that, wouldn't I? Okay then, try this assessment of the decision to award Tipperary a free.

"It was – without doubt – a harsh decision."

And who was convinced of that? None other than Nicky English, the man who was allegedly fouled! He wrote that in his book and that's good enough for me. Fair play to him for being so honest, by the way. That goal gave Tipperary a cushion and while we battled on as best we could, they held the lead all the way to the finish, eventually winning by 1-16 to 0-15. I felt especially sorry for Christy Heffernan that day. He gave Bobby Ryan a fierce hard time in the first half, but we didn't make anything like enough of the advantages he created.

It was also a day that marked the end of an era for a family that had done so much for Kilkenny over almost thirty years. There had been a Henderson on the Kilkenny team – quite often two of them at the same time – since the 1960s but the 1991 final brought the end of the line as it was John's last game in the black-and-amber. Older brothers, Pat and my great hero, Ger had done more than their fair share of brilliant defending over the years too as did John right up to the very end. It was a pity that he didn't go out with an All-Ireland medal but it wasn't to be. Still, he had won three All-Irelands prior to that, which is a fair haul for any player.

You always look back after an All-Ireland defeat and wonder what might have happened, but in all honesty, we could have no real complaints at the end of 1991. Okay, so maybe the free that brought Tipperary's goal in the final should not have been awarded, but who would have won if the decision had gone our way? Who knows? Realistically, the odds would have favoured Tipperary who were a more experienced outfit.

While the crucial call on that free in the All-Ireland final went against us, the whole season would have been a write off for us if Pat Delaney had decided I over-carried before booting the ball to the Wexford net in the Leinster semi-final. Instead, we got a vital break and made it count all the way to the All-Ireland final but, on balance, we could have no complaints about not ending the year as All-Ireland champions.

Tipperary had been the more impressive team all through that summer, beating Limerick easily, dethroning 1990 All-Ireland champions, Cork in an epic Munster final replay and wiping out Galway in the All-Ireland semi-final.

It was as if their name was on the title from a long way out and they weren't going to be denied. As for Kilkenny, it was disappointing to lose the final but, deep down, we felt it was a temporary setback. There was a sense that things were coming together nicely and that if we stuck together and worked hard a return to power wasn't that far away.

We were right. Glory days beckoned.

CHAPTER 5

DOUBLE EVENTS CAST THEIR SHADOWS BEFORE

By the spring of 1992, the Kilkenny public were growing very impatient. They hadn't seen the Liam MacCarthy Cup in Kilkenny hands since Liam Fennelly had captained the team to win the All-Ireland in 1983, which seemed like a different age.

By Kilkenny standards, it was a very long time indeed. In fact, it was the widest gap without an All-Ireland win since the ten year wait of 1947-1957. Between 1984 and 1991, Liam MacCarthy visited Cork three times, Galway and Tipperary twice each and Offaly once. It was as if Kilkenny had offended him in some way and he wasn't keen on coming back.

Okay, he flirted with the idea in 1991 but eventually settled for another year in Tipperary. By mid-February 1992, there were few signs that he had any intention of re-acquainting himself with Kilkenny anytime soon.

Back then, the National Leagues started in October, and while we beat Laois in the opening game, we took a big hammering from Tipperary in the All-Ireland final re-match in Thurles in early November. That might have been put down to post All-Ireland hangover but we had little excuse for what happened in the first League game of 1992 against Limerick in the Gaelic Grounds.

We were beaten out the gate and down the Ennis Road. Limerick led by eleven points at half-time and went on to win by 1-18 to 0-7. I went off injured around the three-quarter mark and because we had been doing so badly up to then, Ollie Walsh had understandably used all the allowed subs (three at that stage) so we had to play with fourteen men for the final fifteen minutes. I don't think we would have won with twenty players that day, let alone fourteen.

The defeat left us fourth of six in Division 1A and looking nervously towards the relegation door, rather than in the direction of the semi-final places. To say the least, Ollie wasn't best pleased with us.

We had two games to save ourselves from relegation and we managed to do that, beating Offaly by two points and Down by seven up in Ballycran. It took us to third place on the 1A table, not good enough to keep us going in the competition.

Once we had avoided relegation, Ollie kept telling the media that the championship was our target all along and that we weren't overly concerned with dropping out of the League. He was right with the first part – the championship was the big ambition – but our League form hadn't exactly flashed out warning signals to all our rivals that we were going to be a mighty force later on.

In fact, by the time we reached the Leinster final, many people thought we were ripe for the plucking by Wexford. We beat Offaly by six points in the semi-final, thanks to a solid performance in the final 20 minutes after trailing by three points at half-time.

A huge amount of hype surrounded the Leinster final against Wexford, much of which was brought on by the presence of Cyril Farrell in their camp.

Cyril was the man who masterminded three All-Ireland titles with Galway in the 1980s and was rightly regarded as one of the smartest hurling men around. Galway had beaten Kilkenny in the 1986 All-Ireland semi-final and the 1987 final so, presumably, Wexford reckoned he could help them plan an ambush for us. It was an interesting move.

Having felt so hard done by a year earlier, Wexford regarded this as their big chance but, if it was, they didn't take it. More accurately, we didn't allow them to take it. More than 40,000 people turned out for the final in Croke Park expecting a real ding-dong struggle but instead they got a game where the outcome was never in any real doubt.

We hurled well within ourselves, yet still led by three points at half time and pressed on comfortably in the second half to win by ten points. It was a fierce let down for Wexford but, in fairness, we had played very well. Maybe something big was on its way.

We beat Galway in the All-Ireland semi-final, a day I really enjoyed as things ran very kindly for me. I played in a variety of positions but it was when I moved to full-forward in the second half that the chances really started coming. It was all square in the third quarter before we pressed on from there to win by four points and set up an All-Ireland final date with Cork, the champions of two years earlier. They had dethroned Tipperary in Munster which was probably the performance of the championship so they went into the All-Ireland final as favourites. Nothing new there, of course. It was the same ten years earlier but it counted for nothing as Kilkenny beat them easily. We felt in 1992 that while Cork had many of the players that won the All-Ireland in 1986 and 1990, we could more than match them. After all, we had enjoyed no luck whatsoever against Tipperary in 1991, yet were only four points adrift at the finish. A year on, we had a lot more experience.

All-Ireland final day was wet, windy and miserable. Every player hates the wind but when it's accompanied by rain, it piles on the problems. Of all days, you hope to avoid that on All-Ireland final Sunday. We played against the elements in the first half, under strict instructions from Ollie to keep everything as tight as possible. Playing with the wind is always a big advantage but it won't win individual battles, nor will it decide who's quicker onto the breaking ball or who gets in the hooks, tackles or blocks. Quite simply, it's an aid but no more.

We gave a text book exhibition of how to play against the wind in the first half that day. We restricted Cork to eight points but, crucially, we scored 1-2 so, in effect, the conditions had minimal impact. I scored the goal from a penalty just before half-time with a shot which would not have been my usual penalty-taking style. I'd always aim for a spot about a foot or eighteen inches below the bar on the basis that it's the most difficult part of the goal area to protect. But, with the wind blowing into my face that day, I decided to go lower, much lower.

Liam Fennelly did his best to get me a new ball, slipping one into a towel while I was drying the other one but the Cork boys spotted it and started yelling at the referee, Dickie Murphy. He made sure I stuck with the original ball which was, of course, that bit heavier than usual because of the wet conditions. It would have been easier to strike a new, dry, ball but Dickie, helpfully alerted by screaming Cork defenders, was having none of it. Funny enough, I could have sworn I saw a bag of balls in the Cork net so I can only assume that the one Ger Cunningham pucked out after each score or wide was not always the one that had gone dead.

Anyway, I wasn't going to let little sideshows fluster me. I drilled the shot low, skidding the ball off the wet surface and it whizzed into the net. Despite the conditions and the concern that if it were saved, Cork would have got a big psychological lift, it never crossed my mind to go for the safe option and take a point. For a start, I always believed that you had to go for a goal from a penalty. Three men in the goal and you're hitting the ball from 14-16 metres range (yes, penalty takers are good at gaining ground before they make the strike!), you have to go for it.

Besides, I was under orders from Ollie to go for a goal if the chance arose. As a former goalkeeper, he knew how hard it is to stop a well-hit shot from that range.

In a sense, that goal in the '92 final was worth more than three points. Cork had huffed and puffed but, for all their effort, they were only three points ahead after having the elements behind them. The goal left us well-placed for the second half, although just as the wind hadn't done a whole lot for Cork, we knew it would be the same for us unless we got our game working properly which we largely did.

The rain eased off and while the wind was still strong, it was easier to play than in the first half. Still, it was a day for tough men and they don't come much tougher than John Power. He scored a crucial goal in the second half, bursting through with a few Cork backs hanging off him before booting the ball to the net. Liam McCarthy got another and while Cork made a real fight of it, we were not going to be denied.

We won by four points after out-scoring Cork by 2-8 to 1-4 in the second half but our doggedness in the first half was probably just as important as it meant that we weren't left chasing a big lead.

Irrespective of how many All-Ireland medals a player wins, the first is always extra special. You have joined an exclusive club and whatever happens from there on, that sense of achievement can never be taken away from you. I went on to win four more All-Irelands and while they were all distinctive in their own way, the 1992 win holds a special place in my memory. It had to. Still two months short of my 21st birthday, I had completed the All-Ireland medal set, senior, U-21 and minor. By the end of the year, I had my second All-Star award. Not bad for that skinny little lad who used to love banging the ball off the wall back home in Gowran.

If 1992 was special in that it brought me my first All-Ireland senior medal, 1993 was something else altogether as I won Leinster and All-Ireland medals, an All Star award and, to crown it all, picked up the Texaco Hurler of the Year award.

I also received a lower-profile but hugely satisfying honour that year. The now-defunct *Sunday Press* launched the Players' Player of the Year award scheme in the early 1990s. It was a novel idea and involved players voting for their choices as provincial and overall players of the year.

Only players from a particular province could vote for their provincial winner while the overall winner was chosen by votes from all over the country. I won the Leinster and National Award in 1993 which was extra special, because I was chosen by fellow-players as opposed to journalists or the general public.

Because it was run by the *Sunday Press*, publicity for the scheme was confined to one paper only, but that in no way took away from the fact that the players loved the idea and were happy to submit their votes.

Still, the Texaco award was as the ultimate individual honour as the scheme had been running for many years, catering for all the main sports, so I was delighted to join the select group of hurlers who were in that particular club. The award usually went to someone from the All-Ireland champions but that wasn't the case with Kilkenny in 1992 when a Cork youngster by the name of Brian Corcoran won it. Yes, that Brian Corcoran!

It was some achievement at a number of levels. He was only 19 years old and still in his first season. He was also a corner-back. Now, that should not matter but history has shown that men who occupy the No. 2 and No. 4 jerseys don't tend to win the big individual awards very often. Brian broke the trend in 1992, having made his first big statement in the

Munster semi-final when he did a great marking job on the 1991 Hurler of the Year, Pat Fox.

When I won the award in 1993, I became the first Kilkenny man to get it since the great Frank Cummins in 1983. Mind you, the prospects of any Kilkenny man being Hurler of the Year in 1993 looked flaky earlier in the year when we somehow managed to get ourselves relegated to Division 2.

We were in a six-team group with Tipperary, Limerick, Down, Offaly and Antrim and after winning two of four games, it all came down to the last round where we played Down in Nowlan Park. Young supporters might be amazed to learn that there was indeed a time when Down were a big threat, not just to Kilkenny but to everyone else too.

The Spring of 1993 was definitely such a time. We were level on points with them going into the game in Nowlan Park, with the winners to qualify for the knock-out stages and the losers to be relegated. Surely, the All-Ireland champions were in no danger of losing to Down and being relegated. Yes, we were.

Sunday, 21 March 1993 is still regarded as one of the most famous days in Down hurling history. Understandably so, because they beat us by a point (1-12 to 1-11) after scoring four late points to wipe out a three point lead and edge home by one. We had been well-warned in advance because apart from winning two of their previous four games, Down had come very close to beating Tipperary up in Ballycran. They eventually lost by three points but felt hard done by after some crucial refereeing decisions went against them.

They hurled superbly against us, battling like demons for every ball. Basically, they wanted the points more than we did and fully deserved to get them. We had no excuses. It wasn't as if we were well below full-strength or anything like that. In fact, we had nearly all of the 1992 All-Ireland winning team on duty but if we ever got a lesson on how reputations count for nothing if you don't raise your game, we got it that day. Offaly and ourselves were relegated; Down and Antrim stayed in Division 1.

Now, while Ollie Walsh would not have been one to place a big emphasis on the League, he wouldn't have expected Kilkenny to drop into Division 2 either and certainly not six months after winning the All-Ireland title.

Still, in an odd sort of way, it might have been the makings of us for the rest of the season.

We now knew exactly where we stood. Equally importantly, so did others, so unless we got our act together, the championship season wouldn't last very long. Ollie had us exactly where he wanted us. Mind you, so did Offaly in the first round of the Leinster championship in late May, when they led us by two points with five minutes left. They had been through a disappointing League campaign too, but were much sharper than us for most of that first round game.

We had scored only 1-9 in 65 minutes. But then along came the chance to turn the day around, and we took it. I found John Power with a pass and he was flattened as he broke in on goal. Penalty. Over to me. I struck the ball well, it flew into the net and we were back in business. I landed a long range point from a free afterwards, leaving us two-point winners.

We were lucky to make it. Offaly had half-back, Roy Mannion sent off eight or nine minutes from the end, forcing them to re-jig the team. It left them with five forwards and, significantly, they didn't score from there on. It's a game I recall fondly as it went very well for me. I scored 2-4 of our 2-10 total and always felt as if I could do damage when the ball came my way.

If the gods were with us for the Offaly game, they were even closer friends in the Leinster final against Wexford. Of all the close calls we survived throughout my career, the 1993 drawn Leinster final is one that really stands out.

For a start, the standard of hurling was very high. We were defending All-Ireland champions while Wexford had just come off a three-match League final epic against Cork which they lost in the second replay. Three years later, thirteen of the same team played in the All-Ireland final when they beat Limerick which gives you a fair idea of the talent at their disposal in that period.

A great contest ebbed and flowed but with seven minutes remaining it was Wexford who appeared to have made the final break when they pulled four points clear. It was looking ominous for us but we plugged on anyway. Eamonn Morrissey, who scored 2-3 in one of his best games for Kilkenny, pointed twice and I fired over a free to leave us one short.

The equalising point was probably one of the best ever scored in Croke Park. Liam Simpson, Bill Hennessy and Adrian Ronan were all involved in a sweeping move, which presented Morrissey with the chance and, given the form he was in that day, the finish was a formality.

Somehow, we had rescued ourselves from what looked a desperate situation. The Wexford players were devastated and they showed it. You could see it in their body language as they left the field. They had given everything and yet were caught at the end. It would be hard for them to lift their game for the replay, whereas we were so delighted to have got a second chance that we couldn't wait for the next day.

We won the replay easily enough a week later in front of a crowd of nearly 42,000. That's the thing about the Kilkenny-Wexford rivalry. It will always draw the crowds when both sides are going well, which was the case twenty years ago. Okay, so Wexford weren't winning any titles but who's to say that if they had beaten us in 1993, they wouldn't have gone on to take the All-Ireland?

Instead, we won the two-in-a-row, beating Galway by five points in the final. It was a solid, if not exactly spectacular performance by us. We led by three points at half-time, Galway came back to take the lead, we battled back to lead again and then PJ Delaney scored the vital goal which put us four points clear a few minutes from the end. I finished off the scoring with a point from play.

As in 1982-83, we had won the All-Ireland double and would, of course, go on to do same a decade later. I was happy enough with my own performance in the 1993 final, even if I didn't score as much as in previous games, yet in the following day's papers, there were a number of references to how I had been off-colour.

The pressure was beginning to build. Unless, I scored 2-7 to 2-8 in every game, I almost had to explain myself. What did people expect? I landed some pressure frees against Galway, worked as hard as I possibly could, yet people seemed to want more. The 1993 final would later be used to support the theory that I didn't play well in All-Ireland finals, an argument which simply doesn't hold up.

As far as I was concerned, All-Ireland finals – or any other games for that matter – were never about how much I scored. My role was the same as everybody else's – work hard for the common good and hope everything gelled as a unit. However, as the years passed it seemed I was only being judged on how much I scored.

In 1993, I was quite happy with my contribution in the All-Ireland final. And whatever the knockers thought, I had another All-Ireland medal, a third All Star and a Hurler of the Year award by the end of the year.

If I had been told at the end of 1993 that it would be seven years before Kilkenny would win their next All-Ireland title, I would have assumed it was the delusional ramblings of someone who hated us. Granted, we had lived fairly dangerously in Leinster over the previous few seasons, but we had survived every time. Wexford and Offaly were right on our heels but there was still no reason to believe that over the next few seasons we would slip from No. 1 to No. 3.

That's exactly the path we took. It's hard to rationalise what happened in 1994 and 1995 when Offaly trimmed us into oblivion in Leinster. Their four point win in the 1994 semi-final was not an accurate reflection of their superiority – they should have won by a lot more. Worse still, their eleven-point win in the 1995 Leinster final didn't come anywhere near telling the full story of how dominant they were that day either.

It says something about a team's performance when they are flattered by an 11-point defeat but such was the case with us in 1995. We never saw it coming. How could we, for God's sake? We sailed through the League like a team whose batteries had been re-charged since being knocked out of the championship in June the year before.

Our march to the final included putting Offaly in their place in the League semi-final in Thurles. They had won the 1994 All-Ireland so there was a real edge to the League semi-final. We both knew it was likely we would be meeting again in the championship so there were markers to be put down. We sunk them deep into the Semple Stadium turf (at least it looked like that at the time), hitting Offaly for four goals and winning by six points (4-8 to 0-14). I scored three of the goals on a day when most things went right for me.

Much was made of our relatively easy win, yet Offaly had scored more often than we had. You don't lose many games when you score four goals but we managed only eight points, a low return by any standards. Still when we beat Clare by 2-12 to 0-9 in the final, we looked well set up for the Championship.

Who would have thought leaving Semple Stadium in early May after we had beaten Clare by nine points that four months later, they would be All-Ireland champions for the first time in decades. We restricted them to two points in the second half of the League final and didn't really have to do anything special to win.

Perhaps the first real sign that something wasn't quite right with us came in the first round of the Leinster Championship when we were incredibly lucky to come out of Dr. Cullen Park with a win over Laois. It took a great save from Joe Dermody, who had come on as a sub for the injured Michael Walsh to deny Laois a victory they probably deserved. We scraped across the finish line, winning by two points after trailing for much of the way.

Don't get me wrong. Laois had a lot of fine hurlers, men like Niall Rigney, Cyril Duggan, Bill Maher, Joe Dollard, Fint Lalor and Ricky Cashin but we would have been expected to win more comfortably than we did. We looked a lot sharper in the semi-final against Dublin, winning even more easily than the 4-13 to 2-10 scoreline suggests. We led by 4-12 to 0-6 with a quarter of an hour left and as we throttled back a bit, Dublin scored 2-4, which gave the scoreboard a decent look without in any way threatening us. Eamonn Morrissey scored 2-4 that day in a golden spell before having to go off injured.

For a second successive year, Offaly awaited us in the final, them as All-Ireland champions, us as League champions. In theory, it should have been quite a showdown. Our win over them in the League semi-final made us favourites to win again but, boy, did we get a right shock.

Much was made afterwards about how we were almost drowned by a deluge just after we came out for the pre-match warm-up. What we did probably wasn't very smart, although I don't think it had any real bearing on the actual game. We were having our puckaround just as the torrents began to fall. We kept going for a while but as the downpour got heavier, we decided to cut our losses and dashed over to the dug-outs for shelter. Offaly had taken a look out but quickly retreated to the dressing-rooms and waited for the thunder shower to pass.

We were pretty miserable in our wet jerseys but if it was going to have an impact, you would have expected it to be in the first half. We actually did okay in the first half and were only two points behind at the interval. However, the second-half turned into the ultimate nightmare. It was something similar to the first half of the 2012 Leinster final when Galway ran riot against Kilkenny. Offaly steamrolled us.

They led by 2-14 to 0-5 on the hour mark, by which stage any prospect of a Kilkenny win had long since vanished. I got two late goals to take the bare look off the scoreline, but it still made pretty alarming reading for us: Offaly 2-16 Kilkenny 2-5. It was Kilkenny's biggest defeat in a Leinster final since 1976 and was also the first time in history that Offaly had beaten Kilkenny in successive Leinster finals. Not a day to remember then.

Not a year to remember either, even if we had won the League. Winning the League is a nice appetiser for the championship, but it can never be more than that, especially in Kilkenny where you're judged solely on how you do in summer and autumn. At the end of 1995 one word dominated our report card – failed.

In reality, we were slipping. The peaks of 1992-93 seemed a long way off, obscured from view by the heavy dark clouds brought in by two clear-cut defeats by Offaly. There was a lot of frustration in Kilkenny, which helped nobody's mood. Ollie decided his time as manager was up. He stood down and was replaced by Nickey Brennan.

Now Nickey was – and is – such an enthusiast for all things hurling and all things Kilkenny, but he would probably be the first to acknowledge that he got the manager's job at a bad time. Things were beginning to stir in Wexford while Offaly were still a major power, so even before we even looked outside Leinster, major threats abounded on our doorstep.

Ever so slowly and surely, Liam Griffin was beginning to get a tune out of Wexford, whom we were drawn to play in the first round of the 1996 championship. We were still favourites to win, largely because Wexford hadn't beaten us in the championship for eight years, while they had also taken a bit of a tanking against Galway in the League semi-final two months earlier. Still, they had reached the knock-out stages and with Griffin working hard on convincing them that they could achieve anything they targeted, their mood changed in the weeks before the championship.

To add to our concern, I pulled a hamstring a week or two before the game and shouldn't have played because I wasn't even at half power. On top of that, John Power couldn't start the game because of a chest infection. I was bandaged from hip to ankle in an effort to somehow get through the game but I was so badly restricted that it was all a bit pointless. Suffice to say, playing against defenders like Liam Dunne, Ger Cushe, Roy Guiney and Larry O'Gorman was not recommended unless you were in the whole of your health. And that's before you came in contact with Seanie Flood, one of the toughest and strongest defenders I have ever encountered. He was unbelievably powerful in the pull, especially along the ground.

It was fiercely disappointing for him to miss out on the 1996 All-Ireland final through injury. Still, he did well afterwards when 'Dancing at the Crossroads' became the anthem for Wexford's glory run through the championship! Mind you, it didn't make up for missing the big day but no one in Wexford has forgotten how much he contributed to making it happen in the first place.

You'd have to say Wexford didn't look like future All-Ireland champions the day they beat us. They led by five points at half-time but we cut the margin back to one in the third quarter before they kicked on again and a goal by Billy Byrne set them on their way to a three-point win. I had to go off in the second half simply because I wasn't able to run. It was the right call but, as luck would have it, we got a few close-in frees in the last six or seven minutes which I would have fancied having a crack at. We needed a goal and weren't creating the chances in open play. I was almost on one leg and while it all but cut me out of the game in general play, it wouldn't have made that much difference from a free. Wexford should have been further ahead, but instead, we were still within striking distance right at the end. So if only I had a chance from one of those frees ... who knows how 1996 might have turned out.

Watching Wexford build brick-by-brick throughout the summer only served to add to our frustration. We were pleased for Wexford on the basis that if we couldn't win the All-Ireland there was no one we would have preferred to see doing well than them, especially the long serving lads like George and John O'Connor, Billy Byrne, Tom Dempsey, Martin Storey and Seanie Flood.

Still, the competitive instinct in a sports person wants to win everything and there were plenty of times during the summer of 1996 when I thought to myself; 'if only that hamstring hadn't gone'.

There were no such regrets at the end of 1997 for the simple reason that we got two bites of the championship cherry, and still came up short. The 'back door' was opened for the first time in 1997, albeit in a more limited way than nowadays, as the beaten Leinster and Munster finalists were the only provincial losers to get a second chance.

Not everyone agreed with the change at the time, on the basis that it might take away from the Leinster and Munster finals, since both the winners and losers would go through to the All-Ireland stages anyway. Mind you, the players were all for it for the very obvious reason that it offered another route to the All-Ireland championship.

As for impacting on the Leinster and Munster finals, there was no need to worry about that in 1997. Between them, the two finals drew nearly 100,000 people to Croke Park and Thurles for Kilkenny v Wexford and Clare v Tipperary.

We got an early glimpse of what to expect in the Leinster semi-finals which attracted over 52,000 to Croke Park for Kilkenny v Dublin and Offaly v Wexford. Dublin were showing real promise under Michael O'Grady at the time and while we started well, they hit back with two goals and led by five points at half-time.

Play was held up for a period to allow an overspill of supporters to cross from the Cusack to the Hogan Stand. Dublin felt that it broke their momentum somewhat and that they would have been further ahead at half-time if it weren't for that. They were still ahead, heading into the final ten minutes, but PJ Delaney and myself got in for goals and we ran out seven point winners, which certainly wasn't a true reflection of the actual game.

It must have been a strange experience for Dublin's top scorers, James 'Shiner' Brennan and Eamonn Morrissey, as only a few years earlier they had been tormenting Dublin while wearing black-and-amber jerseys. However, since both were based in the Capital, they transferred to Dublin, something that was quite common in hurling down through the years as quite a few Kilkenny men wore the blue jersey.

It's different nowadays with motorway all the way from Kilkenny to Dublin, but back then, travelling up and down all the time must have been very wearing.

Wexford beat Offaly in the other semi-final in 1997 to set up the first Kilkenny-Wexford Leinster final for four years, only this time the roles were reversed. We were All-Ireland champions in 1993, now Wexford were the kingpins and the favourites.

A crowd of nearly 55,000 turned out for the final, with Wexford supporters out-numbering ours by about two to one. There's massive support for Wexford hurling when they're going well and with the county still aglow after the previous year's All-Ireland win, they were determined to make Croke Park a purple and gold fortress.

Not that it fazed us and by half-time we were five points clear and looking good. However, the balance changed dramatically in the second half. Wexford improved everywhere and the introduction of super-sub, Billy Byrne, then 37 years old, but still as deadly as ever, made a massive difference. The old warrior scored 1-2 which effectively won the game.

It was a strange sensation watching Wexford being presented with the Bob O'Keeffe Cup. They were obviously delighted with what they regarded as unquestioned confirmation of their superiority in Leinster after winning the two-in-a-row but, from our perspective, we were thinking that we might come across them again in the All-Ireland final.

As it happened, the 1997 All-Ireland final was a re-run of the Munster (Clare v Tipperary) rather than Leinster final but we weren't to know that as we left Croke Park on that mid-July evening.

Two weeks later, we were back in action in the All-Ireland quarter-final against Galway in Thurles. Then, as now, you never quite knew what to expect from Galway. They could blow hot or cold, depending on the mood. As it happened they did both that day, in a game which was a brilliant advertisement for the new championship format.

It's also a game I look back on with huge satisfaction as just about everything went right for me. Mind you, it needed to, as Galway set us a target which should have been too much. Kevin Broderick, Liam Burke and Joe Cooney scored first half goals to leave Galway leading by 3-9 to 1-6 at half-time (we were ten points down just before the break). I had scored Kilkenny's goal, but despite a rousing speech by Nickey Brennan at half-time, pegging back a nine-point lead two weeks after losing the Leinster final looked like a bridge too far.

It wasn't. Remarkably, we won the second half by 3-9 to 0-7. We scored exactly the same amount as Galway had in the first half but, crucially, conceded two points less. There are days when you feel that you can't go wrong, and this was one of them for me. Whenever I made a run, the ball came my way, the breaks fell in my direction too and the longer it went, the more I felt I could do.

Nigel Shaughnessy was marking me for some of the time, before being replaced by Padraig Kelly. Shaughnessy was a good young wing-back, who had won All-Ireland minor and U-21 medals and would have been regarded as a stylish defender. But, for some reason, he tried to turn it into a physical battle. He gave me the odd dig here and there, presumably trying to put me off my game but I never minded that. I always preferred to be marked by someone who was trying to turn it into a physical confrontation rather than someone who left it all to skill. Nigel was a skilful hurler and would probably have done a lot better by marking me on that basis rather than niggling away all the time. In fact, he played right into my hands by doing that.

It wasn't especially rough or anything like that, but I felt from early on that he was more interested in stopping me than from stopping the ball getting to me. It was a risky strategy. After all, the more often a forward gets possession, the greater the chance that he'll do some damage.

The second half of the 1997 quarter-final was as good a performance by Kilkenny as I was ever involved in. It wasn't that Galway collapsed, but rather that we moved up a few gears. Even then, they responded when we went two points clear after myself and Michael 'Titch' Phelan scored goals. Three points put them ahead again but we struck for a fourth goal from Ken O'Shea. We won by 4-15 to 3-16 in a game that got rave reviews in the media. Rightly so. It had just about everything and was all the sweeter from our perspective because we had staged such a great recovery. I ended up on 2-8 but, even more importantly, the nature of our win against a very good Galway team suggested that we were genuine contenders for the All-Ireland.

Of course, the semi-final was always going to be a completely different type of game. Clare were at the peak of their considerable powers at the time, and after losing their Munster and All-Ireland titles in a defeat by Limerick the year before, they were one driven force in 1997. They had beaten Cork and Tipperary in Munster so you can imagine how obsessed they were with adding Kilkenny to their list of victims.

They managed it too but I often wonder what might have been if fate and Davy Fitzgerald hadn't intervened so spectacularly.

We lost full-back, Liam Simpson and full-forward, 'Titch' Phelan to injury before the game which was a massive loss. We needed to have everyone aboard for the big test but instead Nickey was forced into carrying out pre-match repairs. Ten minutes into the game, we were six points down but we battled back and cut the margin to two.

What happened next may have had a huge bearing on the game. We were awarded a penalty which I took with ferocious power. I thought the net would shake but Davy Fitz somehow blocked the ball in as fine a save from a penalty as I have ever seen. When you have a penalty blocked you always ask yourself if you could have hit it harder or more accurately into that unmanned area under the crossbar. On this occasion, I was quite happy with everything except, of course, Davy's unbelievable save! That was Davy, always capable of producing the stunning save at a crucial time.

A goal at that stage might have made a huge difference to the course of the game. Instead, the save lifted Clare and they increased the lead to ten or eleven points in the second half before we staged something of a recovery. I got in for a goal and by the end, the margin was down to four points. Clare were rattled in the closing minutes but we had left ourselves with too much to do after falling so far behind earlier on. And then there was that penalty save from Davy!

Anyway, Clare were on their way to a second All-Ireland title in three seasons and we had established an unfortunate record as the first team to lose two championship games in the one year. It wasn't exactly where Kilkenny ever thought they would find themselves.

Still, when you lose two games in the championship, you can have no excuses. You can always offer reasons why one game went against you but not two. When that happens it's best to accept the reality that the team just isn't good enough, something we had to do in 1997.

CHAPTER 6

MY TIME-OUT CONTROVERSY

It was a mistake and I regretted it pretty quickly. There I was at the age of 27, having just announced that I was quitting hurling. It didn't make sense to the Kilkenny public, who couldn't understand why I'd walk away from the black-and-amber at such a young age for an inter-county player; it didn't make sense to the wider hurling community who were just plain baffled by my decision and, very shortly after I'd announced my retirement in early February 1998, it didn't make much sense to me either. A bad call all around then.

Gone at 27? Why? The first week in February was a relatively quiet time in the GAA world that year so the media jumped on the story, dissecting it from every angle and as the competition grew to produce explanations as to why I'd quit, so did the fanciful theories. Mind you, there were even more far-fetched stories circulating outside the media as to why I jumped ship.

Maybe I was a bit naïve, but I didn't think it would create such a stir. That changed within a matter of hours of me doing an interview with Brian Carthy 'live' on RTÉ radio early one morning, where I explained why I'd quit. Rumours have been rumbling for some time and when I heard that stories would appear in the morning papers, suggesting that I was ready to go, I decided I might as well tell it straight – otherwise it would have dragged on and I would have been pestered for a response. I said in the interview that my appetite for hurling had gone and that I'd always promised myself that once that happened I'd be out of the game like a shot. Hurling – then or now – is no place for anybody not totally committed to the cause.

I probably didn't handle it all that well. I would have liked to hold off for a while so that I could tell some key people in Kilkenny precisely what I was doing and why I was doing it, but once the newspaper stories broke, I felt I had to act straight away rather than allow the speculation to continue. Besides, I wouldn't have got a minute's peace. Not that the RTÉ interview brought any sense of calm. In fact, it fed the frenzy in a way I would never have imagined.

After the radio interview, my phone started ringing. And ringing – and ringing. Friends, colleagues, acquaintances, people I didn't know but who had met me somewhere, people who never met me but felt they knew me and many, many others from all walks of life sent goodwill messages. It was all a bit overwhelming. Humbling too. Lots of journalists were chasing me and while they would have heard my explanation on radio, they wanted to hear it from me again. They also wanted to delve into the decision, beginning every question with 'why'. I took as many calls as I could but after a while it just all became too much. Hell, a hurler had retired. Why all the fuss? Was there nothing else happening in the great wide world?

My retirement was one of the lead items on the six o'clock news on RTÉ television that evening and over the next few days I remained the focus of attention. I hadn't realised how popular hurling – or hurlers – were but then things had changed a fair bit over the previous few years. Various circumstances had come together to raise the game's profile.

Clare and Wexford returned from the wilderness in 1995 and 1996 respectively, winning All-Ireland titles. Guinness came aboard as All-Ireland sponsors in 1995 and led a big marketing drive for hurling. The 'back door' opened in 1997 to allow the beaten Leinster and Munster finalist to re-enter the All-Ireland race. They were all important elements in widening hurling's appeal.

A few days after I'd announced my departure, I saw an article in a paper which detailed how I had done in the twenty-five championship games I had played since making my debut in 1990. Details like that wouldn't be something I'd be aware of, but now that it looked like my final innings, it made interesting reading. I had scored a total of 18-110, of which 14-28 came from open play, the rest from frees and '65's. Kilkenny had won seventeen, drawn one and lost seven of the twenty-five games, accumulating two All-Ireland and three Leinster titles. In addition, we had won two National League titles.

My personal haul was pretty big too. I had won the Hurler of the Year award in 1993 and six All Star awards, including five-in-a-row in 1991-95. Looking at it from the outside, there was no reason in the world why I should walk away from the game that had been such a huge part of my life since I was a kid.

But then, things often appear different from the other side of the fence. That's something I'm always very conscious of when I look at any situation nowadays. Yes, I was still at the peak of my powers as a hurler, but there were niggling little issues which were draining me. Kilkenny hadn't won a Leinster or All-Ireland title since 1993 and frustrations were growing rapidly in the county. I felt I was carrying a huge responsibility every time I went out to play and while I was well able to carry the load for a while, it gradually began to wear me down. I was doing all I could to make things happen but it never seemed to be enough as far as some sections of the Kilkenny public were concerned.

And then there were the rumours. I was supposed to be fighting with various people in the club after we lost the 1997 county final to Dunnamaggin. I was also supposed to be against Kevin Fennelly's appointment as county manager after Nickey Brennan left at the end of the 1997 campaign.

It all got too much. I was running my own business at the time (DJ Carey Enterprises) and obviously that carried its own pressures. Pretty big ones too, at times. I'd be taking a free in a game on Sunday, trying to block out the fact that I needed to get ten thousand pounds in on Monday to keep the business ticking over. Pressure? The free wasn't but the thought of chasing down money on the following day weighed heavily. It was all very fine selling goods but would you get the money in? And would it be on time? And what if it wasn't? Meanwhile, there's a free to be taken, a game to be won and critical eyes watching my every move. It all got to me in the end.

I'd started the business at the age of 22, having worked in sales since I left secondary school. My first full-time job was with Cadbury (I'd worked part-time in Dunnes Stores while still in St. Kieran's College) and I then moved on to MF Kent, Three Rivers Oil and Moynihan & Moynihan in Cork. It was while I was with Moynihan & Moynihan that I got the idea to go out on my own, selling various hygiene products and chemicals.

Running a business was brand new territory for me and, with it, came pressures that I hadn't experienced before. I was learning as I went along and, at times, the demands were intense as I juggled to keep various balls in the air. There were occasions when it got very stressful. Trying to balance the books was mighty difficult and however hard I worked at putting it to the back of my mind so that it would not interfere with my hurling, it just wasn't possible.

Nobody can separate their work and sporting life to the degree where they don't interact. So if my overdraft facility was overheating in a week before a big game and I was trying to get money in to cool it down, hurling had to take its place in the queue of priorities.

Eddie Keher was my bank manager at the time and, as you would expect from such a great man, did all he could to smooth things over. He was a real gem. In those times, bank managers had more discretion than they do nowadays and Eddie always used his very fairly. He helped me in every way possible but there was only so much he could do.

Eventually, the books had to be balanced.

So while hurling might be the most important thing in my life on a Sunday afternoon, I knew that come Monday morning, it was back to the stresses of running a company where a lot of people depended on me. I was, to some degree, in over my head from the start. I had no formal training for running a business which made it all the harder. Learning as you go along is all very fine but you make mistakes and they can be costly. Having said that, I had plenty of good times too, but the stress was there all the time.

The more people you have working for you, the more demanding it gets. You say to yourself: "if I have ten people working, we'll sell five times as much as if there are two people on the road". But what happens when some of the ten aren't doing as well as you thought they would? What happens when some fella is supposed to be out selling but he's actually at home with his feet up? It's easier to keep track nowadays, but mobile phones were in the early stages of development when I went into business so contacting sales people was difficult, especially if they didn't want to be reached.

I hated having to deal with staff when problems arose. By nature, I'm not remotely confrontational so I dreaded having to call someone in to talk about their work or, more specifically, their attitude to work. On the hurling field, I'd go through ten swinging hurleys and a posse of scary defenders if I thought there was even an outside chance of scoring a goal, but I was completely different in business, certainly when it came to dealing with people who were working for me.

I made the mistake of holding on to a few for too long but then I hated letting anybody go because I knew how much it would impact on their lives. Telling someone there's no future for them in your company is a horrible thing to have to do. Well, at least it was for me. This wasn't some specialist HR person full of all the jargon but DJ Carey, the last man in the world who wanted to be in that position. Still, I had to do it a few times in order to stabilise the business. The thing about a small business is that very often the last person to get paid is the owner. That can become a nasty habit. Pay the staff, the bills, the other invoices and then, if there's anything left, pay yourself. It's not like doing a nine to five job for someone else where the money is in the envelope every Friday. I was often the last to be paid in my own business because that was the way it had to be at times.

I was poorly equipped to make hard decisions about staff. If someone wasn't doing well with sales and it had reached a stage where I knew it just wasn't going to work out, I'd call him in for a chat, hoping that he would sense what was coming but mostly he didn't. God, I hated that. You know something has to be done – and really the only solution is a parting of the ways – but you have to spell it out. It definitely wasn't something I knew how to handle, largely, I suppose, because it's not in my nature.

The situation was more difficult because I did a lot of hiring from within the GAA world so if someone had to be let go, it added to the awkwardness. Of course, I had people who worked out great too. Willie O'Connor, who was with me from the start, was superb. So too was Tommy Dowd, who went on to launch his own business after he left me.

Did I regret setting up the business rather than being just a regular employee somewhere else? Absolutely not, but I would have liked to have known at the start what I knew a few years later. It's the story of life, I suppose. I would have been better off with a smaller crew and running things more tightly. I expanded quite quickly and that brought its own challenges.

Being DJ Carey, well-known Kilkenny hurler, certainly helped to get me through doors but as anyone in the sales business will tell you, success is largely down to the quality of what you're selling, the price you're asking, the service you're providing and how you deal with people. There was nothing especially exclusive about my business. It wasn't a niche market or anything so there was always going to be lots of opposition and, over the years, it all became very competitive. And let's be honest, if you're buying toilet rolls or hygiene products, you don't really care whether or not your supplier is a well-known sportsman. A toilet roll is a toilet roll! All that matters is the price, the quality and the service.

Anyway, back to my decision to quit in 1998. The stress of running a business was taking its toll but there were other factors too. I was feeling the pressure of being expected to be a match-winner every time I played, whether for Kilkenny or Gowran. What did people expect? That I would score 2-8 or 2-9 every day? I did it against Galway in the 1997 All-Ireland quarter-final (scoring 2-8) but that was quickly forgotten when we lost to Clare in the semi-final.

Kilkenny supporters are pretty passionate about their hurling and they weren't a happy lot around the end of 1997. The previous four All-Ireland titles had been shared between Clare (2), Offaly and Wexford while the four Leinster titles had been split evenly between Offaly and Wexford. Kilkenny were down the line and the fans didn't like it. Naturally, those at the centre of the perceived hurling recession were coming under intense scrutiny.

There was serious unease in Kilkenny at the time and I felt that I was being blamed – in part at least – for not doing enough to turn things around. What more I could have done, I don't know. Kilkenny supporters found it hard to accept that Wexford and Offaly were the dominant forces in Leinster and I suppose they felt entitled to look for scapegoats. As one of the higher-profile players, I was an easy target.

On top of that, Gowran lost the 1997 county final to Dunnamaggin. Things didn't go well for me that day and naturally I was as disappointed as anybody else that we didn't manage to win the two-in-a-row. Again, I felt I was being held responsible to some extent for the defeat. Some lads will always get blamed when a team loses a county final and county players can expect to ship most of the load.

A few things went on in the background which added to the mix. My brother, Martin, who had been in goal when we won the county title for the first time in 1996, didn't want to play there in 1997. He was a very talented goalkeeper and would later get on to the Kilkenny panel but, in 1997, he wanted to try his luck as a forward.

Kevin Fennelly was the manager and it fell to me to tell him that Martin didn't want to play in goal. Maybe Martin thought it would make more of an impact coming from me or that Kevin would accept the reasoning behind the decision if I made the case. He didn't. As a former top class goalkeeper with Kilkenny and Ballyhale, there was nothing Kevin didn't know about the position so he wanted Martin to stay between the posts. However, Martin was hell bent on a change. Kevin said he would respect that and let him challenge for a position outfield. Martin had a go at that but it didn't work out and by the time we were coming to the latter stages of the county championship, he wanted to be considered for goal again.

However, the position was filled by Ollie Carter, a cousin of Charlie, who was doing well, so there was no way back in for Martin. The beat on the gossip drums claimed that I was annoyed with Kevin over not restoring Martin to the goalkeeping position for the county final. Not true. Martin had made his choice and it hadn't worked out so he had to live with the consequences. In fact, there would have been no one more vexed with him than me that he didn't want to continue playing in goal. That was his best position and, as far as I was concerned, that's where he should have been. Why he wanted to play in attack was beyond me, but once he had made his mind up, I supported him, even if I had a strong suspicion that it wouldn't work out. I had no issue whatsoever with Kevin over sticking by Ollie but, of course, once gossip starts, it's impossible to control it. And when we lost the final, the question of whether Martin should have been in goal was brought up again. It certainly wasn't raised by me, but because my brother was involved, I was dragged into the gossip.

In the great world of GAA, the club is closer to people's hearts than the county so what happens locally often has a greater impact on a community than events on the bigger stages. Fathers, mothers, brothers, sisters, uncles, aunts, cousins ... they all have a view on what happens in a club. And, of course, they are all right. So when we lost the 1997 county final to Dunnamaggin by three points, all sorts of stories began to do the rounds. DJ Carey v Kevin Fennelly over the goalkeeping and other issues were among the main ones. We were supposed to have been at each other's throats, which was complete and utter nonsense.

In fact, I was very friendly with Kevin. In late September that year, we even travelled together to Spain for the Ryder Cup in Valderrama. Kevin got to see a lot of more of the golf than I did because I picked up food poisoning early on in the trip. So while Seve Ballesteros and the European team were battling their way to a narrow win, I was back in my hotel, spending most of my time in the toilet and cursing my bad luck! It wasn't exactly the happiest trip for me, but the fact that I travelled with Kevin shows how well we got on.

Kevin had appointed me club captain in early 1996, a year we went on to win the county title for the first time after beating James Stephens in a replayed final. That gave me the chance to captain Kilkenny in 1997 so why on earth would I have anything against Kevin? Besides, I never had a problem with managers because I saw my role as a player and always ensured I stayed on my side of the line. Still, rumours have a nasty way of becoming fact in some people's minds.

Kevin had been with us as far back as 1992 when we won the intermediate title. Four years later, we won the county senior title for the first time. It was a huge achievement for the parish, one of the most special days in its history. We beat James Stephens in a replay in front of 15,000 people in Nowlan Park. The atmosphere was unreal and the game lived up to all expectations. We had a big lead at one stage but 'The Village' – managed by a certain Mr. Brian Cody – came back and drew level. It looked as if they were primed to finish the job but my brother, Jack popped up to score a late goal which swung it our way. I scored 2-4 of our 3-9 total so I was pretty happy with myself, especially as I was captain. Bringing the Cup back to Gowran was one of the most memorable events in my sporting life. People in the parish never thought they would see the day when Young Irelands, a club that was only formed in the early 1950s, would be Kilkenny champions, so you can imagine the excitement and sense of achievement everyone felt when we returned home with the Cup.

A year on when we lost the county final, the mood changed. People felt it was one we let slip and naturally I took a fair share of blame because I hadn't shot the lights out. And then I was supposed to be unhappy with Kevin which piled more fuel on the rumours fire.

So when Kevin was appointed county manager in late 1997 and I announced my retirement in January 1998, the conspiracy theorists added two and two and got a bit more than four. They decided I wouldn't play under Kevin.

Honestly, it would make you laugh if it hadn't been so frustrating. Ever since I was a kid, all I wanted to do was play hurling for Kilkenny and the idea that I would quit the panel over something like that was too daft for words. Apart from anything else, I always kept strict demarcation lines between club and county.

It was also claimed that I was unhappy with some of the things that went on in the county final. No doubt about it, some harsh stuff was dished out that day and I certainly felt some key decisions went against us but, again, the notion that it would cause me to walk away from the Kilkenny jersey was ridiculous. By the way, that county final marked the arrival of a certain Noel Hickey on the big stage. Noel, still a few months short of his 17th birthday, played at left corner-back for Dunnamaggin and looked very much like a youngster who was destined for a great future which, of course, proved to be the case.

We just didn't perform in the county final. We had gone very well all year but, for whatever reason, it didn't happy on county final day.

A few weeks later, we finished the year on a high, beating James Stephens by seven points in the county League final. I scored 2-9 that day and while it was nice to finish the season with a title, we were still fiercely disappointed over not winning the county final.

Another rich source of gossip after the county final arose from me not staying on the pitch for the presentation of the cup to Dunnamaggin. I meant no discourtesy but I was just so fed up with everything that I got out quickly.

When the final whistle sounded I shook hands with the Dunnamaggin players before heading for the dressing-room. I got changed as quickly as I could and headed for home with the cheers of the Dunnamaggin supporters ringing in my ears. Good luck to them – it was their day. I thought nothing of it at the time but, of course, my quick exit was noticed. Various motives were associated with it, all well wide of the mark but, hey, what's another piece of loose talk?

After we won the League final a few weeks later, I switched off for a while but when January came around, I didn't feel the usual yearning to get back hurling with Kilkenny. In fact, I felt so drained I just wanted out. It was a horrible feeling but it just wouldn't go away.

When I announced my retirement, there was supposed to be a lengthy menu of reasons behind the decision. There wasn't. It was simply a combination of factors and little things relating to work pressures and the responsibility I felt every time I played for club and county. Behind it all were the nasty rumours and gossip. I felt mentally exhausted by it all. After all, I had been hurling non-stop for club, college and county since I was a kid and, basically, my batteries were flat.

I never expected the reaction to my departure would be so overwhelming. Letters, faxes, and messages of support in many and varied forms arrived in their thousands from all over the country. I had travelled to a lot of counties over previous years presenting medals, attending functions and doing coaching sessions so a huge number of people knew me. It really was heartening to get so much feedback from people all over the country.

As ever, the gossip continued. Bizarrely, it was suggested that I had given up hurling in order to try to become a golf professional. I had taken up a golf two years earlier and got my handicap down to seven despite not playing all that much but there's one hell of a difference between that and reaching the next level, let alone becoming a pro. Still, that was the story. I wanted to try my hand as a professional! How ludicrous can you get?

Another theory was that I was about to take up work in Mount Juliet Golf Club. Again, no truth whatsoever but it did the rounds, fuelled no doubt by a totally inaccurate report in one newspaper. I'd normally laugh it off as nonsense which is best ignored but this was different because it led to customers wondering if I was going to leave my business. Did the people who peddled the various lines about my so-called plans ever think of that? Did they care that their loose talk might damage my business? Seems not.

And then, of course, there were the whispers that I had retired in order to make money. Apparently, it was all a cunning plot so that I could hold the county board to ransom, quietly demanding a substantial fee if they wanted me to hurl for Kilkenny. I must say, I was annoyed by all the wild stories. None of them had a grain of truth but once they were out there, some people were always going to believe every last bit of tittle-tattle. Imagine going to the Kilkenny county board and demanding money to return to the panel. I reckon that would be a short conversation! And as for some rich individual or company splashing out to coax me back, well it just wasn't going to happen. Anyway, I would never have considered such a proposal, even if it were made. I always regarded hurling for Kilkenny as an honour and a privilege so the idea that I would have to be paid for it just didn't enter the equation.

Thankfully, not everyone was thinking solely in hurling terms and were instead interested in me as a person. Indeed, I have to mention one man especially, who contacted me after I retired. Stan Kiely of Kiely Meats in Waterford phoned me one day and, in his matter-of-fact way, said: "are you alright boy?" He was really asking me was I okay financially and in myself. A great Kilkenny supporter, Stan wasn't talking about hurling now. He just wanted to know was I okay generally and was there anything he could do to help. I really appreciated the gesture. It was sincere and genuine and put me as an individual first rather than thinking of me purely as a Kilkenny hurler.

Once the initial blitz of media coverage and speculation had subsided, I hoped everything would settle down and I could get on with my life as an ex-hurler. However, there was one small problem. Actually, it started out small but grew quite rapidly and, very soon, I couldn't possibly ignore it.

The truth was that I wanted my hurling career back. I was missing the game a whole lot more than I thought I would. As the National League approached I began to think to myself: what the hell have I done? Why have I quit? How am I going to manage without hurling? My batteries may have been low earlier in the year but why not re-charge them and get back on the road? I suppose the realisation that I would no longer be part of something I found so enjoyable and so rewarding kicked in very quickly once the stark nature of my decision became apparent.

The League didn't start until the second Sunday in March that year but then the action came thick and fast. And with it, came my desire to be part of the scene.

I went along to a few Kilkenny games and the more I saw, the more I realised I had made a terrible mistake. The game that had defined so much of my life had no intention of letting go. There was only one solution – get back in there.

I wasn't in any way embarrassed by the quick about-turn. I knew I would be welcomed back by Kevin and his co-selectors, Dick O'Neill (my fellow club man) and Mick McCarthy, so now it was a question of just getting on with it. News of my return was announced and it was then decided to hold a press conference in Langton's in order to get all the questions out of the way in one clear-the-air session.

Ned Quinn, then Kilkenny vice-chairman (and current chairman) made it clear to the assembled media at the start that there was absolutely no question of financial incentives being involved and pointed out that although it was then the last day of March, I still hadn't claimed expenses for the previous year. Still, the whispering persisted, as I knew it would. That's the trouble with denying a rumour. Those who believe a rumour won't take any notice of the denial while those who haven't heard it up to then begin to wonder if it's actually true.

The heading on the *Irish Independent's* report on the press conference the following day ran: "Kilkenny refute Carey 'cash to play' rumours."

Great! Cash to play and Carey. Put the two together and you're feeding the giant rumour monster again. Ned thought he was doing the right thing by making it clear that there was no question of me being paid to come back, but all it did was add to the gossip among those who wanted the rumour to be true.

Still, I knew the truth and was glad to have put a difficult period behind me. I could now get back to doing what I liked best – hurling for Gowran and Kilkenny.

As it happened, Kilkenny weren't going particularly well in the League at the time. In fact, by the time I got back into action in a Kilkenny jersey as a sub against Laois in Nowlan Park in mid-April we were still looking for our second win.

I came on with 13 minutes remaining and scored two points but it didn't stop us losing by five points after finishing on a measly 1-5. It was a poor performance, not one you would normally associate with Kilkenny. And certainly not in Nowlan Park. We hit 2-13 against Waterford down in Walsh Park in the final group game a week later but still lost and ended bottom of the table with only one win from five games.

As ever, some critics were lying in wait for me, mischievously suggesting that my retirement and return, plus all that went with it, had been an annoying distraction for everybody else and had contributed to the poor form shown by the team during the League. I doubt if it had anything whatsoever to do with it but there you go.

The reality was much simpler but more serious. Kilkenny just weren't performing. It was to be the story of the year. We never really played well in 1998, even if we eventually ended up in the All-Ireland final.

Many Kilkenny supporters still regard the 1998 All-Ireland final as one that got away but I'm not sure that's actually the case. At no time that year did we play with consistent fluency and while we might well have won the All-Ireland, it certainly wasn't one of those years when you'd feel you really did deserve it. We gave Dublin a serious trimming in the Leinster quarter-final, winning in Parnell Park by 4-23 to 0-14.

It looked a lot better than it was. We led by just a point at half-time and while we won the second half by 3-14 to 0-3, it was more a case of Dublin imploding rather than us doing anything especially well. Anyone who doubted that would have changed their minds two weeks later when we nearly came unstuck against Laois in the semi-final in Croke Park.

Laois hadn't beaten Kilkenny in the championships for decades but it certainly looked as if there was every chance that gap was about to be closed when they led by three points with fifteen minutes remaining. What's more they were hurling really well and fully deserved their lead. Not for the first time, lads like Niall Rigney, Bill Maher, Declan Rooney and the Cuddys were putting it up to us but just when it looked as if Laois might press on and win, they lost their way.

They didn't score for the final fifteen minutes and a goal by Ken O'Shea settled us down before we went on to win by 3-11 to 1-14. We were mighty relieved but it was not an encouraging performance, certainly not one that would have our supporters running to the bookies. We beat Offaly by five points in the Leinster final but, to be honest, we were bad and they were worse. You certainly won't find this game challenging for inclusion in any list of classic Leinster finals. In fairness to Charlie Carter, he had a great day, scoring 1-5 and I got 2-1, both goals coming from frees. For me, the day was summed up by a 20-metre free which I mishit but still managed to squeeze the ball over the goal line.

We didn't think we would see any more of Offaly that year, especially when we heard a few days later about the bust-up which saw Babs Keating resign as manager. Besides, Offaly were headed in Clare's direction in the All-Ireland semi-final and, frankly, didn't look anywhere nearly good enough to trouble the reigning champions.

So much for that theory. Two months later, Offaly were All-Ireland champions having beaten both the Munster (Clare) and Leinster (Kilkenny) champions in one of the great revival stories that the 'back door' made possible. We reached the final by beating Waterford, rather luckily it must be said, on a blustery August afternoon in Croke Park. We won by a point (1-11 to 1-10), which shows what a dour game it was.

You don't win many championship games, let alone an All-Ireland semi-final, by scoring 1-11 but somehow we managed it that day. Both sides missed lots of chances and while the swirling wind made it one of the most difficult days I can remember in Croke Park, we should have done better.

Because we had beaten Offaly in the Leinster final, there was a general expectation among the public that we would repeat it in the All-Ireland final but the dynamic had changed significantly in the intervening two months. Firstly, Offaly were reinvigorated by the win over Clare in the third leg of their semi-final trilogy and were always going to be a different proposition in the final than they had been a few months earlier.

Secondly, they were men on a mission ever since the Babs controversy (he described them as playing like 'sheep in a heap') which erupted after the Leinster final. It was typical Babs – calling it as he saw it even if it didn't go down too well with the Offaly players or public. I'm sure he meant no harm but everyone in Offaly took umbrage at his comments and he really had no option but to resign.

I felt a bit sorry for Babs to be honest. I always had – and still have – great time for him. He's a real character who tells it as he sees it, even if it's going to get him in trouble. He's one great Tipperary man and nobody did more to change their fortunes in the mid-1980s than him. When he was appointed manager, he did an awful lot more than run the team. He was also heavily involved in the Supporters' Club, which raised a lot of money through various golf classics and other functions. It was all pumped into the team to make sure they had the best of everything. In fact, Tipperary set a standard in that regard at the time which took others a long time to catch up on.

Babs was a right devil on the sideline, always up to something in an attempt to get an advantage for Tipperary. I remember a National League quarter-final between ourselves and Tipperary in 1994 which, for some daft reason, was played in Croke Park. There was a big controversy about it at the time as it seemed illogical to bring Kilkenny and Tipperary all the way to Croke Park for a League quarter-final. Still, the GAA insisted on it going ahead as part of a double-header with Clare and Antrim.

Anyway, at one stage during the game we got a sideline and I jogged over to take it. Babs was sitting on an Esso sign (he worked for them at the time) and, as I was carefully placing the ball, he said: "DJ, I'll have an even fifty with you".

I didn't know what he meant at first but then it dawned on me. He was using a bet to apply a bit of subtle pressure! Actually, not so subtle but there you go!

I said: "You'll give me fifty pounds if I point it and I'll give you fifty pounds if I miss? Is that it?"

Now, I'm no betting expert but 50-50 that I'd point a sideline seemed heavily weighted in favour of Babs. Of course, all he was trying to do was distract me and as he was explaining in the ins-and-outs of the bet, the referee ran over and booked him. The referee obviously thought he was abusing me which wasn't the case at all. He was just trying to put me off my stroke in his own mischievous way. I didn't point the sideline, by the way! It was typical of Babs. Always up to some devilment. He was though – indeed he still is – a great hurling man, who did an awful lot for the game as a player and manager.

That did not extend, however to managing Offaly after the 1998 Leinster final. His replacement, Michael Bond slotted in quickly and effectively. The players felt they had a number of points to prove and, by All-Ireland final day, Offaly were convinced they could beat us. The way they hung in against Clare in the first game of the semi-final trilogy, got the rub of the green with the early finish in the replay when it looked as if they were going to be beaten and then shot to new heights in the third outing, had them perfectly primed for the final.

Now here's a question: was it the first All-Ireland final to be decided by an outbreak of flu? Brian Whelahan was only barely fit to start for Offaly due to a flu bug and didn't look anything like his old self as Brian McEvoy whizzed up and down the left wing in the early stages. Our impressive No. 12 scored a few lovely points and looked as if he might even be on his way to the man-of-the-match award.

Bizarrely, Kilkenny's Brian was going so well on Offaly's Brian that it might have actually cost us the All-Ireland.

Why so? Conscious that flu-stricken Whelahan was having big problems with his defensive game but equally aware that it would be a huge psychological blow to Offaly if the great man was taken off, Bond switched him to attack where he turned in one of the most remarkable performances of all time.

He scored 1-6 (1-3 from open play and 0-3 from frees), the goal proving the clincher at a time when Offaly were two points ahead. We didn't score for the last six or seven minutes and could have no complaints about the outcome. We led by two points at half-time but lost the second half by 2-8 to 0-6. That's a pretty comprehensive margin by any standards and it was enough to give Offaly a six-point win.

Losing to a team you have beaten earlier on in the championship is always a miserable experience but to lose to opposition who had a change of manager since you last played them made it all the more deflating for us. They were the ones who were supposed to have difficulties, yet we ended up having the bigger problems on All-Ireland final day.

The Leinster title win meant little to us once we'd lost to Offaly in the All-Ireland final. Again, the criticisms rained down thick and fast, but even the sharpest tongues were ignoring one simple reality: we weren't going well at the time. Offaly beat us fair and square and it's most unlikely we would have beaten Clare if they had reached the final. For while Clare might have dropped back a little from the peaks of previous years, they were still a mighty powerful force and would probably have been too good for us.

We'll never know of course. But what we do know is that for a fifth successive year, Liam MacCarthy did not winter in Kilkenny. Bob O'Keeffe did but he kept a low profile, knowing that he didn't count by comparison with the VIP that Offaly were hosting.

On a personal level it had been one hell of a strange year for me, going from retirement to a return, to a Leinster title success, to an All-Ireland final defeat. No surprise but I didn't get an All Star award either! I couldn't wait to see the back of a season that left Kilkenny supporters as frustrated as those of us who were at the heart of the action.

CHAPTER 7

A NEW BEGINNING

What a difference a year makes. Kilkenny ended the old Millennium deep in frustration after losing the 1998 and 1999 All-Ireland finals but launched the new one on a spectacular high. We needed to because if we had lost the 2000 All-Ireland final we would have gone down in history as the first Kilkenny team to lose three successive finals.

That definitely was something we did not want on our report cards. Losing two in a row was bad enough. Prior to that, it hadn't happened to Kilkenny since 1945-46 but they won in 1947 so the previous two defeats presumably didn't seem as disappointing.

You can imagine the pressure we were under going into the 2000 final. There was a feeling among many Kilkenny supporters that instead of trying to avoid becoming the first team from the county to lose three finals in a row, we should have been bidding to become the first team in almost 90 years to win the treble. It was a fair point. If we were good enough to beat Offaly in the 1998 Leinster final we should have been good enough to do it again in the final.

As for the 1999 final against Cork, now there was one we really did mess up. I always take the view that whoever wins the All-Ireland deserves it so I'm not trying to take anything away from Cork for their 1999 win, but even they would admit that we made it easier for them than they would ever have anticipated.

I still regard that day as one of my biggest disappointments and I know that most of the other Kilkenny lads feel the same way. Everything had gone so well up to then that we felt really good about ourselves going into the final. It was Brian Cody's first year in charge so there was a new sense of energy around the place, which was very evident in the Leinster championship. We ran a good National League campaign too, winning all but one of the divisional games before losing by three points to Galway in the semi-final.

Leinster was a doddle. We hit Laois for 6-21 after leading by 5-12 to 0-4 at half-time in the semi-final and blew Offaly away in the final. We were a driven force that day, desperate to make some sort of amends for the 1998 All-Ireland final defeat. I scored two goals in the first half, separated by one from Charlie Carter to leave us eight points clear at half-time.

Just as they had done in the 1998 All-Ireland final, Offaly moved Brian Whelahan into the attack for the second half but it didn't have the same impact this time. Brian McEvoy and Henry Shefflin added two more goals in the second half as we ran out easy winners, 5-14 to 1-16. Having scored a total of 11-35 in two games, we felt really comfortable in ourselves, confident that we were well primed for bigger tests.

The All-Ireland semi-final against Clare was an altogether tougher assignment but we rose well to that challenge too. Clare were beginning to dip a little from the heights of their glory years but were still very hard to beat. They knew how to survive, how to hang on in there when things weren't going well and then make a push at the right time.

They did that at the beginning of the last quarter when Stephen McNamara scored a goal but we countered a few minutes later when I managed to get in for a goal which settled us down again and we went on to win by four points.

It looked like the perfect way to reach the final. Clare had given us a genuine test but we came through it. Cork, under Jimmy Barry-Murphy, had re-emerged as Munster champions for the first time in seven years, before beating Offaly in the All-Ireland semi-final. They had also beaten Clare (Munster final) so the All-Ireland showdown was a clash between two teams who had both beaten the All-Ireland champions of the previous two years.

The difference was that we had All-Ireland final experience, whereas it was new to all the Cork players, except Brian Corcoran. Not that it made any difference on the day. In the weeks running up the game, there was a feeling among Kilkenny supporters that we couldn't be beaten. It was like a sense of entitlement, a belief that because we had lost the previous year's final, we were destined to win this one.

That certainly wasn't the mood in the camp but we did feel that if we played to our full potential we would win. Unfortunately, on the day, we didn't do ourselves justice and lost. Not coming close to our best was the most frustrating aspect of it all. If you lose on a day when you play well but come up against a superior force you have to accept it.

Cork were certainly a very good side but we didn't reach anything like the level we were capable of. As in 1992, conditions were bad but they were the same for both sides so I'm certainly not using that as an excuse for why we lost. We led by four points at the three-quarter mark but tightened up from there on and lost by a point, 0-13 to 0-12.

We had scored a total of 13-52 in our three games prior to the final but were restricted to twelve points by Cork so you can imagine how disappointed we were. You don't lose many games when you concede just thirteen points but you sure don't win many if you only score twelve. The day didn't go well for me personally but then most of the other Kilkenny players would have felt the same about themselves.

Still, with the scoring rate so unusually low, a four-point lead heading into the final quarter should have been enough to see us home, especially since we, not Cork, had experience of playing in a final but, for whatever reason, we lost our way in the final ten minutes.

Naturally, you begin to question yourself when you lose two All-Ireland finals in a row but, at the same time, a lot of positive things were happening. The squad was improving all the time – Henry Shefflin had enjoyed an excellent debut season – and deep down there was a feeling that we weren't that far away from getting it right.

It was Brian Cody's first season in charge so while the players had lost two-in-a-row, he hadn't. He learned a lot from the 1999 campaign and, come the following season, we were ready for anything.

The 2000 All-Ireland win was special for a number of reasons. Apart from avoiding the ignominy of being the first Kilkenny team to lose three finals in a row, we ended a seven year wait for the title. That's a very long time in Kilkenny, especially when we had been in two finals in that period.

Winning the 2000 title brought a huge sense of relief to the squad, but I'm not sure it was valued by the Kilkenny supporters in the way it should because we won it without beating anyone from Munster. I can't see why that should have made a difference but it did for some people. We beat what was put in front of us, which is all any team can do.

We put down an early marker that year when we beat Cork by four points in the first round of the League. A huge crowd turned out in Nowlan Park so the atmosphere was much more intense than you would normally get at an early season League clash. The game itself was pretty intense too. Cork played well but we played better. You could sense the determination in the team right from the start. Winning wouldn't make up for the All-Ireland final defeat but it would flash out a statement to all our rivals that we meant business for the new season.

For some reason, our performance levels dipped a little after that and we lost to Waterford and Wexford, defeats that cost us a place in the League semi-finals. It was a bit worrying but, at the same time, we took the Cork game as our benchmark going into the championship. As in 1999, Leinster was easily won. We had plenty to spare against Dublin and Offaly before lining up against Galway in the All-Ireland semi-final. They were going well that year, having won the League. They beat Tipperary in the League final and repeated the success in the All-Ireland quarter-final so clearly they were a force to be reckoned with.

They led by a point at half-time in the semi-final but we outscored them by 1-11 to 0-5 in the second half. I enjoyed the day immensely. Lots of things went my way, including a break early in the second half when I got in for a goal.

We would have expected to be playing Cork in the final but Offaly, in typical style, tore up the script. They turned in a brilliant performance in the other semi-final, beating Cork by three points. We had beaten Offaly by eleven points in the Leinster final but after what happened in 1998, we were deeply apprehensive about meeting them for a second time.

We felt that we were a better side but Offaly always had the knack of delivering a huge performance when the mood took them. Besides, they had obviously improved since July as they proved conclusively when beating Cork.

Most of their All-Ireland winning team of 1998 team were still aboard and with their confidence renewed after the Cork win, Offaly were ready for all-out war. Thankfully, we never gave them a chance to wage it. We blitzed them from the start. I got in for an early goal and added a second some minutes later after Henry's Shefflin's shot had been stopped on the goal line.

I nearly added a third goal late in the half but was denied by Offaly goalkeeper, Stephen Byrne who made a great save, only to see the ball break to Charlie Carter, who whipped it to the net. We led by ten points at half-time and while Offaly rallied for a period in the second half, we were never in any trouble, running out thirteen point winners (5-15 to 1-14). Incredibly, we scored 5-3 more than in the previous year's final.

It was some day for the Carter-Carey-Shefflin full-forward line! We scored 4-10 between us, enough to win most games but the outside lads added 1-5 just to make sure.

I won the man-of-the-match award and was later named as Hurler of the Year, which was very satisfying after the disappointments of the previous two years. I had taken quite a bit of stick after the 1999 final when much was made of the fact that I hadn't scored. It was just one of those days when little went right for any of us but 2000 was completely different.

Granted, we hadn't beaten any Munster team but so what? That was down to the fact that their top two, Cork and Tipperary, had been beaten by Offaly and Galway respectively so all we could do was beat the teams that had eliminated Munster's best.

We won all our games comfortably in a season I really enjoyed. My game was going well, the squad was strong and determined and with a lot of good young talent beginning to push its way through, we felt that, having finally made the breakthrough, the good times would continue to roll.

They did, although not without some setbacks, including 2001 when Galway stuffed us. Still, in the overall scheme of things, 2000 turned out to be the launch year for the most successful era in Kilkenny's history.

What's more, we launched it in style, winning the All-Ireland final by the biggest margin since Tipperary's win over Antrim in 1989. It turned into something of a watershed year for Offaly. We beat them easily again in 2001/2001 and quite a few times afterwards too.

In fact, Offaly haven't beaten Kilkenny in the championship since the 1998 All-Ireland final, a sequence of events that few would have envisaged back then. They had been Kilkenny's toughest Leinster opponents throughout the 1980s and 1990s but the 2000 All-Ireland final ended all that. It also restored Kilkenny's sanity after losing two successive finals. A new beginning had unfolded.

CHAPTER 8

YOUR COUNTY NEEDS YOU

The question rattled me, even if I knew it would be raised.

In the week before the 2002 Leinster final, Vincent Hogan of the *Irish Independent* phoned to ask would I do an interview with him. I wasn't on the Kilkenny team at the time but Vincent said he would like to talk to me anyway.

We met in Langton's and after a quick, casual chat, we got down to business. He switched on his tape recorder, looked at me and asked the first question: "Is it the end for DJ Carey?"

To be honest, it was something I had been asking myself for a while, but there's a big difference between asking yourself a question and somebody else raising it, especially when your answer is going to appear in the country's biggest selling daily newspaper.

"Vincent, I genuinely don't know," I replied.

I wasn't fudging it or trying to be evasive – I was just telling the truth. I went on to explain that there were a lot of things going on at the time which were making it very hard for me to concentrate on hurling. On top of that, I wasn't anywhere near full fitness after suffering two setbacks. I had been in an accident in Tallaght some months previously where my car got hit from behind by a lorry. I felt okay initially but after a few weeks, I started getting a strange pins-and-needles sensation in my neck, especially when I was relaxed.

I got it checked out and the examination showed that a disc in my neck was damaged. Then, towards the end of April, I got a burst appendix. Talk about bad luck coming in pairs. At that stage, I reckoned the year was a write-off and since I was going to be 32 years old in the following November, there was every likelihood that if I hadn't hurled in 2002, my career was over.

I hadn't even played with Gowran up to mid-summer that year. The week before the Leinster final, I trained with Gowran and boy, was I feeling the strain. I went home afterwards, sat down for an hour because I was hardly able to move. Let's put it this way – my body wasn't exactly telling me to head back to the big time any time soon. I was under a lot of pressure at work too, driving long distances, sitting in the car for six or seven hours a day and not really feeling like a man who could do a whole lot as an inter-county hurler.

Still, I knew I could have gone back to the Kilkenny panel at any time. No guarantees, mind you, but Brian Cody made it clear all along that he would like to have me back. He was very encouraging but I just didn't feel up to going back into the grind. Anyway, I was way behind everyone else in fitness and even further behind the standards I always set for myself.

If I went back in half-heartedly, it would have been unfair on everyone. Brian would probably have come under pressure to play me and I'd be under pressure to perform even if I wasn't fully fit. It could end up being lose-lose-lose for Brian, for me and for Kilkenny. That was the last thing I wanted.

People were asking why I hadn't returned as a squad member, maybe coming on at some point in the second half of games but I had no interest in that. I had to be able to play a full game or no game. This business of being half-fit but hoping to make an impact as a sub when the game had slowed down a little didn't appeal to me at all. It had to be all or nothing. You're either fit to play or you're not.

Shortly before I did the interview with Vincent Hogan, I had issued a statement effectively ruling myself out for the season. I did it to end all the speculation and to make life easier for myself, Brian and the squad.

I was being asked about my future everywhere I went and I wanted to end that. I'm sure Brian was being asked too so it made sense to clear the air. I felt the interview in the *Irish Independent*, which was due to appear on the day before the Leinster final, would further explain my position, although I did leave the door slightly ajar when Vincent asked me what would happen if Brian formally invited me back in. I said I couldn't see myself returning but added: "never say never".

That was exactly how I felt. I had no idea what was going to happen so that's all I could say. Besides, Kilkenny were going well without me, having won the National League in a close call against Cork in the final. Andy Comerford was captain and doing a fine job, the squad looked strong and were improving all the time so everything appeared to be well set for a big run at the championship. Training had gone very well under the harder regime which applied as a result of the bad performance in the previous year's All-Ireland semi-final against Galway, so confidence was high as the summer approached.

The Kilkenny lads certainly seemed to be tipping along nicely when they beat Offaly by nine points in a Leinster semi-final which was played in Thurles because of the redevelopment work in Croke Park. It was back to Croke Park for the final against Wexford, a game which turned out to have a big influence on my career.

I watched it from the stands and, like every other Kilkenny supporter, my heart was in my mouth all the way through. Kilkenny were lucky to win by two points. Wexford missed some good chances and had Liam Dunne sent off four minutes from the end for a pull on Martin Comerford. Henry Shefflin pointed the resultant free and with an extra man for the last few minutes our lads hung on. We had beaten Wexford easily in 2001 but this one was very different. They were in our faces all day, harrying, hustling and generally doing what Wexford were always capable of doing around then – making life tough for any opposition when their mood was right. Kilkenny scraped to victory (0-19 to 0-17) but it certainly was not a performance to send people running to the bookies to back us for the All-Ireland. Most unusually, we didn't score a goal, something that hadn't happened to a Kilkenny team in a Leinster final for a very long time. Worse still, we hadn't looked like scoring a goal.

Still, Kilkenny had won so I felt it would be put down to one of those days when Wexford really put it up to us and forgotten about, once preparations began for the All-Ireland semi-final. Brian obviously had other ideas. On the Monday after the game, he phoned me and asked would I think of coming back into training. I told him I would be well off the pace but he pointed out that the All-Ireland semi-final was still almost six weeks away. He wanted me back in, working as hard as possible for a month or so and then see how things were going.

"If you're not right, you're not right and you won't be playing," he said in his matter-of-fact way. I knew that. He was keen to have me back but there were no guarantees. Not that I wanted them. I would either make the team on the basis of how I was going in training or not at all. That has always been Brian's policy anyway and, in this case, it was also very definitely mine.

I decided to give it a shot and set about putting in six weeks of manic training under Mick O'Flynn's supervision. Mick was a great trainer and I knew that if I put in the work, he'd help me make up for lost time. My only fear was that in trying to cram in as much as possible, I might pick up an injury. That's where Mick's expertise came in. He devised the correct programme in great detail and the tough grind began.

It was one hell of a slog over the first few weeks. Mick and myself would arrive at training early to get in some work before the other lads came in and we would stay afterwards to do a bit more. Jogging, sprinting, twisting, turning ... on and on it went. Then it was straight into the training games, complete with all that involved! Welcome back DJ, but nothing soft going here. This is Nowlan Park and we're getting ready for an All-Ireland semi-final! Gradually, I could feel the old spark returning. With each passing week, I felt sharper and more energetic until I was at a stage where I felt ready for action if Brian picked me.

I was conscious that coming back after the Leinster final might cause a bit of resentment in various quarters but there was nothing I could do about that. It wasn't my call to return – in fact I was resigned to missing the year but Brian obviously felt that if I got fit enough in the six weeks between the Leinster final and the All-Ireland semi-final, I could have a role to play. He was the boss and was making a call.

Not everybody agreed that it was the right one. I was criticised by some texters in a phone-in to the local radio station in Kilkenny. They seemed to think that by returning to the panel, I was trying to grab someone's place at the glory end of the season. In reality, all I was doing was responding to an invitation by the manager to give it a go. But, as I've written elsewhere, there are always people who see ulterior motives in everything.

It was a most unfair depiction of events. I had put my heart and soul into Kilkenny hurling since the late 1980s, so to portray me as some sort of opportunist who turned up around All-Ireland semi-final time was nasty.

Anyway, all I could do was to keep the head down, work hard and if Brian and the selectors thought I was worthy of a starting place for the All-Ireland semi-final, so be it. As it happened, they did.

There was huge interest in the semi-final against Tipperary. They were the reigning All-Ireland champions and while they had been beaten by Waterford in the Munster final, they had got back in the groove with a good work-out against Antrim in the All-Ireland quarter-final. There was every chance that the Munster final defeat would have hardened their determination to save the season and with Nicky English in charge, they were always going to be well-primed for the return to Croke Park.

Kilkenny-Tipperary championship meetings were scarce back then – in fact the 2002 semi-final was the first since the 1991 All-Ireland final which Tipp won. And since the 2002 game was a clash between the All-Ireland champions of the previous two years, it attracted attention well beyond Kilkenny-Tipperary borders.

In Kilkenny, there was also big interest in the make-up of the team. Naturally, there was speculation as to whether I would get a starting place and when the team was finally announced, it showed one change in the forward line: I was in for Charlie Carter. I was a bit surprised to be honest. I thought I would be on the bench but obviously Brian was prepared to take a chance on me.

Replacing Charlie wasn't exactly what I wanted but, as I've always said, club stuff goes out the door when you're in black and amber territory. It's Club Kilkenny then and nothing else matters.

I was very apprehensive going into the semi-final. However well training had gone and however fresh I felt, there was a massive difference between what I had been doing and what I was about to do. Hurling with the club and training with the county was one thing but lining out in an All-Ireland semi-final against the defending champions was altogether different.

The curious thing about a game surrounded by high expectations is that, very often, the build-up can be better than the real thing. Not this time. The game lived up to its billing in every way. In fact, earlier this year, the game was ranked at No. 2 by the *Irish Independent* in their selection of the best fifty hurling games ever played in Croke Park. That's quite a tribute to the game.

It's sometimes difficult to assess a contest when you have been involved, but this really was something special. It was level at half-time before we pulled two points clear, only for John Carroll to force in a Tipperary goal. Shortly afterwards, Jimmy Coogan came on for us and it proved to an inspired substitution. Jimmy scored 1-1, which proved crucial in what was a fantastic shoot-out on the run-in. There was only a point between us fairly late on but we added three more points to win by 1-20 to 1-16. It was Kilkenny's first championship win over Tipperary since 1967 and only our second in eighty years.

The day had gone quite well for me. I nailed a '65' early on and despite not having done very much hurling all year – and certainly none at that level – I felt reasonably comfortable all the way. But then I had gone in fresh, which was a help once the rest of my game came together.

I was especially happy with my role in Jimmy's goal around the hour mark. I found a bit of space, cut in and headed for the Tipperary goal. I have always held the view that a diagonal pass is far more effective than a straight pass because if the receiver is coming in at an angle, it's harder to defend against him. You'll see a lot of blocking and hooking nowadays because players are running in straighter lines which makes it easier for defenders.

Anyway, I spotted a black-and-amber jersey (I hadn't a clue who was wearing it) out of the corner of my eye. I got a good handpass away and bang – the ball was in the net. Jimmy had taken the chance with great confidence for a goal which probably won the game for us.

I finished the day with four points (two from '65's and two from open play) but, more importantly, I felt that I had contributed in a lot of other ways too. In the end, it's not about the name of the scoresheet but rather the number of scores.

In a sense, it was hard for me to take it all in. Six weeks earlier, I was saying it was most unlikely I would return in 2002, if indeed at all, and now I was back in the All-Ireland final. It shows how a season can turn around so very quickly. What's more, I had done my bit to get Kilkenny through the Tipperary test. Those who criticised me for coming back after the Leinster final fell silent – or at least I presume they did. Mind you, you can never be too sure.

Having beaten Tipperary, we were always going to be favourites to beat Clare in the final, even if they had beaten Munster champions, Waterford in the other semi-final. It was a much-changed Clare team from the outfit that won the All-Ireland titles in 1995 and 1997 although some of the old war horses were still there, as determined as ever. Davy Fitz, the Lohans, Seanie McMahon, Colin Lynch, Jamesie O'Connor and Niall Gilligan brought huge experience to the Clare team of 2002 but we probably had greater overall balance.

I always thought that the Clare team in the second-half of the 1990s never got the credit they deserved. If ever there was a team moulded in the manager's personality it was Clare. Hard, driven, obsessive, ruthless. Big men with big hearts. Ger Loughnane types. That Clare team didn't score many goals but they compensated with points and, of course, by keeping the giveaway rate down at the other end.

When we played them in 1997, they beat us fair and square. I would have loved to have taken on the Clare team of that time with the Kilkenny team that came through afterwards – it would have been some showdown.

Clare were unlucky that there was no second chance in 1996 after losing to Limerick in a classic Munster semi-final. Their season was over by mid-June but if the All-Ireland qualifiers were in place at the time, there's every chance that they would have retained the title.

In 1998, Clare were unfortunate not to beat Offaly. They were probably heading for a win in the All-Ireland semi-final replay which had to be re-fixed because of the premature ending to the game when the referee made a mistake with the time-keeping. So when Clare look back on those years, they will probably feel they should have won more than two All-Ireland finals.

Then again, it took a remarkable save from Davy Fitz in the final minute to see them through against Tipperary in the 1997 final, so maybe things balanced out after all. There's no doubt that Clare took training and general preparation to a new level, one which everyone followed quite quickly. Maybe not down to every last detail, but in a general way, where it was accepted that old ways had to be updated and refined.

The Clare team of 2002 wasn't as powerful as its predecessors of 1995-97 but we were still very wary of them. Luckily, we got an early break when I flicked the ball to the net after Henry's Shefflin's shot for a point dropped short.

I always operated on the basis that nobody ever knows where a chance will come from, but if you put yourself in the right position, you can get lucky more often than you might think. Striking has improved enormously over the last ten to fifteen years but when I was coming through the ranks, I worked off the idea that a shot from outfield might be mishit and fall short.

By timing your run in towards goal, you'd be surprised how often things broke your way. That's what happened early in the 2002 All-Ireland final when Henry, one of the most reliable strikers of a ball in hurling history, didn't quite get the connection right as he went for a point. The ball looped across the goal and I was in the right place to get a flick on it and direct it to the net. It looked great on TV – almost like something that might have been rehearsed but that was far from the case.

We won fairly easily in the end after resisting a Clare revival early in the second half. Much was made afterwards of a point I scored from out near the sideline in the second half. I'll admit it looks good on the video but, to be honest, it's overrated. I carried the ball away from Ollie Baker, balanced it on the hurley and fired it over the bar from close to the sideline. It looked fairly spectacular but then I had no choice but to play it off the hurley as I had already caught it once.

Was it something I set out to do? No, it wasn't. For a start, I won possession in a central position but somehow ended up near the sideline.

Yes, of course it was nice to land a point like that but I'd get just as much satisfaction from making a score as taking it. I was lucky enough to do both in the 2002 All-Ireland final which has gone down in my memory as one of those really great days that I look back on with real pride.

All the more so, since it came only two months after I was wondering if I would ever hurl for Kilkenny again. The year ended on a double high as Gowran won the county title and I picked up my 9th – and last – All Star award at left full-forward.

I had won my first award eleven years earlier and, in between only missed out in 1996-98-2001. I won them in four different positions: three each at full-forward and left full-forward; two at left half-forward and one at right half-forward.

The 2002 award proved just how important performances in the latter stages of the championship are in the All Stars selection. I had played only two games for Kilkenny, yet picked up an award. I certainly wasn't complaining, but I'm sure there were lads who would have felt that their consistency throughout the year should have counted for more than two games, even if they were the biggest two of the year. I couldn't disagree with them.

By the end 2002, I was back in business, going well for club and county. What's more, Kilkenny were still improving. Surely, there was more to come.

CHAPTER 9

TROUBLE AT THE CAPTAIN'S TABLE

This is it, the moment I had always dreamt about ever since I picked up a hurl as a tiny young lad back home in Gowran. It was shortly after five o'clock on the evening of 14 September 2003 and I was standing on the Hogan Stand, waiting to accept the Liam MacCarthy Cup from GAA President, Seán Kelly.

We had beaten Cork by three points in the final, having earlier hit Tipperary for 3-18 in a 12-point win in the semi-final. We had won the League, the Leinster and All-Ireland titles. Surely, this is as good as it gets.

It was my second year as captain, having also had the privilege in 1997. However, that wasn't a good year for Kilkenny. We won no titles and ended the season close enough to disgrace for our pathetic effort against Limerick in the National League semi-final. It certainly wasn't the best year to be Kilkenny captain.

Six years later, everything was so different. We were on top of the world after a brilliant season, during which the only defeat we suffered in thirteen League and Championship games was against Tipperary in a Divisional NHL game. Even then, we avenged it, not once but twice in the League final and All-Ireland semi-final.

A remarkable year and now I was about to lift the Liam MacCarthy Cup as Kilkenny captain. It's a very special moment in the lives of the relatively few players who get to experience it. I was about to join an exclusive club.

But even as I accepted the cup, I knew there were those who believed I should not have been captain, people who felt I should have refused the greatest honour that can be bestowed on a county player. I've written elsewhere that I disagree with the Kilkenny system of picking a captain where it falls automatically to a player from the county champions but that's the way it's done so those who are opposed have to accept it for as long as the majority want to stay with the long-standing tradition.

It's well-known how I came to be captain in 2003. My club mate, Charlie Carter was nominated for the honour after we won the 2002 county title. I had my turn as captain back in 1997 so there was no question of me being nominated again. Some people might have liked to turn it into some sort of rivalry between myself and Charlie but it was nothing of the sort. It was his turn – plain and simple.

The problem was that, in 2003, Charlie was in and out of the team. That obviously caused some issues, not least for Charlie, who thought he should have been a regular. When he wasn't, he became very frustrated and eventually signed himself off the panel during the Leinster championship. As the only Gowran man on the team, I took over as captain.

At face value, it was all very simple but, in reality, it was anything but. Indeed, it became very awkward for me as I got caught in the crossfire, despite having no involvement whatsoever in any of the circumstances that led to me being appointed captain.

The first indication that the whole captaincy thing might develop into a problem arose on the day of the 2003 League final. Unusually, it was fixed for the May Bank Holiday Monday and, equally unusually, was played in Croke Park. It turned out to be one of the best League finals ever played, a thrill-a-minute classic which yielded a total of 10-27. We won by 5-14 to 5-13 after recovering from an eight-point deficit just before the hour mark.

Charlie wasn't chosen on the starting fifteen so I captained the team for all the preliminaries. Charlie was brought on in the second-half and made quite an impact as we battled back to snatch victory. The real Kilkenny captain was now on the field and, when we won, the honour of accepting the trophy and making the presentation speech rightly fell to him.

Mind you, the Croke Park stewards were obviously – and understandably – baffled by it all. They had seen me lead the team out and assumed I was captain for the day. Within seconds of the final whistle, one of them came over to me and began ushering me towards the Hogan Stand to accept the trophy.

I said to him: "No, no, Charlie is captain. He'll be taking the cup." Charlie seemed to think I might continue as captain and head for the presentation but I said to him: "go on. You go up and pick up the cup, you're captain."

Charlie did his thing, made his speech and we headed home as League champions, delighted to have won such a dramatic game. Still, the nagging question of what would happen for the rest of the season persisted. Would Charlie be on the starting fifteen?

Shortly afterwards, Guinness hosted the launch of the All-Ireland championships in Croke Park. All the captains from the competing counties were there for the usual photo call and media interviews. Charlie attended in his capacity as official Kilkenny captain but I was there too, having been invited by Guinness.

I had been involved with Guinness and their championship sponsorship since 1995 so I was at all of their launches over the intervening years. I had coached the actor who made one of the early Guinness advertisements for the championship. I couldn't appear in the ad myself because it was promoting an alcoholic drink. However, I had done various other promotional work with Guinness over the years, including attending their championship launches. The Kilkenny captain of any particular year would also be there but nobody took any notice because the media knew of my involvement with Guinness. However, because of what had happened in the League final, the media became curious about the dynamic between Charlie and me.

There wasn't any issue whatsoever between us as far as I was concerned and I presume it was the same for Charlie. He was captain and would lead the team, provided, of course, that he was playing. That decision rested with Brian Cody and his selectors, Noel Skehan and Johnny Walsh. I don't know if Charlie was surprised to see me at the Guinness launch. In fairness, he may not have known that I was always invited by them. If he didn't, it would indeed look strange that two Kilkenny men – one who had led the team out for the League final and one who accepted the trophy –

were at a championship launch attended by all the captains from around the country.

I did some interviews at the launch, not as Kilkenny captain but as a Kilkenny player who had been invited by the sponsors. Charlie talked to the media as Kilkenny captain. We made no distinction, but I suppose it might have appeared a little bit odd to anyone who didn't know of my involvement with Guinness.

Anyway, I thought no more of it as we got down to the serious preparations for the Leinster championship, where we started out against Dublin in Nowlan Park on a Saturday evening in early June. Since Charlie hadn't been chosen on the team, I was back as captain. We won easily (3-16 to 0-10) in a game that would be quickly forgotten except for the dramatic fall-out which followed. Brian brought on two subs, John Hoyne and Walter Burke. Charlie was left on the bench all evening and, on the following Tuesday, he told the County Board he was leaving the panel.

Naturally, it was a big story – KILKENNY CAPTAIN QUITS PANEL. Charlie didn't let me know he was planning to leave but when news of his departure broke, I phoned him and we talked for a while. I asked him if he was sure he had done the right thing. Why not take a bit more time to think through it? Things might look different in a few days. He said his mind was made up and he would not be coming back.

Did he do the right thing? In my opinion, no. He was playing well, even if he hadn't got a run against Dublin. He reacted to that by deciding to leave the panel. Am I going to second guess Brian Cody and his decision not to bring on Charlie in that game? No. I'm not. Maybe, he felt there was no need to make any changes in a game we were winning easily. He would never have been one to bring in subs for the sake of it. For instance, he used no subs against Wexford in the 2003 Leinster final and brought in only one against Tipperary in the All-Ireland semi-final, so it wasn't as if he acted out of character in the Dublin game. Still, Charlie obviously felt that as captain and one of the most experienced players on the team, he should have been brought on, which is understandable. We all see things differently. It was a matter for Brian and Charlie and had nothing to do with the rest of us.

I was sorry to see Charlie leave the panel. We had hurled together for club, college and county since we were kids. There was no better combination than the two of us when we were going well and we enjoyed many a great day together. We had a great understanding of each other's play, always knowing exactly where the other would be at any given time.

If he was out the field and got possession, he knew exactly the type of ball I liked – high and hanging. He'd deliver it perfectly, time after time. And when I had the ball, I knew instinctively the angles that Charlie would run. We made an awful lot of scores for each other over the years and would probably have continued to do so with Kilkenny if he had stayed around in 2003.

With Charlie gone, I was going to be captain for the rest of the season and suddenly the rumours began. Apparently, I was happy to see Charlie go. It was even suggested to me that I should have either withdrawn from the panel as a mark of support to a Gowran team mate or else go to Brian and urge him to ask Charlie back.

There was absolutely no way, I was going to do either. Club loyalty is fine when it involves club affairs but when it comes to county matters, there can be no parochialism. There's a much bigger world at play now. I wasn't a Gowran player when I was with the county squad, I was a Kilkenny player, who happened to be from Gowran.

If I had quit the Kilkenny panel, what would it have achieved? It would have generated lots of controversy and nothing else. Quite rightly, Brian would have left me sitting at home. There was no way he would have come after me. I would, in fact, have done absolutely nothing for Charlie but would have seriously damaged Kilkenny by whipping up a controversy that would have run for ages. Imagine the headlines! The only ones who would have gained from it would have been our rivals. Helping them and disrupting our own was not what I was about as a Kilkenny hurler.

As for going to Brian and trying to persuade him to invite Charlie back, well that would have been a short conversation! The words 'you must be joking' might have been used very early on. No, the best thing for me to do was keep the head down and hurl on as best I could. You must remember too that I was coming towards the end of my career. As it happened I got two more years out of it, but if I had walked away in the summer of 2003, it would have been all over.

Now here's a thing. If Charlie had stayed on, I believe he would have got game time during that championship and would have lifted the Liam MacCarthy Cup as captain. He saw it otherwise, made his decision, left the panel and got on with his life.

What disappointed me was there were some in the club who thought I should have gone out in sympathy with Charlie. It never even crossed my mind.

I don't know how many people Charlie talked to before deciding to leave the panel. He certainly didn't talk to me. If he had I would have tried to talk him around or, at the very least, urged him to think it through very, very carefully on his own.

If I was ever to give a piece of advice to anyone about making a big decision it is this: don't take too much notice of what people who are on your side say. Whether that's family or friends, it's not a good idea to allow yourself to be over-influenced by them. In most cases, they are operating off the version of events that you have provided so their judgement will, understandably, be coloured by that. They are taking their cue from what you have told them. They are emotionally involved and will generally side with your take on events. In effect, they will reinforce that view, rather than challenge it. It's far better to take a step back, sit down and coldly analyse the situation.

Phone someone who won't be automatically on your side but whose opinion you trust. You might not like what they have to say but at least they are looking at it objectively, rather than listening to your side of the story and telling you what you want to hear.

Some of the biggest kicks I've got in life have been when people questioned how, or why, I did something in a particular way. When you're questioned, you look at things differently. You look at yourself differently. In the end, you're all the better for the questioning having taken place because it made you think.

There were certainly a few questions whizzing around in my direction in 2003 when I found myself caught up in a situation which wasn't of my making after Charlie opted out. Was there anything I could have done to smooth things over between Brian and Charlie? No. Brian was making decisions, based on how he saw things as manager; Charlie made his decision based on how he saw things as a Kilkenny captain who wasn't getting a start and who hadn't been brought on in a game we were winning easily.

There was nothing anyone could do to square that circle, although it might have solved itself if Charlie had stayed around.

The only close call we had in the 2003 championship was against Cork in the All-Ireland final. We beat Wexford comfortably in the Leinster final and then had an unexpectedly easy victory over Tipperary in the All-Ireland semi-final.

After the intense battle of the previous year, we were expecting another massive test and it turned out that way in the first half, by the end of which Tipperary led by two points. The second half was completely different. We out-scored them by 3-9 to 0-4 in those 35 minutes to win by twelve points. It was something similar to the 2012 All-Ireland semi-final, in that Tipperary did very well until half-time only to fall away in the second-half.

The win set us up for a repeat of the 1999 decider against Cork, although much had changed for both counties in the meantime. We had won two of three All-Ireland finals while they had gone through some very turbulent times, especially around the end of 2002 when the players went on strike.

However, once Donal O'Grady came in as manager, the scene improved very quickly and by September 2003, they were a powerful force. Indeed, it took a very solid performance by us to wear them down. A scoring burst that yielded 1-3 put Cork ahead in the second half but we remained calm and worked our way to victory. A goal by Martin Comerford five minutes from the end proved crucial. He was outstanding that day, scoring 1-4 from open play from a total of 1-14. He was the obvious selection as man-of-the-match.

I've always thought that Martin never quite got the credit he deserved. He was brought aboard for the 2002 season and made an immediate impact. He could do just about anything: win ball in the air or on the ground, get scores, create scores and generally make a nuisance of himself around the opposition square or further out, depending on how the game was going. He was a great target man which added to the balance of an attack where we had plenty of runners.

He certainly caused lots of problems for the Cork defence in the 2003 All-Ireland final and for many others in the years that followed.

Captaining Kilkenny to an All-Ireland win will always be a major highlight for me, even if the honour came about in circumstances I wouldn't have wanted. Still, you have to take whatever chances come your way and I was fully at ease with myself over how I came to captain Kilkenny that year.

As I left the Croke Park pitch on that Sunday evening, clutching the Liam MacCarthy Cup, I certainly didn't think it would be my last All-Ireland final win. We had captured the two-in-a-row and while Cork made it very hard for us in the final, there was no reason to believe that even if they improved in the following year – which they did – we couldn't move up another notch too.

That's the way we always look at things in Kilkenny. However high the peak we've reached there's always a higher one to take on. There has to be. It doesn't always work out, of course, as happened in 2004 and 2005.

CHAPTER 10

DID I COST KILKENNY AN ALL-IRELAND TITLE?

Sometimes I wonder if I cost Kilkenny the 2004 All-Ireland title. More especially, I wonder if my indiscipline cost Kilkenny the All-Ireland.

Now, a lack of discipline wouldn't be something that people associate with me – or indeed that I'd associate with myself – but on this occasion, I'm afraid I didn't maintain the high standards I should have and it may have had consequences.

I'm not talking about anything that went on in the final against Cork, which turned into an absolute disaster for us, but rather something that happened three months earlier. The week before the Leinster semi-final against Wexford in mid-June, I played golf in a pro-am at the K-Club.

I was due to train with Kilkenny that night so I teed off early enough to give myself plenty of time to complete the round of golf and head for Nowlan Park. The best laid plans and all that. Bad weather delayed the golf and as the day dragged on, it became clear that the times just weren't going to add up. There was no way I could finish the golf and still make training.

What was I to do? Walk off the course in an event I had been invited to a long time before? Miss training with Kilkenny? Now, while I was no great fan of training, I never, ever took short cuts. Training was there for a reason. It had to be done and, all through my hurling life, I treated it as seriously as it deserved. Cut corners and you're only fooling yourself.

However, on this particular occasion, I felt I had no choice but to skip training. I phoned Brian Cody and told him I wouldn't be able to make it down that night. Typical of him, he made no fuss.

"Right so, DJ."

I felt bad about it but what could I do? Besides, it wasn't as if I had a history of dodging training. In fact, I fairly rarely missed a session over all the years.

Anyway, I thought no more about it after my phone call to Brian but when the team for the Wexford game was announced on the Friday night, I wasn't included. I had been carrying a bit of knock some weeks earlier but, as far as I was concerned, I was fully fit to play. Brian had other ideas. He never mentioned the missed training session but I have no doubt it was behind his decision to leave me out. Effectively, he had dropped me for a breach of discipline.

What's more, he was 100 per cent right. I might have been on the Kilkenny team for fourteen years, won lots of titles and awards, but I was still an ordinary member of the squad and, as far as Brian was concerned, I had let the side down by putting around the greens of the K-Club rather than putting in some hard work in Nowlan Park. There had to be consequences.

No one paid any great attention to my absence from the team because it was put down to me carrying some sort of niggle or other. I've never gone for that line when I hear about a player being left out. You're either fit to play or you're not. If you can't start a match, who's to say you will be any use if you're brought on?

I was well fit to play against Wexford that day but was dropped. Plain and simple. Brian put me in my place and I could have no complaints. Nothing personal, just business. And in the case of Brian Cody, nothing comes before the business of doing what he thinks is right for Kilkenny.

He doesn't show favours, doesn't do grudges and certainly isn't into sentiment. That applies whether you are DJ Carey, Henry Shefflin, Tommy Walsh or someone who has just come on the panel straight out of minor. Everyone is treated the same.

Some people said that he was wrong to start Henry Shefflin in the 2010 All-Ireland final against Tipperary because there was doubt over how

Henry's knee would stand up to such a big test after he had been all but ruled out of the game a few weeks earlier. The implication was that he had been picked because he was Henry and had been on every championship team with Brian since 1999.

Rubbish. He was picked because he was Henry alright: the same Henry who had done so much over the years to make Kilkenny the force they were. As it happened, his knee gave way early on in the final and he had to be replaced, but I still think Brian was right to start him. Henry had put in an unbelievable amount of hard work; the knee had stood up in training so why not let him take his chance?

Certainly, there was no question of sentiment in Brian's decision just as there wasn't any shown to me when he dropped me in 2004. Anyway, I took my place among the subs against Wexford and settled back for what I thought would be a relatively straight-forward win. Now, Kilkenny never, ever took Wexford for granted but the form book was pointing very much in our favour at that time.

We were double All-Ireland champions and had beaten Wexford by eleven points in the 2003 Leinster final. We did exactly the same with an understrength team in the League two months before the 2004 championship game. However, Wexford were a different outfit in June. They matched us point for point throughout the first-half and even when a goal by Eddie Brennan put us four points up early in the second half, we never looked like we were going to pull away.

Wexford were in one of their really stubborn moods which they did so well from time to time and dug in for a real battle. In fact, they led by a point with ten minutes left. I had come in for Jimmy Coogan just before the hour mark. It was all square heading into stoppage time when I got a chance for the lead point from open play. I nailed it, but there were still a few minutes to go and, right at the death, Michael Jacob scored a goal after a sideline cut from Adrian Fenlon hadn't been cleared.

Final whistle: Wexford 2-15 Kilkenny 1-16. We had lost in the Leinster championship for the first time since the 1997 Leinster final in the most dramatic circumstances. I felt very badly about it. I'm not saying that if I had been playing all the way through, we would have won but, at the same time, I might have sneaked a point or two somewhere along the line.

Suffice to say, I wasn't contributing to the cause by sitting on the bench for nearly an hour.

It was my own fault. I had broken the discipline code and, by doing that, may well have cost Kilkenny a place in the Leinster final. Now, instead of preparing for the final and staying on the direct route in pursuit of the All-Ireland three-in-a-row, we were headed for the 'back door'.

Suddenly, the season had taken on a completely different complexion. We were now going on the scenic route to the All-Ireland final. We got there in the end but, in light of how badly we played in the second half against Cork, I can only assume the long journey had taken its toll. We beat Dublin and Galway easily in the qualifiers, the latter surprisingly so, since they were well-fancied that year. However, they caved in completely in the last quarter. We were only four points ahead with twenty minutes to go but cut loose from there on, out-scoring Galway by 3-7 to 0-1. Were we that good or Galway that bad? It was a combination of both, I guess.

Clare gave us a real fright in the All-Ireland quarter-final. We were five points up ten minutes into the second half but they battled back and a late point by Jamesie O'Connor brought it level.

It says a lot for the pressure we were under that James McGarry was man-of-the-match after making some brilliant saves. In fairness, we were at a severe disadvantage for much of the second-half after Tommy Walsh was sent off for a fairly harmless foul that drew a yellow card. The trouble was he had also picked up one earlier so he found himself heading for the dug-out.

If Tommy felt bad about leaving us short-handed, he certainly more than made up for it in the replay which we won by five points (1-11 to 0-9). He turned in an unbelievable performance. Clare set themselves up defensively, which led to much lower scoring than usual. You don't win many championship matches scoring 1-11; then again you don't lose many by conceding 0-9. In fairness to Clare, they came at us with a plan on both days and made life very hard for us.

Henry Shefflin got a right scare in the replay when he took the butt of a hurley in the eye, but thankfully, the damage didn't turn out to be as bad as was first thought and he was back in action for the semi-final against Waterford eight days later. What's more, he brought his A-game to Croke

Park, scoring two goals from open play as well as nailing several frees. It was some performance so soon after getting such a serious scare.

We won by 3-12 to 0-18, with all the goals coming in the first half. To be honest, it was not a good performance. Waterford had scored more often than us and since they were without John Mullane, who was suspended, you wondered what would have happened if he had been playing. It was our third game in fourteen days so we put our listless second-half effort (we only scored six points) down to that.

There was probably more to it than a busy schedule. With the exception of the Dublin and Galway games, where we really let loose, we hadn't functioned at anything like full power all year. Still, we had reached the All-Ireland final against Cork, who had also come through the 'back door', after losing to Waterford in the Munster final. Cork hadn't been tested at all by Antrim or Wexford in the quarter-final and semi-final so it was difficult to gauge where exactly they were by comparison to the previous year when we beat them by three points in the final.

Personally, I have always remained convinced that if we had played Cork on the Sunday after we beat Waterford, we would have won. We had played five games since losing to Wexford and while we didn't really fire against Clare or Waterford, we had still built up decent momentum.

Now, we had a five week wait for the All-Ireland final. In theory, that should have suited us but after being so busy up to then, the long gap was probably a hindrance. Something similar happened Meath footballers in 1991. Granted, they had a lot more games than us but they kept rising to the challenge week after week until they reached the All-Ireland final.

The final was some weeks away and everyone thought the break from highly-pressurised games would do them good. Instead, they didn't play anywhere near full potential against Down in the final and were beaten.

It's safe to say we didn't do ourselves justice in the 2004 All-Ireland final. Correction – we did ourselves a great injustice in the second half, a period which we lost by 0-11 to 0-2. The idea that Kilkenny would score only two points in 35 minutes in any game, let alone an All-Ireland final, might look bizarre but that's exactly what happened. Both points came from Henry Shefflin, from a free and '65'. Yes folks, we didn't score once from play in the second half. Between us, the starting six forwards scored

0-4 from open play in the entire game; myself, Eddie Brennan and John Hoyne drew a total blank.

So what happened? It's impossible to know. We missed a lot of chances in the first half but were still a point ahead (0-7 to 0-6) at half-time. The second half was a total nightmare. Cork piled on the points and we failed to respond in any meaningful way. Bad and all as our performance was, we were still in with a chance of rescuing something until Donal Óg Cusack made a great save from Henry around the hour mark. A goal at that stage might have re-ignited us but once that chance passed we were gone.

We lost by 0-17 to 0-9 and soon found out that it was Kilkenny's biggest defeat in an All-Ireland final since 1964 when they lost to Tipperary by fourteen points.

It was a shocking day on all fronts. I didn't realise it at the time but it would also turn out to be my last All-Ireland final. What a way to go out. It meant that I lost my first (1991) and last (2004) All-Ireland finals – still, I was lucky enough to win five in between.

Would it all have been so different if we had beaten Wexford three months earlier? Would our season have settled into the routine to which we had become accustomed, rather than taking us on a new route? Would we have beaten Wexford if I hadn't got myself dropped for missing training? We'll never know the answers to any of those questions but I have to say that 2004 is not a year I remember with any fondness. Apart from anything else, it was the first year that we didn't win a Leinster, All-Ireland or National League title since 1997.

Still, the great thing about hurling for Kilkenny is that you always believe in the future. Things go wrong from time to time in sport so it's important to view it in the right way. A particular incident can't be revisited or a lost match replayed but there are always new games to be played, fresh challenges to be taken on.

That's how we looked at life heading into 2005. That being the case, the best way to rehabilitate ourselves was to go out and win the League. Brian always treated the League seriously on the basis that if you were hurling well in spring you were more likely to hurl well in summer. I agree with him. If a game is worth togging out for, it's worth winning. Otherwise, why bother?

We hurled very well in the 2005 League beating everyone except Clare in the group games. Clare beat everyone except Galway to set up a final which was a repeat of the previous year's All-Ireland quarter-final. The League final was played in Thurles on May Bank Holiday Monday and we were expecting another gruelling test from Clare. Anthony Daly had been setting them up in a way that was very hard to break down and that again proved to be the case in the first half of the League final which ended level.

Maybe the fact that this was our fourth game against them in less than ten months was helpful but, whatever the background, we found the key to their defensive locks in the second half, opened the doors and flooded through. We won by 14 points in what was very impressive performance.

Everything looked in place for a big championship season but after scalding Offaly in the Leinster semi-final we got a real fright against Wexford in the final. I missed it due to injury and, like every other Kilkenny person in Croke Park, looked on in a state of shock as the first 25 minutes ran away from us.

Wexford were carrying on from a year before, only this time they were putting considerable daylight between us as they raced into a seven-point lead. It was a real test of character for Kilkenny and the lads responded well, but it wasn't until the last quarter that they finally took control. We won by three points.

For a few years back then, provincial champions had to play in the All-Ireland quarter-finals so, in real terms, we were no more advanced than Wexford.

It was still hard to know where we stood as an All-Ireland force and the quarter-final against Limerick did not provide much enlightenment. We led by eight points before half-time but Limerick were back within a point of us in the third quarter. We saw it through in the end, winning by five points, but it certainly wasn't an impressive performance. For a second successive game, we hadn't scored any goals, which was most unusual for Kilkenny, especially since we had hit Offaly for six in the Leinster semi-final.

It was claimed afterwards that we had been complacent against both Wexford and Limerick but nothing could be further from the truth. It's always easy to come up with that line when a fancied team doesn't win impressively. The truth was somewhat more concerning. For whatever reason, we just weren't firing.

"After the havoc wreaked on Clare in the League final and on Offaly in the Leinster semi-final, Kilkenny suddenly look human," wrote Colm Keys in the *Irish Independent* after the Limerick game.

Still, we had reached the All-Ireland semi-final through the direct route, which was all we could have done and all we needed to do. Ours was the second quarter-final on a double-header that also included Galway against Tipperary so we didn't see much of that game. We heard all about it later, in particular, how Galway had turned in a first class performance which overturned a six-point deficit in the final ten minutes.

We had beaten Galway easily in the qualifiers a year earlier but we knew full well that would count for nothing in the semi-final. After all, we beat them comfortably in the 2000 semi-final too, only for them to overwhelm us a year later. That's Galway for you – certainly when it comes to playing Kilkenny anyway. You never know what's coming next. Neither, it often seems, do they.

Off-field events were to have a major influence on the 2005 semi-final. Noel Hickey had contracted an illness after the Leinster final and was ruled out for the rest of the year. Indeed, there were concerns at the time that he might not hurl anymore, but thankfully he made a full recovery and was back to his very best the following year.

Noel was a huge loss to us, especially since Galway chose that particular semi-final to produce one of those wild, manic performances that can devastate any opposition. Playing Galway when they are in that mood is like being sucked into a tornado and blown all over the place. All you can do is hang on and hope you're still intact when it blows itself out.

The 2005 semi-final has gone down as one of the great classics which I suppose it was if lots of scores is the yardstick used to measure the quality. In all, it produced 9-36 with Galway winning by 5-18 to 4-18. Little did I know as I headed out on that pleasant August Sunday that it would be my last time to play in Croke Park and the last time I would wear the Kilkenny jersey. What was it someone once said? "You never know when it's all going to end."

Galway led by 5-17 to 3-12 after 57 minutes before we mounted a massive rescue operation which, in the end, left us one score short of survival. I have no doubt that if we had another three or four minutes, we would have won because Galway were hanging on desperately with one eye on the clock. Put it another way, if we hadn't leaked so alarmingly in the mid-section of the second half, we would have won.

Galway full-forward, Niall Healy helped himself to three goals that day and, inevitably, John Tennyson, who replaced Noel Hickey at full-back, took some criticism from Kilkenny supporters. It was easy to pick on John, who was only twenty at the time. It was also downright unfair. Healy had one of those days that wherever he went, the ball followed him and while he made the most of it, I'm sure he would be the first to admit that every break went his way.

I'll give you an example. At one stage, Peter Barry was awarded a free and obviously felt that he should have got a few others earlier on. John was coming out to take the free when Peter passed a remark along the lines of: "about time, ref". The free was cancelled, the ball thrown in, it broke towards our goal and, in an instant, Healy had whipped it to the net. Poor John was stranded but there was damn all he could have done as he was on his way out to take a free when the referee changed his decision.

There was always going to be soul-searching after that defeat. It was a second championship setback in less than a year and, inevitably, raised questions about the extent of the re-build required in Kilkenny. I wrote earlier that I didn't think the semi-final would be my last game for Kilkenny or in Croke Park which is true, because I never thought we were going to lose to Galway. However, when it was over and I began to reflect on things, I knew deep down that I wouldn't be back. My future became a matter of huge speculation in the media but I was determined not to let them retire me. I would make up my mind in my own good time, which I did in 2006.

Why not give it another go? Granted, I would have been 35 years old by the time the championship came around, but I had always minded myself and was feeling pretty good. Still, little things had changed.

Ever so slowly – and this happens to every player – the edge gets blunted. You grow a little softer; the relentless obsession which kept you going isn't quite there anymore.

You start thinking: 'I have to go training tonight,' rather than doing it automatically. For years that's how it was for me. Training was a huge part of my life, even if I didn't enjoy it a whole lot. Still, I loved the competitive element, trying to be first in the runs, trying to out-wit lads and always looking for new ways of doing things.

By 2005, I had lost a yard. I was finding it much more difficult to get away from opponents than I used to. I wasn't leading the training runs anymore. Speed was everything to me and once it started to drop a little, my game suffered. It's frustrating when that happens. You can see the gaps but can't quite make them. You know well what's happening – your pace is slipping.

Mentally, I had probably become a bit softer too. Father Time had made his call.

Ironically, one of the days that really convinced me I had done the right thing to quit the inter-county scene came in early summer 2006, sometime after the National League final, which Kilkenny won again. Gowran played Tullaroan and Tommy Walsh was marking me. I can't recall exactly what I scored but it was certainly in the 2-8 or 2-9 range, with both goals coming from open play.

Now, it might have looked as if I was as good as ever and giving Tommy a really hard time but that wasn't the case at all. Both goals came from flicks that were sent through to me. All I had to do was finish them off but when it came to winning my own ball, it simply wasn't happening. The day you can't win your own ball in any part of the field is the day to go.

I know Tommy Walsh isn't exactly the easiest man to play against but, at the same time, I would have loved the challenge in my prime years. By 2006, Tommy probably felt that as well as marking me, he could do a bit more – hence the two goals I got when the ball was flicked through. Tommy had ventured out a bit looking for more action. There's no way I'd get those sort of chances in a Kilkenny jersey.

I would always have been my own biggest critic. One of my cardinal rules was never to think I was better than I actually was. I have to say, that came easily to me. There were games where the media might have given me rave reviews for my performance and I'd be thinking to myself: 'yes, but I could have done an awful lot better'.

I'd look back at an incident where I missed a ball or took the wrong option. Did I miss a free? And if so, why? Could I have done better off-the-ball? I'd always concentrate on what I did wrong rather than what I did right. That way, I knew what to correct for the next day. I never, ever stopped doing that right throughout my career. It meant that when the time was right to retire, I recognised it straight away.

Once my speed had dipped, one of the main anchors in my game was gone. I could have hung around in 2006, probably got a few runs as a sub and picked up a sixth All-Ireland medal but it would have meant absolutely nothing to me. As far I was concerned, I would be there as a player challenging for a starting place all the time or not at all. That super-sub stuff wasn't for me.

It was disappointing that the 2005 season, in particular, ended the way it did. We were beaten in Leinster in 2004 and again in the All-Ireland final on a day when we had no excuses whatsoever, but the 2005 semi-final was a bit different. Galway deserved to win, having taken so many of their chances, but we made it a lot easier than it should have been in the second half when we would normally be coming on strong.

Galway out-scored us by 3-5 to 0-3 in a fifteen-minute spell which, even they would admit, was pretty unusual. Even after that, we very nearly saved the day. Not quite though. Galway saw it through and we had to live with the fact that after scoring 4-18, we were still out of the championship. I wonder how many times that has happened in the history of the championship.

As for me, the curtain had finally come down on my Kilkenny career. It really was a strange day, having started out with such high hopes of booking a place in another All-Ireland final and ending with the curtain coming down on my career. I didn't think about it as I left the pitch because I wasn't one hundred per cent sure about what I would do. There was no question of taking a last look at the stadium from a player's perspective as I headed for the tunnel.

All that was in my head was the crazy game I had been involved in, and the feeling that, if only we had a few more minutes, we would probably have saved it. In the days and weeks that followed, I realised that I wouldn't be coming back. There were lots of examples over the years of players who made a hasty decision after losing a championship game, only to regret it later.

Anyway, I had a fair bit of experience over retirement issues from my own brief exit in 1998. This time, I decided to say nothing, let time take its course and make the call in 2006. When I finally made the break in early summer, I had no idea of the impact it would have on me. Kilkenny had won another National League and everyone was looking forward to the championship and the prospect of replacing Cork as All-Ireland champions.

I hadn't played very much League hurling over the previous few seasons but I would have been training with the panel; now it was different. I hadn't been with them at all in 2006 but it wasn't until I finally announced my retirement that I began to think about how much I would miss the entire scene.

It's something that every player experiences eventually and it can be hard. Well, it was for me anyway. For almost half my life, the Kilkenny dressing-room was like a second home to me. From the Sunday afternoon I arrived in Nowlan Park as a teenager in the autumn of 1988, when Christy Heffernan put out his big hand to welcome me to the county scene, to the sound of Seamus Roche's whistle at the end of the 2005 All-Ireland semi-final, Kilkenny hurling had, to a large degree, defined who I was. I had become institutionalised within the system, the seasonal cycles, the training, the games, the success, the disappointment, the fun, the camaraderie and, most of all, the sense of belonging.

When you are involved in something for seventeen years, it becomes a large part of what you are. But, as and from the summer of 2006, that part was gone. Suddenly, there was a huge void in my life. I knew that retiring was the right thing to do but that made it no easier.

It's amazing how practical things that you never thought about before now become an issue. Instead of getting a Garda escort to Croke Park, where the coach whizzed through the streets largely unimpeded by traffic, now I was driving there. Since Croke Park was redeveloped, team coaches can be driven all the way to the dressing-room doors so you have no interaction with the public.

As a former player, all that changed. That's as it should be, of course, but it takes a bit of getting used to. Driving to a game, trying to find a parking spot a mile or more from the ground, the walk along the streets, the banter and the slagging with supporters were all a brand new experience. I grew to enjoy that but it was strange at first.

However, the big thing for every player who retires is the withdrawal symptoms from what has effectively been a drug. Watching games isn't easy either, particularly when you hear spectators giving out about players, especially the colleagues you have soldiered with for so long. You know well there were days when you were getting the same treatment but that's the way it is and there's nothing you can do about it.

I certainly found it hard to listen to people criticising lads who were my colleagues for so long. Although I was no longer part of the squad, I naturally felt an attachment to the panel, albeit from outside the tent. That's the thing about retiring – when you're gone, you're gone.

You can feel outside the loop when you're injured too but at least it's temporary. Retirement is final. The scene moves on without you, as it should.

I watched the 2006 All-Ireland final from the Cusack Stand and was absolutely delighted at the manner in which Kilkenny got to grips with Cork's game to such a degree that wherever there was a red jersey, there were two black-and-amber ones. I have always believed that it's not the team at the top that changed trends but rather those who are challenging them.

When a team is on top in any sport they will continue doing what got them there. Okay, so they will refine and adapt it but if the basic structure was good enough to get them there in the first place, then obviously it's working well.

Cork's possession game took them to the top in 2004/2005, so whoever was going to beat them would have to come up with something to counteract that. Kilkenny were always going to lead that charge which they did in 2006 when they successfully clogged up the channels that Cork had been so good at using. It demanded an unbelievable amount of hard work but the Kilkenny lads took it on and were rewarded.

I would have loved to be part of a team playing like that – and would have been a few years earlier – but as I watched the 2006 final, I knew my day had passed.

As it happened, the 2006 final was the last really tough one Kilkenny encountered until 2009. A number of circumstances came together after 2006 which worked very much in Kilkenny's favour. The panel was incredibly talented, they had a great manager over them and it all combined with a period in which the standard in the rest of Leinster dropped a lot.

Kilkenny hardly had to break sweat in the 2007 and 2008 Leinster championships, winning both very comfortably. Unusually, they won both All-Irelands by beating teams who had lost in the Munster championship, only to revive themselves through the 'back door'. Kilkenny could play whoever was put in front of them but it was unusual that over that two years period, neither of the Munster champions (Waterford 2007, Tipperary 2008) reached the final.

Waterford made it to the final, via the qualifiers in 2008, but might have had a better chance if they got there a year earlier.

It wasn't until 2009 when Tipperary re-emerged as a really powerful force that Kilkenny got their next big challenge in the All-Ireland final. Mind you, they were ready for it, winning a smashing contest.

The manner in which Kilkenny came to dominate after 2005 in no way surprised me. Everything was in place down to the last detail and made to work as close to perfection as possible. Naturally, I would have loved to be part of it but the legs had made their call a few years earlier. They wanted me in the stands, not on the pitch.

CHAPTER 11

THE BOSS

A few seasons back, I dropped in on Nowlan Park one evening to take a look at Kilkenny training. I do that from time to time just to remind myself of what it was like through so many years, so many good times, hard times but always enjoyable times. It's also interesting to see if, and how, things have changed.

It was a grand fine evening and the lads were having one of the famous in-house games where no quarter is asked, given or expected. I was watching it for a while and reckoned it was pretty much as it always had been. Then, I decided to text the referee. He wasn't dressed in standard refereeing gear, neither was he galloping up and down the field after the play. In fact, he was all but static around the middle of the pitch, moving just a few yards towards one or other goal from time to time.

The referee's name? Brian Cody.

My text ran along the lines of: "You've never changed with the whistle anyway. Still buried deep in your pocket and going to stay there by the look of things."

Brian would have liked that. He always loved the training games to be as close as possible to the real thing, only with a bit of extra edge. Every man for himself and all that. If you can win your own ball in a training game where you've little or no chance of getting a free, you'll do fine in the real thing when the referee has his whistle in his hand, rather than his pocket. Brian's system works. It makes players tougher, harder and better prepared to take whatever comes their way on match day. Let's put it this way – there's not much a player will experience in a game that he hasn't been through in Nowlan Park.

I'll give you an example of how you needed to be able to look after yourself in Kilkenny training. I remember one session where the ash was flying in all directions and as I jumped with Peter Barry under a high ball, he pulled and caught me flush on the middle finger. It was badly dislocated and I knew straight away it needed urgent attention so I ran off the pitch without saying a word to anyone. Mind you, I hadn't even got a free. The whistle never left the manager's pocket! It was hard enough to get a free out of him at any time but there was definitely no way he was going to penalise a fellow-'Village' man! In fairness, I probably didn't deserve a free, although my busted finger, now pumping blood and looking as if had been hit by a sledge-hammer, might not agree.

Almost doubled up with pain, I headed straight for the car, swung out of the car park as fast as I could and sped down to Dr. Bill Cuddihy's house. Dr. Bill was an expert in all types of emergencies and I thought from the way he looked at the damaged finger that it might be serious. He said something about maybe needing an operation but then he gave me an injection and got to work on the finger. His expertise eventually worked and he jerked it back into place. As I said, he was an expert. It still looked a bit of a mess but Dr. Bill assured me it would be okay now that it was back in place.

Happy that the injury wasn't as bad as I thought but still feeling pretty miserable, I wanted to head home but since I was in my tracksuit and my clothes were up in the Nowlan Park dressing-room, I drove back up. The lads were still training but the game was over and they were running around the pitch. I came out the tunnel from the dressing-room, took a look at them and wondered what I'd do next. Heading back in and getting changed seemed like a good idea but they were just approaching the tunnel entrance so I decided to join them. I tucked in with the group, and saw out the rest of the session. I swear to God, I don't think I had even been missed! I was away for about forty-five minutes but training went on, hell for leather, dog-eating-dog and no room for looking around to see who wasn't there. No doubt, it continued as a whistle-free zone as well! I was back running at the end of the session so it was assumed I was okay.

Nobody asked me how I was and I didn't say anything. If I was looking for sympathy, which I wasn't, I was in the wrong place.

Brian was the fifth and last manager I played under in my Kilkenny senior career, having earlier been there under Dermot Healy, the late Ollie Walsh, Nickey Brennan and Kevin Fennelly. I knew little enough about Brian when he took over in late 1998, other than he had been an outstanding full-back in his playing days. I also knew he tried his hand at full-forward for a season.

He had managed his own club, James Stephens for a few years and was known to be a fiercely proud 'Village' man. For some reason, he didn't enjoy a whole lot of success as club manager, certainly not in terms of winning county titles, but then competition was fierce, as indeed it always is in Kilkenny.

My recollection of playing against James Stephens is that Gowran had a very good record against them. We might have been a small country club but we always seemed to lift our game against the city lads. In fact, that probably helped us since there's nothing more that rural clubs in any county like than beating the townies. Cody was in charge of 'The Village' in 1996 when we beat them in the county final replay, taking the senior title back to Gowran for the first time. James Stephens had a very good team at the time, led by Peter Barry, Philip Larkin and Brian McEvoy but we got the measure of them in the replay.

I can't recall if there was any sense of surprise when Brian was appointed Kilkenny team manager to succeed Kevin Fennelly. If there was, it passed over my head. Personally, I always took the view that whoever the County Board appointed as manager was fine by me and I think most of the other lads thought along the same lines.

Kevin only stayed for a year and, between that and the savage way Nickey Brennan had been treated at the end of his reign in 1997, I suspect that not very many were interested in taking on the job in late 1998. Well, would you? At that stage, Kilkenny needed a really strong man to take the reins and drive things on in his own way. In hindsight, Brian was the perfect choice, but since he hadn't led James Stephens to a county title, I'm sure there were many who doubted whether he would make it as a county manager. They won't admit that now, of course!

Anyway, Brian arrived and brought Ger Henderson and Johnny Walsh with him as selectors. He would have played with Ger for years and obviously knew Johnny from his playing days with Ballyhale.

So what was Brian like to work with? He rang me up shortly after he was appointed and asked me generally about things. I'm sure he talked to a lot of other lads too. He was coming in at a difficult time in Kilkenny hurling, even if we were the reigning Leinster champions. Winning Leinster is always important to Kilkenny but unless it's followed up with an All-Ireland, questions are asked and answers expected.

After all, nobody said "well done" to Kevin Fennelly for steering Kilkenny to a Leinster title in 1998. No, all the focus was on the defeat by Offaly in the All-Ireland final. Basically, the year was regarded as a failure.

The first two years under Brian were straight-forward enough, albeit with different results. We lost the 1999 All-Ireland final to Cork and won it a year later, beating Offaly, but then came the crash against Galway in the 2001 semi-final. It was a watershed moment, one which changed Brian's approach.

Galway bullied us off the pitch, dominating us physically in a way we had not experienced over the previous two years. What Galway did was perfectly legal, let me add. It was still bullying, but it worked brilliantly for them. We just weren't ready for what they threw at us. Maybe winning the All-Ireland the year before had made us a little soft mentally, and since neither Offaly nor Wexford extended us to any great degree in the 2001 Leinster championship, we might have thought we were actually better prepared than we were. Besides, we had beaten Galway fairly comfortably in the 2000 All-Ireland semi-final and saw nothing in the meantime to suggest they would be any better a year later.

They were and they showed it right from the off. They never allowed us an inch and won the vast majority of the one-on-one battles which, of course, sowed the seeds for their overall dominance. They had Gregory Kennedy sent off just before half-time but it made no difference, whatsoever. It should have but it didn't. They played with five forwards from there to the finish and kept the scoreboard ticking along from a comfortably safe distance ahead of us. Although it was August, Croke Park was in a terrible state that day. This was before the new surface was put down and, for some reason, the old one had cut up like a bog during the Tipperary-Wexford All-Ireland semi-final replay, which had been played the day before.

The ball regularly got stuck in the sodden ground which added to our frustration on a day when everything was going wrong anyway. Not that the conditions made any difference to the flow of the game. It was the same for both sides, but Galway coped a lot better and from the moment Eugene Cloonan got a goal from a long range free early on, they had the edge.

They led by three points at half-time but, with an extra man for the second half, we should have been able to assert ourselves. We were, after all, the reigning All-Ireland champions so surely we would make things happen. We would if we were let. However, Galway never allowed their pace or tempo to drop and won the second half too (1-9 to 1-7). To be honest, a five-point defeat flattered us. Our goal came very late on when I hit a 20-metre free into the net but all it did was take the grim look off a grim scoreline on a grim day.

Eugene Cloonan scored 2-9 – almost as much as all of the Kilkenny team put together – and it was also the day when Kevin Broderick scored a memorable point. You never like to see the opposition scoring but I always admire true skill, wherever it comes from. Broderick was a lovely touch hurler and he certainly showed it on that occasion when he soloed forward, flicked the ball over Eamonn Kennedy's head as he ran past him, balanced the ball on his hurley before taking aim and firing over a magnificent point. A wonderful score. We were struggling anyway but, after seeing that, I reckoned it certainly wasn't going to be Kilkenny's day.

It wasn't. We all felt really deflated after that defeat, but Brian seemed to take it worst of all. He blamed himself personally for not spotting that maybe little things had changed in the course of the season and that we hadn't reacted to them. It can happen without being noticed and it's only when you come up against a driven force – as Galway were that day – that you realise something isn't quite right. By the time you spot it, there's no way back. It's too late.

Clearly, it hurt Brian very badly, the extent to which became apparent early in January 2002 when we started back in training. After a session in Kilkenny CBS, he called a team talk and we all trooped into the Science lab to listen to what he had to say. He gave what I would regard as the most powerful talk I heard in the seven seasons I played under him.

It really would put the hairs on the back of your neck standing. He said he had looked closely at himself over the winter, in particular, his role in the Galway defeat. He made it clear that he took most of the responsibility but pointed out that others had to take their share too, including every player who lined out against Galway and every sub who didn't. He widened the net to include the County Board too. In fact, just about everyone was made to feel that they had a part to play in the failure, which was probably true. Most of all though, he blamed himself and, from the passionate way he spoke, it was obvious that he believed every word of it.

Players like to see someone else take responsibility when things go wrong, even if it's not always warranted so Brian's reaction to the defeat was spot on.

He hadn't cost Kilkenny the 2001 All-Ireland semi-final but he still put his hands out to take a lot of the blame. He did it straight away in the interviews immediately after the game. Five months later he was still doing it but even as he spoke, we knew that as well as being very honest about how he perceived his own role in the defeat, he was also throwing down a challenge for the future.

Apparently, he had seriously considered resigning but thought better of it (thank God for that).

However, once he decided to stay on, things were always going to be a lot different. Changes would be made, attitudes would be harder, intensity would be greater. It was all driven by the boss, who knew that having publicly blamed himself for the Galway defeat, he was in a position to demand just about anything from us. He was the leader, but all he could do was lead. It was up to us to do the rest.

The Galway game also convinced him of one thing – never play a player who isn't fully fit. A few of the lads carried knocks and niggles into that game but played anyway. No more. From then on, only lads who were 100 per cent right would be playing.

The training in 2002 was much harder than over the previous two years. I missed a lot of it through injury but I knew what was going on. One session had to be abandoned because a few lads got hurt. It was fiercely demanding stuff. And so it went for months. The idea was to make everyone a ball winner who would be self-sufficient and not relying on others. Training was now very serious business. Not much fun, but then it wasn't supposed to be. Whether you held your place depended on how you did in training. There would be no hiding on match days and, by God, they was no hiding in training either. Brian had raised the stakes and only those who went with it survived. Kilkenny's record since then proved just how right he was.

Very few people know Brian Cody well. In fact, I'd go so far as to say that his wife Elsie and family are the only ones who really know him. The many Kilkenny players involved with him over the years know a certain amount about him but no more. He's good for them, good for Kilkenny hurling and, indeed, good for hurling in general, but that's as far as it goes. After that, he's a private man who does his own thing. He keeps to himself, gets on with his job and expects others to do the same.

I'll say this about Brian Cody – if anyone ever tells you that he passed a critical remark in public about any player who was on the Kilkenny panel at any time, they are telling lies. His loyalty to the players, to the jersey and to the Kilkenny brand is unbreakable and he always has the utmost respect for the people he works with, provided of course that they do their job. And if they don't, they are gone pretty quickly. It's that simple.

The idea that Brian would ever bad-mouth a player behind his back is so alien to the man that it just wouldn't happen. I know Brian as well as anyone else who played under him and never heard him being critical of a Kilkenny hurler, past or present. Since I retired, I would ring Brian occasionally before a big game to wish him and the team well but we'd never talk about individual players. Nor would I ask him who he was planning to play or anything like that because I wouldn't put him in a position to have to say: "Well, you know I don't talk about that."

Loyalty to the cause and to the players is one of his great strengths and I, for one, always appreciated it.

Don't get me wrong. If you aren't pulling your weight, you will hear all about it. And it doesn't matter whether your name is DJ Carey or Henry Shefflin or Tommy Walsh, you get it too, if you deserve it. You're part of the Kilkenny squad and expected to act as such. I have to say I never had a cross word with him but that doesn't mean he didn't have his say on various things with me from time to time. Suffice to say, I was asked to step up my game at half-time on a few occasions. And when Brian asks, you know you've been asked! I suppose I would have been regarded as one of the leaders and he made sure that I – and others in the same boat – carried out our responsibilities. Mind you, he expected every player to be a leader in his own way.

The thing about Brian is that Kilkenny always comes first. Inevitably, that involves making decisions that lads won't like, but then no manager can keep everyone happy all the time. There will always be players who think they should be on the panel but aren't, and others who are on the panel but not making the starting fifteen. There's bound to be unease from time to time, but that can be healthy and positive for the overall scene. It's not always possible to keep everyone happy but it's not always necessary either.

I'm sure there are plenty of lads who were fiercely disappointed over either not being on the Kilkenny panel or the team over the years but they had to take it. There can't be a Court of Appeal. The boss has the ultimate call.

And when it comes to the end of a player's career, it can be difficult to know when to let go since everybody wants to go on for as long as they can.

Few people leave any squad fully satisfied. Lads like John Power, Pat O'Neill, Eamonn Kennedy, Denis Byrne and, of course, Charlie Carter would have felt there was more in them and maybe there was. But when a manager makes a call, that's it – you've got to accept it. That's what he's there for. John wouldn't have been happy to have got so little action in 2002 but, on the other hand, it was Brian who brought him back on the panel at the start of 1999. John hadn't been involved at all in 1998 and it would have been easy for Brian to leave him out and go for someone from the younger generation but he didn't and he was proven right. John was brilliant for us over the next three seasons.

Eamonn had been hurling well on the club scene for years but it was only when Brian came in that he finally got his big chance at county level. He took it with both hands in 2000, turning in a great year at centre-back, winning an All-Ireland medal and an All Star award.

He was gone by 2002 and probably felt hard done by. Still, it was Brian who gave him his opportunity at an age when he probably thought the county scene was going to pass him by.

My own brother, Martin was brought into the panel by Brian shortly after he took over. Joe Dermody was No. 1 goalkeeper in 1998 with James McGarry as sub but when Brian came in, he replaced James with Martin.

Shortly afterwards, Joe picked up an injury and James was invited back. Then, Martin got married, went away on honeymoon and James got his chance. The rest is history. James did very well, became first choice goalkeeper and held on to it for many years, becoming one of the best keepers in the business, even if he never received an All Star award. Martin got back as sub goalie but didn't show up for a trial game at the start of one season and that was the end of that. His days on the panel were over.

That's the way it is in Kilkenny, where there are always several challengers for every position. It's the manager's job to sift through them all and decide on a final 30-35. Of course, there will be disappointments but there's nothing the manager can do about that.

You'll always have people waiting in the long grass for the day when things go wrong – or the days when they stay wrong – but Kilkenny's record under Brian Cody meant that he escaped the critics more than most. That doesn't mean they're not out there.

People often ask me what he was like in the dressing-room. I think they expect to hear about this giant of a man bellowing out instructions and generally laying down the law but it wasn't like that at all. Yes, he would make stirring speeches when he had to; yes, he would lay down the law but it was always done in a well-organised way so that everyone knew exactly what it was about and what he wanted. His command in a dressing-room is total, not in a domineering sort of way, but rather as the man who pulls everything and everyone together.

One thing he always hated was empty talk. He had no time for fellas who'd talk a good show and then fail to deliver. You either put up or shut up with Brian. Sometimes, you'd have lads shouting and roaring as if they couldn't wait to knock down the door and get out on the pitch but they mightn't be quite as driven once the action began. They were no good to Brian. In fact, he had no time whatsoever for that sort of carry-on.

And then you had a quiet lad like Noel Hickey. He didn't say a whole lot in the dressing-room but when he did, boy, was it worth listening to. He was brilliant when he spoke out and, of course, the big thing with Noel was that you knew when he got out on the pitch he would back up his words with actions.

The way Noel saw out his career was typical of him. Michael Kavanagh too. Noel was a sub in 2012 and didn't get much action, but he still saw the season through to the end. Michael was the same the year before. These lads didn't start any year thinking they would be subs. Fierce competitors like that always believe in themselves and in their ability to force their way onto a team. But when they didn't, they just got on with it anyway and worked as hard as ever. Cody would have huge time for that sort of spirit and attitude. And rightly so.

When it was my turn to sign off before the start of the 2006 season, I met Brian and said: "that's it, it's time to go." He asked me was I sure and I said I was. He put no pressure on me to stay on but I have no doubt he would have been happy if I had stayed around.

He might have wanted me to play a different role, maybe coming on as a sub from time to time but I had no interest at all in that. He didn't say that's what he had in mind, by the way. He just listened to me and left it at that.

I played from 1999 until 2005 under Brian and enjoyed many, many great days, as well, of course as suffering some disappointments. I'll say this about Brian Cody – he's a brilliant manager and a brilliant person for Kilkenny hurling. It owes him a massive debt.

One of his great strengths is his devotion to the cause, starting with his club, extending to the county and on to hurling in general. Brian would be big into lads performing well for their clubs. Club games are well spread over the weekend, often in double-headers so Brian and his selectors can take in as many as possible. They might not attend them together but it still means that between them they have seen most of the action. By Sunday evening, very little has happened over the weekend than Brian doesn't know about.

He applies a fairly basic philosophy to the job. Get in the best players, train them well and let them hurl. I know a lot has been made of Kilkenny's training matches but I'm sure they are just as intense in other counties. They have to be because if you're not going flat out in training, how are you going to do it in a game? Training is supposed to be preparing you for a match situation so, as far as it's possible, it has to replicate an actual game.

The one thing Brian would never accept in training was a drop in tempo. If your touch was out or the overall quality of hurling wasn't particularly good, he wouldn't worry too much about it on the basis that he knew it was there and would come out at another time. But if the tempo and intensity dropped to even the slightest degree, he just wouldn't have it. He wanted lads rattling into each other, not just now and then but for the full training game. If it wasn't happening he would stop the session and let you know all about it. Very often, that would be followed with an extended run!

Hurling had changed around the time Brian took over as Kilkenny manager. Ger Loughnane had driven Clare in a different direction and it not only brought them great success but also made it clear to everyone else that unless they adapted they would be left behind. Cork came along with their new approach which involved a lot of running and hand-passing. Prior to all that, Kilkenny tended to play their own game and let the opposition worry about them but now we had to re-invent ourselves to some degree.

Training techniques were changing too. Floodlights were being installed at various venues which meant you could do more outdoor work at night. Mick O'Flynn was the trainer for most of the years I was there and did a great job. Michael Dempsey came in after him and brought his own style. He travelled around the country, checking out what others were doing and mixing some of it with his own ideas. One of the changes under Brian was that the selectors became more actively involved in the training sessions.

Prior to that, their job seemed to be essentially about helping the manager to train the team but, under Brian, they had more to do. But then times were changing and Kilkenny was changing with them. Brian recognised the need to adapt.

He looked at Cork's running game and figured out that the best way to counteract it was to block things up. Be in their faces all the time. It worked.

Brian focussed a lot on workrate. The corner-forwards had to be able to tackle as well as the full-backs. Defence began near the opposition goal and continued all the way back. A forward could score four or five points from play and think he had a right good game but if his marker cleared five or six balls without being under fierce pressure, Brian would let him know all about it.

His approach was simple. Every player who comes into the Kilkenny panel is playing to a high standard so it's no big deal for a forward to hit a few scores. However, if he does that and also restricts his marker, now he's in business. Brian has no time for forwards who aren't able to tackle properly or, worse still, think that it's beneath them. Lads like that never last long with him.

I was lucky enough in that I was a good tackler. But then I had to be, because since I was quite small as a youngster, I had to learn how to fight my own corner. If there's one thing Brian dislikes more than bad tackling it's a bad attitude.

Being involved with Kilkenny is a serious business and he simply won't accept any sloppiness. I remember at one stage how a guy who was new to the panel made the mistake of thinking he didn't have to heed what he was being told. We were doing a drill which involved sprinting and picking up the ball at speed on the way back.

The new lad tried to lift the ball one handed on a few occasions and it didn't come off. He was told the drill involved using both hands but he still didn't do it. He wasn't there the following night and was never brought back. Brian obviously didn't like his attitude and cut him adrift.

There was no way Brian would ever tolerate having anyone on the panel who isn't prepared to toe the line. Standards are set and maintained by the group as a whole and once everyone buys into that, the ship is easy to run.

I know people find it hard to believe Brian when he says after matches which were won fairly easily that he expected a fierce battle but it's the truth. It has never mattered to him who Kilkenny are playing next, whether it's one of the big powers or a so-called weaker county. He will treat both exactly the same on the basis that the day you allow complacency anywhere near the dressing-room, it will undermine everything.

It's that attitude that turned Kilkenny into the unbelievable force it became under Brian. People wonder how players who won so much continued to be motivated year after year but the actual winning is a key ingredient in that. The more a player wins, the more he wants to win. The challenge for a manager is to keep the standards up, which Brian has done so consistently.

But then the whole scene is pretty solid in Kilkenny. Ned Quinn would always have been important in ensuring that things ran smoothly between the players, management and County Board. So when some other counties – Cork immediately comes to mind – had all sorts of hassle, we were happy enough with what we had because, in fairness, we were well looked after. I'm sure that applies to this day.

Overall though, I'd say the biggest secret to Kilkenny's success is humility. A lad with four or five All-Irelands doesn't think he's in any way special. And why should he? He was lucky enough to be born with a good talent and just as fortunate to be born in a county that had a history of winning titles. How many medals would some Carlow players have if they were born in Kilkenny? And how many Kilkenny hurlers would have none if they were born to the north in Laois or to the South in Carlow?

That's why it's important to appreciate the chances you get and to remain humble, irrespective of how much success you have enjoyed. The day you forget that it the day you lose the run of yourself.

Happy times for three young Gowran lads:
Myself, Charlie Carter and Pat O'Neill won an All-Ireland minor title in 1988.

I'm flanked by two of my great mentors, Dick O'Neill and John Knox,
men who did so much to help me make the grade.
A few young supporters are enjoying the occasion too!

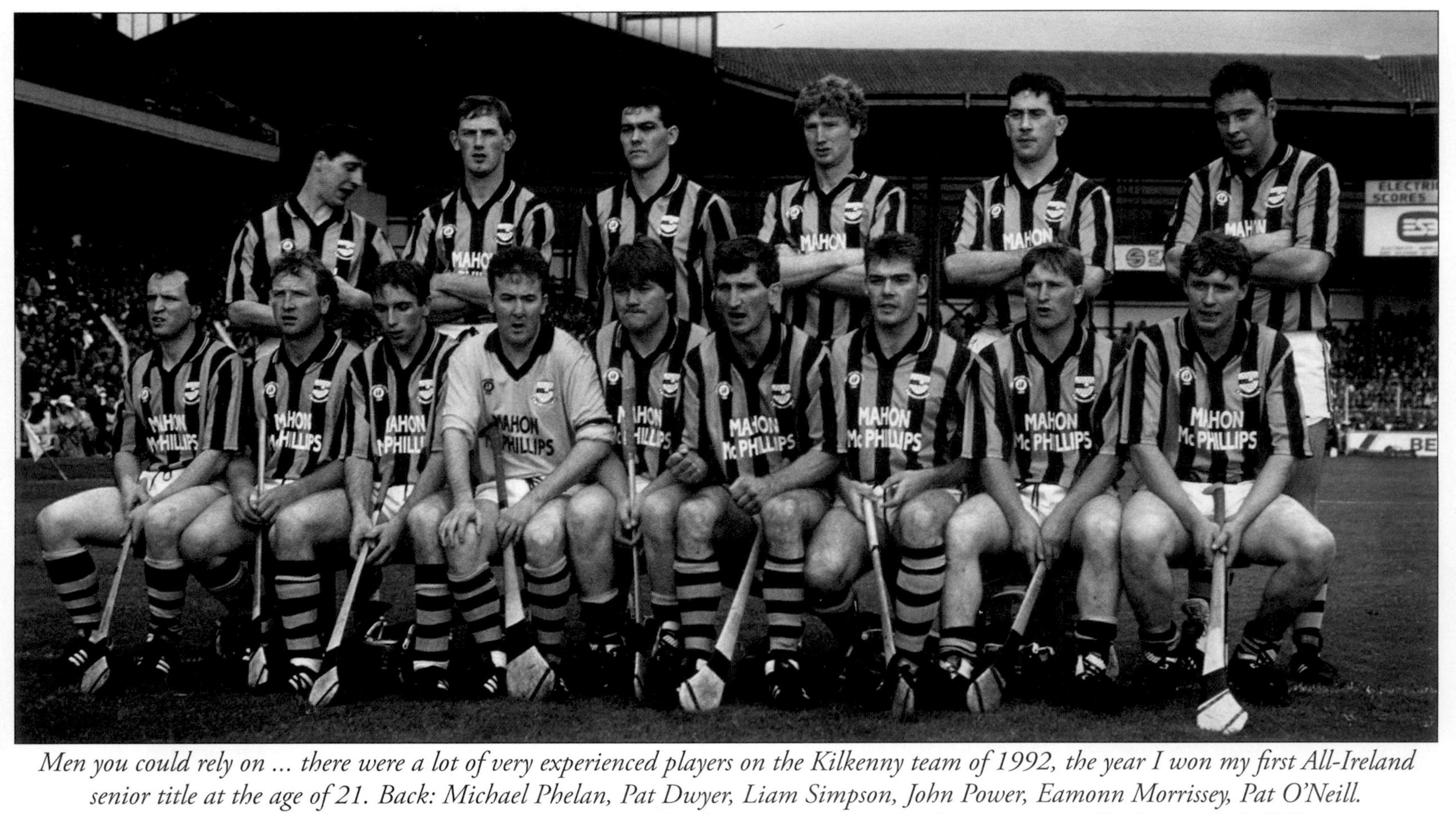

Men you could rely on ... there were a lot of very experienced players on the Kilkenny team of 1992, the year I won my first All-Ireland senior title at the age of 21. Back: Michael Phelan, Pat Dwyer, Liam Simpson, John Power, Eamonn Morrissey, Pat O'Neill. Front: Eddie O'Connor, Willie O'Connor, DJ Carey, Michael Walsh, Liam McCarthy, Liam Fennelly, (captain), Bill Hennessy, Jamesy Brennan, Liam Walsh.

My sons Mikey and Sean help me show off the Liam MacCarthy Cup on our return to Kilkenny after winning the 2003 All-Ireland final.

Christmas 2002 and times are good. I celebrate an All-Ireland win with Kilkenny and a county title success with Gowran along with Dick O'Neill, Charlie Carter and my brother Martin.

The High Priests of Gowran. I have the Liam McCarthy Cup while Charlie Carter has the National League trophy in 2003 after we captained Kilkenny to the double. Charlie captained the team in the League but left the panel during the championship and missed out on the All-Ireland success.

My brother Martin and me with some happy young supporters. That's my son, Mikey, under my right arm.

And I lived to tell the tale! I'm taking on Michael O'Halloran, Liam Doyle, Frank Lohan, Davy Fitzgerald and Brian Lohan in the 1999 National League final against Clare.

On my way to a first Leinster title. Dublin's Sean Kearns gives chase in the 1991 Leinster final which we won narrowly.

What an 11-a-side this lot would make. A splash of county colours at the 1999 launch for the All-Ireland championships. Martin Storey (Wexford), Kevin Broderick (Galway), Tony Browne (Waterford) and Conor McCann (Dublin) join me in the front row. Niall Rigney (Laois), Brian Corcoran (Cork), Joe Quaid (Limerick), Brendan Cummins (Tipperary), Anthony Daly (Clare) and Brian Whelahan (Offaly) are quite a back row!

Bill Maher (Laois) was determined not to let me escape in the 1999 Leinster semi-final.

My long-time sparring partner, Brian Whelahan moves in on me during the 2000 All-Ireland final. A brilliant hurler, he was also one of the most sporting opponents I came across.

Happiness is ... scoring an early goal against Offaly in the 2000 All-Ireland final.

Croke Park was my second home for a long time.
I celebrate winning the 2002 All-Ireland final.

A dream come true! I lead Kilkenny in the parade for the 2003 All-Ireland final. We beat Cork by three points.

You did fine, DJ. Brian Cody is pleased after we won the 2002 All-Ireland final. Earlier in the year I thought my career might be over.

As good as it gets! I hoist the Liam MacCarthy Cup after captaining Kilkenny to the 2003 All-Ireland title.

I had some great battles with Wexford over the years. Here, I'm coming under pressure from David 'Doc' O'Connor in a Leinster championship game.

Club is personal. I had same great days in the red-and-white of Young Irelands, including senior county title wins in 1996 and 2002. I made a comeback to play special junior this year.

I played in four All-Ireland finals against Cork between 1992 and 2004, winning two and losing two. Jerry O'Connor, Ben O'Connor and John Gardiner lead the chase on this occasion.

It wasn't easy to escape from Brian Lohan but I have the run on him in this clash during the 2005 National League final.

The last time I figured on a winning Kilkenny team. Limerick's Stephen Lucey and Brian Geary are on my case during the 2005 All-Ireland quarter-final in Croke Park.

Galway defenders everywhere in the 2005 All-Ireland semi-final which was my last game in the black-and-amber

I am always happy to help out anywhere if I can.
Here, I offer a few tips to Wicklow hurlers in April 2007.

Rough times in the rough at the K Club during a Pro-Am. Lots of grass but where's the ball?

Well deserved, Henry. I present the Hurler of the Year award to Henry Shefflin at the 2012 All Star awards banquet. RTE's Marty Morrissey looks on.

We can still do it, lads. I join Nicky English, Charlie Carter and Damien Fitzhenry for a charity game in Newbridge in August 2013.

CHAPTER 12

TEN YEARS – FIVE MANAGERS

Dermot Healy must have taken one look at me, decided I was a handy little hurler but needed fattening up if I wasn't going to be blown away, the first time I ventured out with the seniors.

I was in Leaving Cert year in St. Kieran's when I was first called onto the Kilkenny panel in late 1988 after we'd won the All-Ireland minor title. Dermot had taken over as senior manager and, just as I turned eighteen, I was among his first recruits.

On evenings when we had county training, I'd finish school at around four o'clock and since the session would be in Kilkenny later on, there was no point going home to Gowran and coming back in again. Dermot reckoned that some of that time could be put to good use by sending me down to Langton's to eat. I was small – very small – at the time so he obviously felt that filling me up on Langton's finest would prove to be a good investment.

I had no objections. So, a few evenings a week, this scrawny little fella would arrive in Langton's, order himself a fine meal, eat it as his leisure and relax before heading off to training. Steak, chicken or fish – they all looked – and tasted – good to me! I'd eat again after training but then I was a young, growing lad, not given to counting calories or bothering about what was supposed to be good or bad for me. I ate when I was hungry and thought no more of it. I don't know whether Dermot could spot the fruits of his plan straight away but even if he didn't, I was very definitely enjoying them.

I'm not sure what dietary experts would make of the two-dinner policy but it suited me fine. In fact, I always maintained what I suppose would be regarded as an unusual approach to eating before a game. Some lads would eat virtually nothing on the day of a game but I'd have to top up with the full works a few hours before throw-in, even on All-Ireland final day.

Maybe it was my way of coping with nerves. Some lads would be sick in the hours before a game which, I suppose, was how their systems coped with the nervous tension. Pat Dwyer was a typical example. Poor Pat could eat nothing at all on the day of a game but would still go out and hurl a storm. How he did it I'll never know. If my stomach wasn't full, I couldn't function at all.

Mention of Pat, he was some full-back, probably one of the most underrated of all time. He had brilliant wrists and was a bloody nightmare for a forward. I spent many an evening on him in training in Nowlan Park and, as was my wont, I always played from the front. I'd get out ahead of him; the lads out the field would spot it and fire the ball into me. I'd collect it but what happened next was interesting, not to mention frustrating, for me at least. I lost count of the number of times I'd throw up the ball, getting ready to hit it and suddenly it was gone.

Pat would time his flick to perfection and because his wrists were so good, he'd knock the ball twenty or thirty yards down the field. I bet you there isn't a forward he ever played against who doesn't have similar stories of Pat's unbelievable ability to get the ball away, just as you were ready to pull the trigger. It was fierce frustrating. You'd think you had done everything right when – bang – the ball was thirty yards away. At least I only had to suffer from Pat's skill in training but opposition full-forwards got it all the time in games. What's more they didn't always realise what was happening so an awful lot of them got caught over the years. I'd be watching from the other end of the field and thinking to myself: 'good man, Pat, you've done it often enough to me in training'.

He'd be doing in on an empty stomach too! I'd have to eat a full meal before we left the hotel, however big the occasion. Usually, I'd eat chicken or fish but I had the odd steak too, even if the advice would be to avoid it. I knew what made me feel comfortable going into a game and a full stomach was very definitely high up that list, so I never ignored what my body was telling me, whatever the expert advice said.

Maybe it came from Dermot Healy's 'fatten him up' policy all those years ago. I was lucky in that it didn't matter what I ate, I wouldn't pile on the weight. Obviously, I put in all the hard work in training but some lads can do that and still find it hard to keep the pounds off, especially in the closed season. That was never a problem for me – I was always naturally thin.

At one stage I was fierce fond of sugary things too. I remember being down in Jim Bolger's house on one occasion – it was around the time he was training Cois na Tine for Niall Quinn – and we were having a cup of tea. We were sitting there chatting about hurling (Jim loves hurling as much as racing) and after he poured the tea, I scooped two spoons of sugar into the cup. He looked at me as if I had tipped in a handful of performance-enhancers.

"How many cups of tea would you drink in a day," he asked.

"Don't know. It depends on the day, I suppose. Maybe six or seven".

"Six or seven? And you put two spoons of sugar into every one of them?"

"Yea, I do. I love it."

He paused for a second, stared at me and said: "keep that up, DJ and you'll have diabetes in no time".

I never put a grain of sugar in my tea from that day to this.

I put lots of sugar in my tea down in Langton's in those early days when I used to head down after school. Dermot Healy wouldn't have approved, I'm sure, but the main thing from his viewpoint was that I was getting plenty of nourishment before going to training. The fact that he even thought about it showed how clued in he was to the individual needs of different players. That was very much the style he brought to his management.

He was big into detail. I used to do some part-time work in Dunnes Stores around that time and he fixed it so that it wouldn't clash with training. He knew I wanted the bit of part-time work and quietly went about mixing it in with the hurling so that there was no clash. He was always very conscious of things that might be impacting on players' lives outside sport. It was very intelligent management. After all, a happy hurler is a better hurler and little things can make a big difference.

His desire to bulk me up a bit was well justified. He was a modern manager, always up to date with the latest trends. He was big into elaborate stretching exercises, which was fairly new to the scene at the time. One of the drills involved two lads lining up with their hands on each other's shoulders. The idea was that you pushed hard enough to stretch the leg muscles. You weren't supposed to move – or be moved from the original spot but obviously nobody told Ger Henderson that. Either that, or Ger ignored him.

Ger, my big hero when I was growing up, was one of the most competitive men that ever stood on a sports field and it even extended to stretching. I was paired off with Ger one evening and we began the exercises. Before I knew it, he had me driven half-way across Nowlan Park and if Dermot hadn't intervened, I would probably have ended up back home in Gowran with Ger still pushing away furiously.

Dermot's knowledge of the game was tremendous. He had done a wonderful coaching job in Offaly in the first half of the 1980s, joining Andy Gallagher and the rest of the lads up there in their drive to make the big breakthrough. It eventually happened in 1980 when they won the Leinster title for the first time, followed by an All-Ireland win a year later.

By the time Dermot left, Offaly had won two All-Irelands and four Leinster titles, some achievement for a county that had won neither title prior to 1980. What's more, Offaly would continue to be a major force for a very long time although, sadly, things have dropped off considerably for the county team now, although their clubs do very well.

When Dermot finally took over back home in Kilkenny, there was an expectation that more riches would flow our way. It was never going to be that simple, of course. He stayed for two years (1989-90) but we lost to Offaly on both occasions, the second by sixteen points which, of course, led to convulsions in Kilkenny.

Dermot wanted to change the system of choosing selectors after that, making his own choices as opposed to nominees from the county champions. It all looks so perfectly reasonable now – no manager would consider taking over without being allowed to bring in his own men – but it was different back then. Old habits die hard and that particular one still had a few years left in it. More's the pity because it cost us a really talented manager.

Anyway, Dermot left, far too soon in my view. He deserved to get a longer run but he was a man of deep principle and conviction which he wasn't prepared to compromise. Like all other counties, Kilkenny eventually changed the policy on choosing selectors but have still maintained the perk for county champions whereby they automatically provide the captain.

I benefited twice from that, thanks to Gowran's successes, captaining Kilkenny in 1997 and again in 2003 after Charlie Carter quit the panel during the Leinster championship. I had the privilege of leading Kilkenny to an All-Ireland win in 2003 so I know all about the honour it is for any player to lead his county.

The fact that I twice captained Kilkenny as the representative of the county champions leaves me in a good position to comment on the system. I regard it as wrong that any player gets to be captain on the basis that he happens to be playing with the best club in the county in a particular year.

Sure, it's an honour for the club but is it deserved? County champions enjoy the glory and the bragging rights that come from winning the title. That's fine since it's the pursuit of being the best they can that keeps every club going. County champions also get the chance to move on to provincial championships and, for some, there's the great experience of playing in the All-Ireland final in Croke Park on St. Patrick's Day.

That's fine too, but I cannot for the life of me see how winning a county title entitles a club to automatically have the county captaincy the following year. Surely, a captain should be there for his leadership skills and other qualities, not simply because he happens to play for the top club. At the very least, it's got to be somebody who is guaranteed to be on the starting team.

What if the champions have no one of leadership material on the county team? They still get to nominate one of their own who may be totally unsuited to the role. To me, it's a cheapening of the captaincy and I would love to see the system changed in Kilkenny, a county that leads the way in so many other ways.

And then, of course, there's the blatant unfairness involving a player from a club that's not good enough to win the county title. It doesn't matter how consistently excellent he is, or how long he has been on the team, he will never get to be captain.

Tommy Walsh is a perfect example. Tullaroan have more Kilkenny senior titles than any other club in the county but most of them were won more than fifty years ago while their last success was in 1994. Now unless things change fairly soon, Tommy will have gone through his entire career without captaining Kilkenny just because Tullaroan didn't win the county title.

To me, that's downright unfair. Tommy has been on the Kilkenny team for the past ten years and is one of the best wing-backs the game has ever seen, yet he will probably end his career without captaining his county. I have no problems with anyone who captained Kilkenny over the last decade – good luck to all of them, they didn't make the rules – but there's something wrong when a man like Tommy Walsh doesn't get a chance because of a regulation that most other counties have long since scrapped. In all honesty, how can anyone in Kilkenny look Tommy Walsh in the eye and say: "Sorry, Tommy, you don't deserve to be captain." I'm using Tommy as an example for obvious reasons but others have – and will again – missed out in the same way.

Only for I was lucky enough to get to be captain twice, people would say I'm making the point because I missed out. I got my chance, once as first choice by club and then as replacement for Charlie in 2003, but it was all down to what my Gowran colleagues had done on the pitch in the previous years and nothing to do with whether or not I was suited to the role. There's no sense to that.

I would regard the system of picking captains in Kilkenny in the same way as denying the team manager the power to pick his own backroom team which, of course, no longer happens. If the new system regarding the choice of selectors had been in place back in 1990, Dermot Healy would probably have continued and who knows how his stint would have turned out.

Not that he needed any further vindication of his talents. What he had done with Offaly was more than enough to prove just how good he was as a coach and indeed as a person.

Next man in after Dermot was Ollie Walsh, a legend from his playing days. He had done well as manager of the Kilkenny junior team, winning a few All-Ireland titles, so he was a fairly logical choice. He was also a great success, winning three Leinster and two All-Ireland titles in his first three seasons in charge. After all he had done in a wonderful playing career, his success as a manager added greatly to the legacy that man left Kilkenny hurling.

Ollie was a real character. His enthusiasm was infectious. Let's put it this way – if Ollie could raise a laugh, he'd do it every time. He wanted to do things with a sense of fun and he managed to balance that brilliantly with the more serious side. He'd laugh before or after a training session but when business was underway, he was a seriously committed man. He knew the game inside out and was good at imparting that knowledge to players.

He called me 'Carey' all the time, not DJ. It was done in an affectionate sort of way but then there was a natural warmth to him in everything he did. Ollie used to make hurleys and always took huge pride in getting them spot on to suit individual tastes.

He knew exactly the sort of stick I liked and he would often arrive at training, call me over and say: "Carey, I made a real beauty for you. What do you think of this?"

The look in his eye as he examined a hurley was that of a supreme craftsman admiring his work and getting a huge sense of satisfaction from making something that would help the Kilkenny cause. I loved watching him with the hurley in his hand. He saw it as a work of art and, yes, he was right – he made me a few right beauties.

I liked a really light hurley. The bas was being made a little bigger around then but the one thing I always wanted was a hurley that felt light in my hand. Other than that, I didn't care very much, unlike some lads who were very fussy. Willie O'Connor could go through ten sticks before he'd pick up one he liked. The thing about Ollie was that he knew instinctively what lads wanted.

There were times he'd tell me he had a beauty in store for me even before he shaped it. He knew from the grain and the weight of the wood what sort of hurley he could make and was brilliant at it.

As a manager, he was first class. He could be stern enough when he had to, but when he was in a mischievous mood, he would be up to all sorts of devilment. We used to drive to most games back then, rather than travelling together by coach. If you passed Ollie on the way home, nothing would do him but to get ahead of you again. I suppose it was as much his competitive instinct as anything else, but you could rest assured that he would find a stretch of road somewhere to put the boot down and fly past you.

His policy as a manager was to mix the serious side with as much fun as he could get into the system. What's more – it worked.

I was too young to remember Ollie as a player but obviously I had heard all about him. Any man who kept Noel Skehan out of the Kilkenny team for so long must have been something special. There were no All Star awards in Ollie's time; however a GAA magazine ran their own scheme during the 1960s and Ollie was chosen on the team for three years. He also won a Texaco Hurler of the Year award in 1967. Noel won the Texaco in 1982.

The interesting thing is that they are the only goalkeepers to have won the Hurler of the Year award, which shows what outstanding talents they really were.

Mind you, neither Ollie nor Noel could have been prepared for a rather amusing incident on the question of great goalkeepers. It came following a GOAL game in Nowlan Park after Kilkenny had won the 1992 All-Ireland final.

John O'Shea of GOAL used to organise fund-raising games between the All-Ireland champions and a Rest of Ireland selection in the week after the final. It was a great idea because it gave supporters a chance to salute the All-Ireland winners back on home ground, while also raising quite a lot of money for GOAL. For a long time, it was easy enough to get players from the rest the country to provide the opposition in what was always a fun occasion. Sadly, it doesn't happen any longer, which is a pity.

Anyway, the game went ahead in Nowlan Park and later on that night, there was a get-together for both teams in Langton's. John O'Shea made a speech and, as was his wont, had a go at this and that before moving on to talk about players – or rather his version of players and their various talents. As with everything involving John, he dealt in straight lines. On this particular night, he was in generous mood and went on about how it was a massive privilege to be in a room with possibly the greatest goalkeeper of all time.

Ollie and Noel were both there, wondering, no doubt, which of them would be handed the supreme accolade. Would it be Ollie, whose senior career spanned three decades (1950s-60s-70s)? Would it be Noel who, after waiting patiently on the bench until Ollie retired went on to be No. 1 for more than a dozen years? Between them Ollie and Noel had manned the Kilkenny goal for nearly thirty years, so they were definitely in serious contention to be regarded as the best of all time.

All the more so, you would have thought when the self-appointed selector was speaking in front of a Kilkenny audience! Except this was John O'Shea and you never knew what he'd say. Anyway, John went on for a while in praise of this wonderful goalkeeper who was in our midst and just as everybody was wondering where Ollie or Noel were about to be crowned, he finished off with an unexpected punch line: "I'm delighted the best goalkeeper in hurling history is here tonight. Ger Cunningham, you're very welcome."

Ger had travelled up from Cork for the game and had just been named 'best goalkeeper of all time' in Kilkenny a few nights after we had won the All-Ireland. Not only that, but the announcement was made in the presence of two of the great legends of Kilkenny hurling. O'Shea was lucky to get out alive that night. Still, the two lads saw the funny side of it. At least, I think they did.

Ollie was in charge for five seasons (1991-95). In addition to winning two All-Irelands and three Leinster titles, we also won a National League title in 1995, easily beating Clare in the final in May. Four months later, Clare were All-Ireland champions and Ollie was gone as Kilkenny manager. Unfortunately, his last two seasons coincided with comprehensive beatings by Offaly in the Leinster semi-final and final and he left after the second defeat in 1995. There was no second chance in the championship back then. One defeat and the season was over, sometimes as early as mid-June.

We were all stunned by Ollie's untimely death from a heart attack in March 1996 at the age of 58. Ollie had taken a month out to consider whether he wanted to continue as manager after the 1995 Leinster final and, for whatever reason, he decided to stand down. He would, no doubt, have continued to be closely involved in the game he loved but, sadly, he didn't get the chance. It was a terrible shock that a man who had managed us with such passion, knowledge and enthusiasm for so long had died so suddenly. He really was a hugely popular character and a brilliant hurling man in every respect. I learned an awful lot from him and enjoyed every minute of the time he was involved with the team.

Next into the managerial chair was Nickey Brennan, a man whom I knew well from 1990 when he coached us to an All-Ireland U-21 title. Nickey was a busy man on a number of fronts, having served as county chairman for three years in between the U-21 win and his appointment as senior manager. That probably put him at a bit of a disadvantage, because little frictions can arise between county boards and players. They are usually fixed up but what was unusual in Nickey's case was that he became team manager after having been county chairman. Other than Brian McEniff in Donegal, I can't remember it happening anywhere else. It wasn't a big issue but it can't be easy to go from being county chairman to manager. After all, the roles are very different.

For instance, I don't think Nickey was best pleased when Eddie O'Connor chose the presentation ceremony after Kilkenny won the 1992 All-Ireland to tell the GAA in no uncertain terms that they should be funding team holidays for the winners. Maybe because of his position as county chairman he had to be seen to be unhappy with the idea because it caused embarrassment for Croke Park to have the subject raised on the steps of the Hogan Stand on All-Ireland final day. It was also very clear that Nickey was on his way up the administration ladder, as indeed proved to be the case when he eventually reached the President's office. Still, while he was working up the political ladder, he never lost his passionate interest in being directly involved in hurling (and football too) and he got his chance to try his hand at senior inter-county management after Ollie left.

Nickey was an excellent coach but the trouble was he took over at a time when the squad was breaking up. We had won All-Irelands in 1992-93 but the scale of the defeats by Offaly in 1994-95 led to a lot of frustration in Kilkenny. Clearly, change was needed because, in addition to Offaly going well, Wexford were lining up for a run while Clare had become the new overall power. The hurling landscape was changing and, worryingly for Kilkenny, there were no apparent signs that we could adapt quickly enough to keep pace, certainly not in the short term.

We had two ordinary years under Nickey, not because of anything he did or didn't do but because that's where we were as a county at the time.

However, some Kilkenny people could not accept that and it eventually led to a very disturbing episode. Indeed, what happened in Nowlan Park on an August Sunday evening in 1997 after we lost a National League semi-final was utterly disgraceful and left a dark stain on the county's reputation for fairness.

A League semi-final in late August? Exactly. For reasons that most of us could never quite figure out then or now, the GAA decided to run the 1997

League divisional games between March and early June, by which stage the Division 1 semi-finalists were known. The League was then parked until August when the semi-finals were played, followed by the final in October.

I think the aim was to have the League final as a big end-of-season showdown, maybe even a repeat of the All-Ireland final. It might have looked like a good idea, in theory, but it never worked out, certainly the idea of parking the competition and returning to it in August. Playing the divisional games in March-June worked well enough. Big crowds turned out and with the championship closer than usual to the League action, there was a real edge to many of the games.

When the divisional games were completed, the semi-final pairings were as follows: Kilkenny v Limerick; Galway v Tipperary.

By early August, Kilkenny and Tipperary were the only two of the four who were also in the All-Ireland semi-finals. We lost to Clare while Tipperary beat Wexford which left us in a different frame of mind for the League semi-final. Actually, it left us in no frame of mind at all for another game. With an All-Ireland final to plan for, Tipperary showed what they thought of the League semi-final by fielding a largely second-string team against Galway.

Who could blame them? They weren't going to risk injury by playing their top team in a full-blooded clash with Galway a few weeks before the All-Ireland final. Instead, they played with a much weakened hand and, unsurprisingly, lost heavily. Mind you, it did nothing for the League to see a second string team playing in a semi-final.

Our situation was completely different. We were out of the championship so it might have looked like an ideal opportunity to go full blast for the League. It might, until you think about how players feel after being knocked out of the championship. It's the ultimate downer and very definitely the end of the line as far as inter-county action is concerned for that year. Yes, I know we used to play League games in October-November up to the late 1990s but that was different. There was a good break after the championship, whereas in 1997, we found ourselves facing a National League semi-final two weeks after losing an All-Ireland semi-final. What's more, we were playing Limerick, who had lost the All-Ireland final a year earlier and who really wanted to win a national title. Besides, they were out of the championship since mid-June.

Professional to the last, Nickey rang me a week or ten days before the Limerick game and asked me to do my best to lift the lads and get them going. As captain, it was my duty to do that but, honestly, it was going to be very hard for me to lift other lads when I was finding it so difficult to motivate myself. Quite simply, we had all switched off. Nickey was probably the only one who hadn't, but he was relying on us, which wasn't a good place to be.

The game turned out to be a complete mess for us. We never raised a gallop and were beaten by ten points. And in scenes that most genuine hurling people in Kilkenny thought they would never see or hear, a section of the crowd turned nasty.

They cheered when Nickey's brother, Canice was taken off and abused Nickey as he left the pitch at the end of the game. Nickey's mother was in the stand that evening and had to listen as a crowd of yobs abused her son. It was horrible and must go down as one of the most shameful episodes in Kilkenny hurling history.

The reality is that Nickey had nothing whatsoever to do with the bad performance. The players – and I include myself in this – had switched off and no manager in the world could have been able to re-start the engine. Maybe we should have been able to get something going but, in fairness, it was ridiculous to play League semi-finals in between the All-Ireland semi-finals and final.

The League is a great way of preparing for the championship but to split it the way it was done in 1997 had to be one of the daftest decisions for a long time. It was the first – and last year – for that particular experiment.

We were the only ones who found ourselves facing a League semi-final two weeks after losing the All-Ireland semi-final and when the game started to run against us – as it was always going to – some people took their frustrations out on the team management.

Because he was Nickey's younger brother, Canice Brennan came in for unfair criticism. Canice was a very versatile player and, consequently, spent much of his career being moved around the pitch as problems arose in various areas. He played in every outfield line at one stage or another. Wherever a glitch arose, Canice was sent in to deal with it. That was a tribute to his versatility but, to some degree, it also left him with no position he could call his own. That's the problem with being so flexible. You can play all over the place but never find a permanent home.

With Nickey as manager, the critics – or rather a small but hurtful section of them – lay in wait for Canice.

As often happens, when a manager has a relation on the team, both lose out. You'd hear the usual guff around 1996-97 that Canice was only on the team because Nickey was manager. Canice had been there before (with Ollie Walsh) and after (with Kevin Fennelly and Brian Cody) but it was only when Nickey and his co-selectors, Richie Power and Pat Aylward picked him that the criticisms flew. It made no sense but then it didn't have to in the eyes of the blinkered. Canice seemed to be some sort of lightning rod for all the difficulties Kilkenny were experiencing at the time which was all wrong.

It was hugely unfair on Canice and Nickey. I recall being disgusted as we left the pitch in Nowlan Park after that League semi-final because no one, least of all the Brennans, a family so steeped in the Kilkenny GAA, should be subjected to that sort of treatment. As a group of players, we had played our part in it by not being more competitive that evening but, in fairness, the circumstances were most unusual. To be honest, I doubt if any team in the country would have done any better if they were asked to play a League semi-final two weeks after losing an All-Ireland semi-final.

I was having doubts about my own future at the time and I can tell you that what happened to Nickey, in particular, increased my sense of unease and disillusionment. It showed that there was a nasty side to the Kilkenny support, which felt entitled to belittle good people when things weren't going well.

Nickey resigned straight away after the Limerick game and who could blame him? He had been treated disgracefully by a county where he did so much as a player, manager and administrator. He was replaced by Kevin Fennelly whom, of course, I knew well from his long association with Gowran, where he was living. Kevin was a superb coach, as knowledgeable a hurling man as you will ever come across. He was also a great man for finding out little titbits of information about what the opposition were up to and how they would approach a game. Kevin would climb the tallest tree and perch on a branch for hours to have a look at the opposition if he thought it would do any good. It worked too because he was brilliant at throwing little scraps of information about opponents.

The one thing that some players probably found hard to cope with was Kevin's straight-talking. He could be critical of players and would let them have it right between the eyes when he thought they deserved it. It was born out of frustration because nothing disappointed Kevin more than if he could see real ability in a player but it wasn't coming out in his game.

He was usually right in his judgements but I suppose there are various ways of conveying that and Kevin definitely went for route one – straight between the eyes. That gets the best out of some people and turns others off. Most unusually, he only had one year in charge of Kilkenny, leaving after the 1998 All-Ireland final defeat. It meant that Kilkenny had three different managers in the 1995-98 period, Ollie, Nickey and Kevin. Who would have thought that such a long period of stability was about to get underway?

It's curious how things turn out. When we were going well against Offaly early in the 1998 All-Ireland final, it looked as if Kevin was on his way to becoming a first season success. If we had won, I'm sure he would have stayed on and who knows how different the landscape might have looked over the next few years? Instead he was gone after one year, leaving a vacancy which was about to be filled by some very big shoes.

I was lucky enough to play under five excellent managers throughout the 1990s and am happy to say I got on well with all of them. But then, I never cared who managed the team, once they were good at the job, which all five were.

They brought different personality traits to the task, but the common denominator was the same for all of them – they possessed a huge passion for Kilkenny to be the best. They channelled it in different ways but then that worked too. Ollie and Brian were the only two to run All-Ireland winning campaigns but that doesn't mean the others didn't do a good job. As I've said, Dermot didn't get a fair crack at all, Nickey was in charge at a time when we just weren't good enough to beat Wexford and Clare and Kevin only stayed one year.

CHAPTER 13

A RUMOUR A DAY KEEPS THE TRUTH AWAY

A true story. I was in a bank one day early in 2013 when a woman started chatting to me. She knew who I was and went on to tell me a story which she thought incredibly funny but left me completely baffled for one very simple reason – it hadn't happened.

She said that I was in a garage owned by her brother-in-law a few months earlier and had introduced myself as DJ Carey. Clearly, she had been told that I had made the introduction in some big shot sort of way, which is about as far from the truth as you could possibly find. It seems I walked in and declared confidently: "I'm DJ Carey." No, I did not.

Apparently, her brother-in-law replied that he wasn't into GAA and had no idea who I was. Now apart altogether from the question of how he knew I was involved with the GAA if he didn't know who I was, there was the small matter of the truth of the story. Which, in this particular case, wasn't even remotely accurate. It was 100 per cent rubbish.

The woman wasn't being in any way aggressive but obviously felt amused by what she regarded as a real put-down by her brother-in-law on this guy who thought everyone knew him. Now, if only she had any idea how little interest I had in being recognised by her or her brother-in-law then or now, she would have been surprised, but anyway she seemed to think it was a very funny yarn.

I couldn't let it go because it wasn't true. I pointed out to her, as politely as I could, that it hadn't happened.

I said: "And do you know why I'm so sure it didn't happen? Because that's not the way I go on. I don't know the man you're talking about and anyway I haven't been in that town for years."

Hoots of laughter. Mrs. Convinced wasn't having any of it. She had her story and was sticking to it.

"You were, you were," she replied cheerily, oozing a certainty which gave the impression she had tapes, pictures, date and time of my encounter with her unimpressed brother-in-law. And then came the really damaging bit.

"And my brother-in-law tells that story everywhere he goes," she added.

I have no doubt she meant no harm whatsoever and thought it funny that I had been put in my place by her brother-in-law. I'm sure she didn't believe my denials but there was nothing more that I could do. Her mind was made up, based on the story from her brother-in-law who, presumably, continues to regale people with tales of the day he put me in my box. That's how nasty rumours start. God knows how many people that pair have told about how DJ Carey thought he was some sort of big shot, instantly recognisable everywhere he went.

At face value, that might seem harmless enough but, in reality, it's not. In fact, it's a dangerous example of how small-town Ireland can throw poison around without considering the consequences. This woman has an obvious talent for gossip and, by the sound of it, so does her brother-in-law. So how many people have they told that I'm a jumped-up ego-merchant who goes around thinking everyone knows who I am? They could be even saying that I was looking for special favours for all I know. And how many people who heard the story from them told it to others?

The trouble is that one untrue story can fan out and multiply. You wonder why anyone would do that sort of thing but you'll never find the real answer. There are always people out there who want to belittle others, people who feel the urge to pretend that have the inside track as seen and understood by them. And when they don't have it, they will make it up. Sure, who will know the difference?

Sometimes, it's to do with familiarity, a sense that because people know you, they own part of you. In the case of the gossipy woman and her brother-in-law, it was twisted somewhat to portray me as somebody I'm not but the potential for damage was still huge.

I always got on well with the majority of Kilkenny supporters (by the way the town where I was supposed to have committed the great sin of egotism is not in Kilkenny) but I was conscious too that the knockers were out there. It was nothing personal, just a state of mind among some people who like to try and bring others down.

I was getting lots of criticism around the mid-1990s when Kilkenny weren't winning Leinster or All-Ireland titles. And since those were pre 'back door' days, the season ended when you lost a provincial game. It was a hell of a lot more frustrating for me and the rest of the Kilkenny players than it was for the public but that was never taken into account.

I'd hear things along the lines that 'his business is nearly gone, that's why he's not hurling well.' Now, I thought I was hurling quite well in those years but it was never enough. With the exception of 1996, I won All Star awards every year between 1991 and 1997 so obviously the GAA journalists thought I was playing well. I had no chance of an All Star in 1996 because we didn't do a whole lot in the League and were knocked out of Leinster by Wexford in the first round on a day I shouldn't have started because of a hamstring problem.

I'd also hear stories about how I was supposed to have fallen out with someone or other. Now, falling out with people is not in my nature but that didn't stop the gossip-mongers. We're back to familiarity again, people letting on they know more about you than they actually do because they are from the same area or the same county. Why let the truth get in the way of a bad story?

I'll give you an example: When Eddie Keher was my bank manager, I'd often call to see him to discuss my business. He lived in a house attached to the bank and sometimes I'd drop in on him at around five o'clock in the evening. We might sit down with a cup of tea and talk hurling for an hour and a half and discuss my business affairs for half an hour. But because I was in with him for two hours, the word would go out: 'DJ's in real trouble; he was in the bank for two hours the other evening. Things must be going bad. He looked terrible when he came out'.

Small town stuff, but horribly destructive nonetheless.

I have always regarded myself as a friendly person who keeps to himself and who would do a good turn if he could. I don't impose myself on others and certainly wouldn't be laying down the law in pubs after games or at any other time either.

I never drank alcohol or smoked and wouldn't have gone into pubs all that often. Correction, I drank once, wolfing down a hot whiskey for a cold. Someone with a finer appreciation of such matters told me it would be good for me. It was the most vile-tasting stuff I ever came across and I certainly couldn't figure out how anybody would actually drink it unless they had a temperature of at least 102! Mind you, it did seem to do some good. Drink played no part in my upbringing which is probably why I never fancied pubs. When you don't drink alcohol, pubs can be boring places. They're okay for a while but then it's time to go.

Let's put it this way – the beginning of the night is a lot different to the end of the night. I have no interest being in a place where's there not a lot of sense around, especially when you know full well that much of what's being said won't even be remembered the following day. When you're drinking a few glasses of Coke or whatever, enough is enough.

I'd go to the pub if the club won a championship or some big game and would enjoy it but not for the full night. Well, not always anyway. Having said that, I never felt outside the loop in Gowran or elsewhere. I did things my way and if others did them differently, good luck to them. We all knew each other well in the group and nobody passed much heed on what others did. It's part of being a team, a sense that you're coming together for a common aim but don't have to live in each other's pockets afterwards.

In any event, I'd often be so wrecked after games that all I wanted to do was go home and get some rest. I put a lot of effort in on the pitch and that's where I liked to leave it. Mind you, I always felt I had a responsibility immediately after a game to sign as many autographs for people who wanted them. In fact, I nearly always remained on the pitch until the last person who wanted an autograph was looked after.

There were days after games in Nowlan Park when by the time I got into the dressing-room, it was empty. Still, I'd be happy that I hadn't left any kid – or adult either – without an autograph. I just couldn't walk away with people waiting. Anyway, as a Kilkenny hurler, I saw it as a duty to mingle with the genuine supporters. After all, the county team represents them so players can't be aloof.

I also saw it as a responsibility to accept invitations to go around the country attending presentation functions. I particularly liked going to counties where hurling wasn't all that strong because I felt it was, in a sense, spreading the gospel.

I was always conscious that a lot of unsung heroes went around the country coaching hurling just for the benefit it might bring somewhere. It had – or has – nothing to do with making money but is done purely for a love of the game and a desire to impart its skills and traditions. Now, as a well-known player, I felt a responsibility to do my bit by attending as many functions as possible whether they were in Carrick-on-Shannon, Carrick-on-Suir or Carrickmacross.

Naturally, there were rumours that I was making a fortune from my travels. I wasn't. I never asked for anything and very often never got anything, not even the price of the diesel used in all the driving. It would have been nice to get a few quid for diesel but, most places I went, I got a clock or some other memento of the visit. At one stage, crystal clocks were all the rage and since I was doing a lot of travelling at the time, I had so many of them that I could have opened a jeweller's shop. Sometimes, I'd be offered money but I'd give it back to the club. I might be biting my lip at the same time but I'd do it. I'd often bring a few signed hurleys for an auction or whatever so the club actually made money from my visit. I was quite happy with that, but it was annoying when things were twisted to give the impression that I was a presentation mercenary on the road every Friday and Saturday night, pocketing hundreds of pounds. Nothing could be further from the truth.

It was different if I was working for a company or a promotion which was designed to make money. In that case, I was happy to accept a fee because I was providing my time for a commercial concern. If they felt I was of value to them, they were obviously prepared to pay a fee in a straight-forward business deal. That's not at all the same as a club asking me to present medals some Friday or Saturday night, even if it was a long way from home.

Despite the clear demarcation lines between business occasions and club functions, the rumours persisted that I was making a fortune. Worse still, some of them were coming from inside Kilkenny. I know of one club in the county where it was suggested that they ask me to make presentations at an awards night, only for a senior officer to pipe up: "no we won't do that. DJ will be looking for five hundred pounds."

Where did he hear that? Since it wasn't true, it had to be a case of listening to rumours and whispers and taking them as true without ever checking. Worse still, they were then spread further.

That's the trouble with a rumour. It can start off among two people but multiply to hundreds very quickly. At that stage it's out of control and there's nothing you can do about it. That's even assuming you know about it in the first place. The more it spreads, the worse it gets.

I can't over-stress how annoyed I was to hear about all the money I was supposed to be making from attending functions. Why would people spread lies? Why would an official in the Kilkenny club say I'd charge five hundred pounds when he had no basis for it? Why didn't he ring me up and ask: "DJ, can you come over here and present medals?" If the date suited, I would have done it and he would have found out that it came for free. Instead of that, he was happy to spread a lie which was damaging me. I'm sure it wasn't malicious but that doesn't excuse him.

A lot of that sort of stuff was going on in the mid-nineties. It's no coincidence, of course, that it was at a time when we weren't winning All-Irelands. People had to find a scapegoat and this fella who was supposed to be making a fortune from going around the country was an easy target.

I'd also hear comments from time to time about how 'Carey is always in the papers'. The inference was that I was organising publicity for myself just to keep my name out there. Another great big, ugly lie!

I was always comfortable dealing with the media and found the vast majority of the sports journalists fair and honourable. It wasn't the same with some other sections of the media, certainly not when they started imposing on my private life but that's another story.

When it came to sports journalists, I had no problem whatsoever dealing with them. I didn't court attention but they all had my phone number and because I was happy to talk to them about hurling, I got regular calls. It followed that my name and picture were in the papers quite a lot and, of course, some people saw that as a case of me pushing myself. It's another example of how perceptions can be all wrong.

Also, at press nights before All-Ireland finals, I'd be one of the players who always did interviews. Some players prefer not to, which is their right, but because I had no problem talking to the media, I'd usually be asked to do my thing. I was happy to do it and if it took pressure off other lads, all the better.

I found the vast majority of sportswriters great to deal with. In fact, the only time I was really put out was after I went into my short retirement in early 1998 when a story appeared in a paper that I was going to work in Mount Juliet golf club. It was one of a number of daft rumours which were flying around at that time. There wasn't a grain of truth in it but it caused me problems because customers and suppliers I was dealing with at the time were left wondering if I was about to quit my business. That's about as damaging as it can get for any business if there are rumours flying around that the proprietor is about to jump ship.

I couldn't understand how any paper could print such a story without contacting me. Even in the crazy days after I announced my retirement, I was still taking calls from journalists so there was no excuse for not contacting me. As I've said, it wouldn't be all that important if it hadn't the potential to damage my business. Was it a case of not spoiling a good (but untrue) story with the truth? You would have to think so.

As media numbers increased over the years, it became harder to deal with them all because if you took calls from everyone, you'd get no work done. Still, I'd deal with as many as I could, especially people I'd known since I started hurling.

The late Peadar O'Brien was in that category. Peadar worked for the *Irish Press* and later the *Irish Sun* and would ring me regularly over many years. On one occasion, he couldn't reach me for one reason or another so he devised a very clever way of ensuring that I phoned him back.

He left a message on my phone which went along the lines: "DJ, Peadar O'Brien here. I'm doing a piece and need to talk to you. Ring me back if I can't quote you."

He left the impression (at least I think it was an impression!) that he was going to quote me on something without talking to me, knowing full well I'd have to ring him. Talk about the old dog for the hard road!

In fairness, I always found him good to deal with ever since I started out with Kilkenny. I rang him back, Peadar got his quotes and we were all happy. It was the same with most others in the sports media and I would like to think they found me easy to deal with too. I saw it as part of a wider responsibility to hurling to promote it as much as possible. Talking to the media was a good way of doing that.

That's why I don't like what's happening nowadays where players are far less available to the media than in my time. I understand perfectly that some players don't want to do interviews but there are still plenty of good talkers out there. If they are happy to deal with the media they should be allowed to get on with it, rather than locking down all access.

Anyway, the media will always have its say and at least in an interview situation a player can control what's appearing. There's a broader issue of course – hurling and football need all the exposure they can get at a time when international sports are on TV all the time and I believe that the top GAA players have a responsibility to do their bit to promote the games.

Yes, of course, they are doing that through the games, but dealing with the media is also important. Players are better educated and more street-wise than ever before, so doing basic interviews is simple for the vast majority of them. For some reason, the culture of the times says otherwise which is a pity. It's also a big loss to the GAA.

CHAPTER 14

SCORING ISN'T EVERYTHING

I never wanted to be a free-taker. People might find that difficult to believe after all the years I spent on frees but it was not something I planned from my early days. Even in St. Kieran's College, I only started taking frees for the seniors in my final year (I was on the team for three seasons) because Adrian Ronan was gone.

Scoring from open play wasn't something I was particularly hung up on either. Again, that may seem strange but it's true. People have the view that if you slot over a few points from play, you're going well but that's not always the case. There were days when I hit a lot of scores for Kilkenny or Gowran, yet I knew I hadn't been as effective as in games when I only got a few scores – or maybe even none – but contributed well in general play.

I always based my game on work-rate. If I had been more selfish about taking scores, I would probably have had a much higher return but the day you start thinking like that is the day your value to a team decreases dramatically. Defending has to start in the full-forward line and work back from there. Everyone thinks that way nowadays but it wasn't always so. There was a time when attackers – certainly the full-forward lines – saw themselves exclusively as score-getters but the game has altered so that you have to be switched on to everything that's happening on the pitch nowadays, irrespective of the number on your jersey.

I got just as much of a thrill out of making a run, tossing out a long handpass or playing a colleague in for a score as I did from hitting the target myself. Having said that, one area where I invariably went for broke was when it came to chasing goals. I would always try for the big one if the odds were any way in my favour, and sometimes even when they weren't because I felt it was worth a gamble.

There are times where a goal is, in real terms, worth more than the three points it adds to your tally. It can have a hugely uplifting impact on a team while deflating the opposition. Not many games are lost when a team scores a few goals so, on that basis alone, it's worth going for the half-chance. Also, I found that the best way to answer an opponent who was trying it on with the odd sly dig or pull was to score a goal.

Some lads think about goals instinctively which I love to see. Eddie Brennan was always in that category. Eddie scored a lot of goals for Kilkenny over many years and made quite a few as well because that was his approach. His high goal tally speaks for itself, but I'll give you an example of how he always had an eye for the bigger picture. In the 2011 All-Ireland final against Tipperary, Kilkenny were five points ahead in the second-half when Eddie broke through into open space where it would have been easy to tap the ball over the bar. Instead, his instinct for goals kicked in. He carried on, passed the ball to Richie Hogan, who fired a screamer past Brendan Cummins in the Tipperary goal. It was a glorious finish by Richie but Eddie's nose for goal had made it possible, when he could easily have stroked over a point.

Suddenly, Kilkenny were eight, rather than six points ahead. The difference might not have looked all that important at the time because Kilkenny were well on top but fifteen minutes later, Tipperary had cut the deficit to three points. It would have been a one point lead if Eddie had taken a point earlier on and who knows how the rest of the game would have played out? Did Eddie's instinct for goal win the All-Ireland? It's quite possible that it did.

I remember watching Eddie and thinking: 'good on you – that goal is down to you, although you didn't score it'. It was a classic example of a man who saw the goal chance and spurned a point.

It was also a case of a player who put the good of the team above his own, even at a time when everything was going well. It was a philosophy I always believed in. Even when it came to free-taking I was happy to hand over to someone else, as happened in 1999 when Henry Shefflin came onto the Kilkenny panel. Now here's another myth I want to explode.

It was implied subsequently that I was disappointed at how Brian Cody appointed Henry as first choice free-taker in his debut season. After all, I had been taking most of the scoreable frees for nearly a decade.

The word was that I wanted to stay as No. 1 free-taker but Brian opted for Henry instead. Yes, he did, but he had my full support. Henry was brilliant on frees right from the start so I was happy to let him get on with it and concentrate on all other aspects of my game. And, if the occasion demanded, as it did from time to time, I was quite happy to go back taking frees.

The 1999 season wasn't the first time I had handed over the free-taking task. Ray Heffernan often took them when we were playing on the same team. Ray was a deadly accurate marksman and a brilliant all-round club hurler with Glenmore but it didn't always go as well for him with Kilkenny. Ollie Walsh reckoned that it would help Ray's overall game if he pointed a few frees early on so he regularly asked me to stand aside. I totally agreed with Ollie. If free-taking helped Ray with the rest of his game, then the team benefited.

The same went for Henry when he came aboard. Brian obviously calculated that taking frees would help settle him into the new surrounds and I had no difficulty at all with that.

Now, while I wasn't at all protective of the free-taking job, I approached it with meticulous care when I carried the responsibility. After all, it's often the difference between winning and losing a game. I worked very, very hard on it in my earlier days, in particular, in order to get into a reliable rhythm. It was more difficult to be a good free-taker back then and harder still in the days when Eddie Keher was the supreme marksman in the 1960s-70s.

In those days, the ball was heavier and less consistent in terms of the line it kept. The modern ball is much more dependable and certainly makes life easier for free-takers. Mind you, I would have an issue with the ball nowadays because I think it's too light, travels too far and cuts out various sectors of the pitch.

I got a lot of help with free-taking from Eddie Keher in my earlier days. He always insisted that lining up properly was the most important thing of all. If the striker does that, it's much easier to make the right connection and drive the ball where he wants it to go. If he's set up incorrectly, then it follows that he will be off-line with the strike.

I had a different style to Eddie but his advice on lining up was still invaluable. I practised free-taking evening after evening, always trying to give myself a new target. I never believed in taking frees from a range of angles. Instead, I would go out twenty or thirty metres from the goal and aim at one of the uprights. Firing over points from various angles out the field is easy enough – especially when you're practising and it doesn't matter if a few go wide but if you set yourself a target of hitting the post, the need for precision is far greater.

Okay, so you're not going to hit the post (not intentionally anyway) from fifty or sixty metres very often, but you should be able to manage it fairly regularly from closer in. Apart from anything else, it's great for the concentration. And if you hit the post once, you want to do it again. Then, the challenge is to see how many times you can manage it off ten or twenty shots. It keeps you engaged with what you're doing rather than lashing the ball over the bar from further out, which can become monotonous.

Another trick I used was to fix a target in my eye-line, usually high up in the netting behind the goal. That way, I was aiming at something small rather than the wide area between the posts. It was all about doing something that would add a bit of pressure during practise, rather than hoisting balls over the bar just for the sake of it, which is relatively easy to do.

I had a fairly good record on frees over the years although one day stands out as a bit of a disaster. Luckily, we won, so it didn't matter but, had we lost, I would have been disgusted with myself.

It was in the 1998 All-Ireland semi-final against Waterford and, unusually for mid-August, a very strong wind whistled around Croke Park. Not only that, but it was swirling violently all over the place. A regular wind is tricky enough but you get used to it and gradually settle into a rhythm. This particular day was totally different. The wind seemed to be hitting the Cusack Stand and doubling back across the pitch, causing erratic gusts which were impossible to gauge accurately. So when I aimed at the right hand post and waited for the wind to swing the ball back in, it rarely did and when I went for the left hand post it didn't work either.

It was one of those awful days when you're hitting and hoping, which isn't exactly the recommended style in the free-takers' manual. A free-taker has to believe that he will nail every shot because otherwise doubts kick in, making the job twice as hard. I missed a few frees in the first half against

Waterford that day, which might have proved costly but, luckily, we won by a point.

In general, free-taking is pretty straight-forward if you have put in the hard work and the practise because they will deliver for you. Whatever the pressure, or however big the game, my routine was the same - line up properly, concentrate and trust myself.

I would tell myself that I had done it thousands of times and this was just one more. 'This is no different to the pitch in Gowran – set your target, set yourself up right and strike the ball cleanly.'

Now I know I probably shouldn't admit this as a Kilkenny man but I was pleased for Joe Canning when he pointed the equalising free in the last minute of the 2012 All-Ireland final. He had missed one earlier on from around the same position and was now facing another free to save the day for Galway. It was the ultimate pressure situation. Point it and Galway have drawn the All-Ireland; miss and they have lost. Joe held his nerve and slotted it over. Free-takers everywhere would have been pleased for him.

In that situation, you have to tell yourself that there's nothing anyone can do to stop you from scoring, ensure the lift is right and make the strike as cleanly as possible. The free-taking instinct in me wanted Joe to point that free for his sake, even if I was obviously hoping Kilkenny would win. They won the replay anyway so all was well eventually from a Kilkenny viewpoint!

The standard of ball-striking is much better now than it used to be but then the sliotar travels much further. In my opinion, it flies much too far. The use of goalies' hurleys out the field, combined with better quality balls and improved striking technique have made some areas of the pitch largely redundant. Lads can drive the ball eighty or ninety yards with a flick of the wrists nowadays while the really long hitters can strike it much further.

I know that it's difficult to stop hurleys being designed to drive the ball huge distances but there has to be a balance. Maybe the answer rests in re-designing the sliotar so that it doesn't travel as far, irrespective of how well it is hit. After all, the longer the ball is in the air, the less real hurling that gets done, which isn't good for players or spectators.

I got a lot of scores during my career which I probably wouldn't get now because the standard of striking is so much better. Let me explain. The chances are that a shot for goal from any reasonably distance will either end up as a point or a wide. In days when striking wasn't as good, you could expect to see a mishit or a short delivery quite regularly so it was up to forwards to be out in front of their men and get to the ball first. I loved trying to do that. I was quick so it often worked out for me.

I even benefited from one such example which involved none other than Henry Shefflin, a man not noted for mishitting the ball. It came early in the 2002 All-Ireland final against Clare. Henry raced down the left side so I moved across towards the other side to try and create space for him. He shot for a point from around forty metres out but didn't connect all that cleanly and the ball dropped short. I cut inside and flicked the ball to the net. It almost looked like a rehearsed move but of course it wasn't.

Back then – and certainly in earlier times - there was also profit to be had by lurking around the goal, sniffing for a mishit but it's much less fertile territory nowadays because most shots are so well hit. That may be good for the overall game, if not for score-poachers.

There's one trend in the modern game that really frustrates me. With so much emphasis on closing down space, there's an unwelcome growth in the number of unsightly mauls where the ball becomes stuck amid a large group of players. Everyone is obsessed with getting it into their hands but very often nothing happens except the ball gets poked over and back in the middle of the skirmish before the referee intervenes to re-start play with a throw-in.

You expect that on a cold, wet day in February or March but not in high summer, yet it happens all the time. It's taking away from hurling as a spectacle.

Skill levels have never been higher but they are coming under attack from other unwelcome developments within the game. I have no doubt that since the turn of the Millennium, Kilkenny did an awful lot to raise standards, certainly when it came to first touch and getting the ball into the hand. Others copied them so the next challenge was to maintain those skills while still managing to create space. It's not easily done.

In a way, hurling has aped Gaelic football, with the emphasis on crowding out the opposition. But with referees leaning very much against the player in possession and blowing for over-carrying, the close-up warfare will continue until there's an overhaul of the rules. It's even ingrained in young players. I have refereed under-14 games where lads were constantly complaining about over-carrying. Everyone wants to get around the player in possession in clusters, doing nothing other than prevent him escaping or playing the ball away. It's pure guesswork as to who is fouling whom but very often the player in possession gets penalised.

As a forward, it's understandable that I would be in favour of anything that creates space but isn't everybody? Are scrambles for possession, with a posse of players poking furiously for a ball that won't come to hand, doing anything to make hurling a better spectacle? I don't think so.

Now, where I have an even bigger complaint is on the rule as it applies to over-carrying. The rule states that the ball may be carried in the hand for a maximum of four steps or held in the hand for no longer than the time needed to take four steps.

Two issues arise here. One, what exactly is the time needed to take four steps, and two, what happens when a player is surrounded by two, three or more opponents and cannot move? If his path is blocked in all directions, he can't take one step, let alone four, yet he's penalised for over-carrying even although there's no way out. Is he supposed to drop the ball on the ground for an opponent to pick it up? Where's the fairness in that? Surely, he must be allowed to play the ball away.

If a player holds an opponent, a free is awarded against him, yet if the ball-carrier is surrounded by three or four opponents and allowed no escape route, he becomes the sinner unless he drops the ball on the ground. If he can't move in any direction, is he not being obstructed?

Besides, if he's prevented from taking one step, how can the referee decide how long four steps would have taken?

Anyway, back to my free-taking days. I loved taking penalties. My plan was simple: drill the ball as hard as possible in the space between opposition heads and the crossbar. If you hit that area with a powerful shot, the chances of blocking the ball are very slim. Some free-takers like to go low, skimming the ball off the ground just in front of the two defenders or the goalkeeper, but I always felt there was a real chance of it being saved. Not so with the properly hit shot under the crossbar. Even if the goalkeeper or defender gets a hurley to the ball, there's every chance it will cannon into the net anyway. That was my theory, which was why I preferred air to ground wars!

My only exception to that rule applied on a wet day. The ground route has its attractions in those conditions as the ball will gather pace off the grass. As I've mentioned elsewhere, I went low with a penalty against Cork in the 1992 All-Ireland final and it worked perfectly. We were playing against the strong wind at the time which made up my mind for me as a high shot would have a little sting taken out of it by the elements.

Naturally, the closer you get to the goal before making the strike, the greater the chances of hitting the net. Now here is one of the shadiest of grey areas, one which the striker is happy to exploit to the maximum on penalties and close-in frees when he is trying for a goal. For example, when I was going for goal from a penalty (which I always did) or from a 20-metre free (which I often did) I obviously tried to get in as close as possible before striking the ball.

I'd take a step or two into the free, lift the ball on the hurley for a split second, toss it up and forward, while on the run. My aim was to be as close as I could to the 13-metre line by the time I hit the ball. It's very difficult to make it in quite that far but it's certainly easy to gain four or five metres. Every free-taker takes the ball well in from the 20-metre line, but is it legal? How long can you leave the ball on the hurley before making the strike? Also, there seems to be no rule about how much ground can be made up between the lift and strike. You won't find free-takers asking for clarification on that one but goalkeepers complain about it and, frankly, it's hard to blame them. They believe that the striker has enough advantages from 20 metres without being allowed to steal four or five more metres on the run. They are probably right too.

Another area of concern is hand-passing, which has become something of a joke in the modern game. It seems to me that the majority of hand passes are throws. The occasional one is penalised by the referee but you wonder why the rest aren't. And when a player is penalised for a throw, he feels aggrieved because he has probably seen several other similar 'handpasses' go unpunished in the same game.

With getting the ball in hand the top priority for all teams nowadays, the handpass has to come under the spotlight. If you looked at a clip of twenty or thirty handpasses, I bet half of them are illegal, yet only a tiny number draw frees. A clear striking movement with the hand should the minimum requirement. If it was – and referees applied it rigorously – it would solve the problem pretty quickly.

Instead, we have a twilight zone where the good old-fashioned throw frequently goes unpunished. At a time when many skills are executed brilliantly, it's a pity to see that happening, especially when it could be quite readily dealt with.

It's important to keep examining rules all the time to ensure that they are achieving what they set to do while, at the same time, providing the very best framework to run the wonderful game in the best possible manner. As far as I'm concerned that's not happening now.

CHAPTER 15

PLAYER POWER

Modern-day players have a lot to be thankful for. Some of the younger lads might not realise it but only for a group who stood up for what they believed in and challenged what had been going on for decades, players would not have the good conditions they now generally enjoy.

There are, no doubt, some in the GAA who still regard the Gaelic Players Association (GPA) as a renegade outfit, intent on destroying everything the great old Association stands for. They see it as trouble and remain deeply suspicious that its ultimate aim is to force the GAA into pay-for-play. It doesn't matter how often they are told that a move to professionalism has never been on the GPA agenda, they still insist on convincing themselves otherwise.

Happily, there are enough enlightened people in the GAA – many of them at the top end of the administration – who see such narrow-mindedness for what it is. That's why such huge progress has been made in the relationship between Croke Park (I use the term loosely to describe the GAA's governing bodies) and the players, but it should not disguise the fact that some in authority would still prefer if the GPA closed its tent and everything went back to the way it used to be.

I best make my position clear early on. I never have, do not now and never will support a call for pay-for-play. By that, I mean a move to some form of professionalism where players receive a fee to play for county or club. Apart from the fact that the GAA could not afford it, it would be a betrayal of the principles on which the Association is founded. I respect those and would fight with everything I have to defend them.

However, opposition to pay-for-play should not be confused with support for a system which recognises that the players are the most important people in the Association. Without them, there are no massive crowds, no big stadiums and no GAA. Generations of players come and go but the principle is the same – at any given time the players are the ones who really matter. Lots of others play an important part too, but the players should always be at the centre of everything. That applies to everyone who puts on a pair of boots from the very top end of the scale down to Junior B.

In general, players don't look for a whole lot, certainly nothing that the GAA can't afford from the income generated by its prize assets who draw the crowds and pack the stadiums. In fairness, the situation is a whole lot better now than it used to be, but there is still no room for complacency because if that were allowed to creep back in, serious trouble would not be far behind.

Time passes quickly and fourteen years seem like a lifetime, but I have no doubt that the founding of the GPA in 1999 was hugely important in shaping the direction that relationships between players and the authorities would take over subsequent years.

I was one of the players who supported the GPA from the start. Donal O'Neill rang me and explained that there was a bit of dissention among players, especially up north. I had been aware of that myself anyway from talking to players around the country, lads who felt powerless to challenge what was going on, although they knew it wasn't right. They felt they had nowhere to bring their grievances except to the very people who were responsible for causing them in the first place, a case of the chicken asking the fox for help. It wasn't something that was particularly prevalent in Kilkenny where we were well looked after, but judging from the horror stories in some other counties, players were being treated like fools.

Mind you, I had my own bad experience on one occasion, when I was out of work for six or seven weeks with a broken leg. For some strange reason, my claim form for insurance got lost a number of times and, in the end, my time to claim had elapsed so I was entitled to nothing. From what I heard afterwards, that sort of thing was rampant around the country, but there were other problems too over gear, travelling expenses, match tickets and even little things like getting into the players' hospitality area in Croke Park after games. You might have played in front of a full house but in the early days you still only got one ticket to get into the players' area afterwards. I'm sure nobody meant any harm by it but it was deeply insulting to players who were putting their heart and souls into everything they did. That included attracting enough people to games which generated the gate receipts that made it possible to develop all the grounds, including Croke Park. Even as far back as 2000, when the players' movement was beginning to gather momentum, gate receipts from All-Ireland championship games reached nearly €9 million. And that was without the income from the provincial championships.

Apart from that, the GAA landscape had changed enormously during the 1990s. Allowing sponsorship of county teams with company names emblazoned on jerseys was sanctioned early in the decade and, later on, Guinness and Bank of Ireland came aboard as sponsors of the All-Ireland championships. The introduction of team sponsorship brought a big financial boost for County Boards, which, in fairness, was badly needed. However, it altered the dynamic for players as they were now walking (and running too!) billboards every time they took to the field. Now, if you are promoting a company in ordinary circumstances, you expect to be paid. It's a simple business transaction. Obviously, that could not apply directly to GAA players for wearing county jerseys with a sponsor's name on them but it certainly raised the stakes in terms of what teams were entitled to as part of the general conditions under which they operated as a group.

Within a few years of allowing counties to acquire sponsors, the GAA moved to extend the market to include brand links with the All-Ireland championship in what were very lucrative deals.

Guinness, in particular, made a huge impact with their classy advertising campaigns and general marketing expertise glamorising the hurling championships in a way that had never been done before.

I have an interest to declare here. I did quite a bit of work with Guinness right from the start of their sponsorship and while I never drank their products (or those of any other alcoholic company either), I loved the way that the company went about marketing hurling as part of their overall campaign. It was slick, modern and presented with such impact that even people with no interest in hurling could not have missed it. I have no doubt it was hugely beneficial for the game. Bearing in mind that Nickey Brennan, who would later go on to become GAA President, spoke in 1994 of how hurling was in crisis and badly in need of a boost, the arrival of Guinness as highly pro-active sponsors was hugely significant.

But then things were changing all over the place. Players saw how that change was bringing so much more money pouring into GAA coffers but they also noticed something else – very little was coming back to them in terms of how they were being treated. It was as if players were cash cows, ready to be milked every day while, at the same time, not seeing any improvement in the food they were being fed in order to produce the milk in the first place. That simply could not last.

All players love what they're doing but lines have to be drawn. Early in my county career I got knocked out in a game against Wexford and was out of work for three weeks after suffering concussion. I was working for Cadbury at the time, a job that depended on driving, but I wasn't allowed in the car because of the concussion. I was told – politely but firmly – that I either wanted to work for Cadbury or hurl but that I couldn't have time off every time I got a belt. Fair enough. They were paying my wages. I'm sure the same thing was happening to lots of other lads all over the country. I understood full well how Cadbury felt. After all, I was no use to them sitting at home nursing a headache for a few weeks.

And then there was the issue of player exploitation. Players appeared to have no rights whatsoever over how they were used for the commercial gain of others. I remember Nicky English raising a very interesting point at a launch of a promotion as to whether companies had the right to use pictures of players without permission for their own commercial gain. It seems they had. And for free as well. The view was once you signed up as a GAA member, you signed away your rights and anyone was entitled to use your name and picture for commercial gain without paying anything for it. How unfair was that?

That area has been tightened up considerably over the years – although not entirely – but back in the 1990s anything went. And when it came to the players, it went all the way to exploitation. The commercial world was becoming increasingly aware of the value of being associated with inter-county-players and was miles ahead of the game by comparison with the GAA. So now the problem was two-fold.

On the one hand, you had the GAA bringing in lots of extra cash through sponsorship deals while many companies were exploiting players' popularity for their own gain. I'd say some companies were having a right laugh at the GAA. I'm not talking about the major backers like Guinness, Bank of Ireland, AIB and Allianz, who were putting big money into competition sponsorship but smaller, opportunist outfits who spotted very quickly that the GAA were very much behind the game in this area.

Meanwhile, the players were caught in the middle with nothing coming their way except the ever-increasing pressure brought about by the higher profile the games were enjoying through increased TV, newspaper and general media coverage which, in turn, led to bigger crowds attending games. The GAA, the business world and the media were all benefiting from the interest surge but the players weren't, not even when it came to the basics.

Here's how daft it was. For example, take Croke Park on the day of a big championship game. Many of the people who were working there were being paid. The public paid their way in and if anyone suffered an injury of any description, they were covered by the stadium insurance. Now the players were the ones who were most likely to suffer injury and while, in theory, they were covered, it was a difficult process to get anything from a system that wasn't especially user-friendly. And even when a payment was made, it quite often came nowhere near providing full compensation if you were off work. Effectively, the entertainers were regarded as second-class citizens by comparison with the audience.

I remember getting bills from the Health Board one time for x-rays because, as you can imagine, my hands, in particular, took a lot of belts over the years so I spent a fair amount of time in hospitals. The Health Board didn't give a damn who paid up – they just sent the bills to the person who was treated and waited for the cheque. And if they didn't get it, they kept chasing you with a little more urgency and menace every time.

It's all very different now. I had to go for an x-ray some time ago after injuring my hand and the bill was sorted out by the club automatically through the insurance. I can only assume that it's the same everywhere. And so it should be.

The GAA's response to the founding of the GPA ranged from lukewarm to cold to freezing. A few more enlightened people in power could see a certain merit in having a formal relationship with the players but many others were openly hostile and would have done anything they could to kill it at birth. They had succeeded in the 1980s when a Players' Association was formed, only to fizzle out after a few years, largely because it was ignored by Croke Park. The players who started the movement did the best they could but times were different. There was much less money coming into the GAA and, besides, players were supposed to be seen but not heard. If the GAA had embraced the concept in the 1980s, the friction and upheaval that accompanied the arrival of the new Millennium would have been avoided. The players' association of the 1980s never stood a chance, not because it wasn't a good idea but because the authorities were sufficiently powerful to freeze it out.

If the launch of the GPA in 1999 sounded alarm bells in Croke Park, a development in the following year sent them into a right tizzy altogether. There was utter consternation in the corridors of power in August 2000 when a £50,000 (€63,500) deal was announced through the GPA between recruitment group, Marlborough and ten players.

It all looks very innocent nowadays when the GAA is swimming in commercial deals but, back then, it was huge news. It left the back pages and moved up front very quickly. Basically, it was to work like this: each of the ten players would receive £4,000 in return for doing a certain amount of promotional work for Marlborough, with the remaining £10,000 going to the general GPA fund.

The deal was announced in early August and the players who fronted the launch were: Brian Whelahan (Offaly), Peter Canavan (Tyrone), Brian Lohan (Clare), Ja Fallon (Galway), Brian Corcoran (Cork), Stephen Melia (Louth), Paul Flynn (Waterford) and Derek Duggan (Roscommon).

They were eight long-serving players spread from across the four provinces, all of whom commanded a lot of respect. Why only eight? It was announced on the day that two others would be named later. The other two? DJ Carey and Brian Stynes of Dublin.

The reason I wasn't at the launch was because it was held on a Wednesday and Kilkenny were due to play Galway in the All-Ireland semi-final on the following Sunday. Now, Brian Cody never interfered in anything I did outside the game but I reckon he would not have been all that happy to see me perched up at the top table for the launch of a controversial sponsorship deal four days before I was due to tangle with the Galway defence. Nor would it have been fair of me to do so, I presume it was the same for Brian Stynes as Dublin were due to play Kildare in a Leinster final replay on the following Saturday.

The Marlborough deal became more than sports page news. It was treated as a massive story in the media, with lots of debate and analysis as to what exactly it meant for the future of the GAA. Talk about over-reaction. You would think we had just announced a breakaway from the mainstream GAA and were planning to run a counter-organisation. Still, I suppose I could see where the media were coming from.

It wasn't so much the deal itself as the implications it might have that captured attention. Was it the first drive towards pay-for-play? It wasn't, of course, but Croke Park were deeply suspicious over anything the GPA involved themselves in. There were even dark murmurings that the GAA might take action against the 'Marlborough Ten' on the basis that we had infringed the amateur status rule. Pure nonsense, of course, since the payments were to be made in return for work done by the players in a straight-forward business arrangement. How could a sporting organisation control what its members did in their private lives? It would have made an interesting case if Croke Park decided to take it on. Interesting, that is, until it was blown out of Court.

Of course the Marlborough deal wasn't Croke Park's only worry. Their real concern centred on the fact that the GPA was gaining in strength and credibility all the time. Unlike in the 1980s, it wasn't going to go away this time. Its time had come and no amount of bleating about threatening the aims and ideals of the Association could change that reality.

That alarmed Croke Park, who reckoned there was no need for the GPA because they had established their own Players' Committee.

It had been introduced some years earlier and consisted of a group of players who were hand-picked by the GAA President of the day. I served on it myself for a while and saw its limitations at first hand. In theory, it was a good idea. A group of current and ex-players would meet a few times a year and come up with proposals which would then be forwarded on to the authorities. Now, if they were acted upon, it would be worthwhile but very often they weren't. Well not all of them anyway.

And, God knows, they weren't very radical. The other big flaw in the system was that the Players' Committee changed every three years in line with the presidency turnover. So, in a sense, it was back to square one every three years. Besides, the committee didn't really command the respect of the broader playing community because it was appointed by the president of the day. Naturally, the presidents were careful who they appointed.

For instance, there was never a chance that the likes of Eddie O'Connor would be called in. Eddie ruffled official feathers during his acceptance speech after we beat Galway in the 1993 All-Ireland final. Never one to mince his words, Eddie chose the highest profile moment of the season to declare that All-Ireland winners and runners-up should be rewarded with a team holiday, paid for by the GAA.

Eddie had a point but, at the time, his comments caused uproar. He was criticised for using his acceptance speech to promote such a demand. But as Eddie saw it, it was the ideal chance to have his say. There was no point saying it after a League game in Ennis on a wet February Sunday. He had a captive audience in Croke Park on All-Ireland final day and in most of the houses around the country and wasn't going to let the opportunity pass to state bluntly that players deserved to be rewarded with a holiday if they got to the All-Ireland final. He was articulating what every player felt.

It's important to give Eddie the credit he deserves for making those comments. I'm sure he hadn't planned it but when the chance arose, he went for it in his own inimitable style. He spoke as he hurled – straight from the heart and with total honesty. Standing on the steps of the Hogan Stand as captain of the All-Ireland winning team, Eddie was looking out over thousands of supporters and felt the time was right to make a stand.

It wasn't a protest or a rebellion, but merely a statement that after all players put into the game, the All-Ireland finalists should be rewarded with a holiday. I doubt if there was one genuine hurling supporter who would have objected. The people who packed Croke Park that day would have been happy for a tiny percentage of the receipts to go to team holidays but the GAA didn't see it that way.

Eddie was asked about his comments by the media at the All-Ireland lunch on the following day where he elaborated further. He pointed out that gate receipts for the final were around £1 million and suggested

£30,000 (€38,100 in today's money) should be put aside for finalists' holidays.

There was such a clear logic to it that most people agreed with him but the GAA authorities saw it differently. They pointed out that since players everywhere were putting in a huge effort, the All-Ireland finalists should not get special treatment. Now, I doubt if players who didn't reach the finals would have problem with Eddie's suggestion but the GAA claimed it wouldn't be fair. How very convenient.

I always admired Eddie for speaking out on the subject. In that sense, he was well ahead of his time. I made my own stand against what was going on when, one time, I refused to run against a dog in a fund-raiser for a team holiday. It took place in Kilkenny dog track and the plan was for a group of us to run against a greyhound in a special novelty race.

I thought it absolutely ridiculous that after putting in such a big effort all year, we were expected to resort to running against a greyhound to help fill the holiday coffers. It was bad enough having to go around pubs selling autographed team photos to raise money – which we did for years – without having to sprint around Kilkenny dog track against a four-legged flyer!

Eddie O'Connor's comment after the 1993 All-Ireland final may well have been a whole lot more important than many people think. Of course, he should not have had to say it. In fact, rewarding players should have been a given, especially once the sponsorship area opened up and more money was sloshing into the coffers. Something of a precedent had been set when the Leinster Council gave a special grant to the Meath and Dublin squads to help their holiday funds after the four-game first round championship epic in 1991. Mind you, those four games were watched by 238,000 people so the players were well entitled to some consideration.

Anyway, back to the Players' Committee. Having served on it for a while, I know it was well-meaning and committed to bringing about improvement but it never had any teeth. All it could do was make suggestions which then went before the GAA authorities. And if they rejected the proposals, there was nothing the Players' Committee could do because it had been appointed from within the very system it felt needed to be challenged. Catch 22 and all that.

The GPA was different. It was totally independent of the GAA and could agitate for change in a real and meaningful way. It had the backing of most players which gave it a strong mandate. And if it got no response from Croke Park, there were various avenues through which it could pursue its objectives, up to and including strike action. Now, that was the last thing the players wanted but the option of going for the nuclear button was always there. It had to be.

The most important point of all was that the GPA had become a major force within the GAA. It was here to stay.

The Marlborough deal led to a clash between the GPA and the Players' Committee which was then chaired by Jarlath Burns, whose long career with Armagh footballers had ended a year before. Jarlath flashed out a statement, effectively accusing the 'Marlborough Ten' of denying our team mates of their entitlements as team members. I'm not quite sure where that came from but that's what he said. He also said that those who accused the GPA of being elitist and 'only representative of a greedy minority' may well have been proven right.

Strong stuff from Jarlath but he had missed the point. And when you look at how the area of player endorsements and rewards for off-field activities has expanded so enormously over the last decade, I think it proves that the GPA initiative of 2000 was no more than a sign of things to come. The world was changing and the GAA would have to change with it. Maybe Jarlath felt that as chairman of the official Player's Committee, he had to toe the official line but I thought his comments were over the top.

I have to say I resented being accused of elitism or greed through my involvement with the GPA, for whom I served a period as President. In all my years playing for Kilkenny, I only put in travelling expenses for three seasons. That was when I was going to Dublin to get treatment from the great AK, Alan Kelly.

Other than that, I was happy to pay my own way because I was doing what I loved. I regarded playing for Kilkenny as an honour and a privilege and would never, ever do anything to interfere with that. Yes, I was actively involved in the GPA but if Brian Cody had come to me and said "DJ, I'd prefer if you had nothing to do with that." I would have respected that. He never did, by the way.

Nothing came above my devotion to club and county and I think anyone who knows me understands that. All of the other players who were driving the GPA were in exactly the same boat, but that didn't mean that we weren't entitled to campaign to make life better, not just for ourselves, but for players everywhere.

The reality was that a wide division existed between administration and players and something needed to be done about it. The idea that somehow that was a smokescreen to hide the real agenda of bringing in pay-for-play was not only wrong – it was insulting. It was also deliberately mischievous as it painted a picture of a group of well-known players trying to steer the GAA towards professionalism for their own gain. The truth was, of course, that if the GPA were to get off the ground, it needed to be led by higher-profile players. However, the battle was being waged on behalf of everybody. Players from the so-called weaker counties couldn't really bring about change; neither could younger players. The leadership had to come from well-known players from the stronger counties which is exactly what happened. Unfortunately, that was turned into a claim that we were out for what we could get for ourselves.

The irony was that once it became clear that the GPA would become a permanent presence on the GAA landscape, things moved on quite quickly. I won the Hurler of the Year award in 2000 and got a trophy; Henry Shefflin won it two years later and got a car from Seat, who were sponsoring the GPA at the time. Good luck to Henry – and to everyone else who got cars – but it showed how times had changed. They haven't stopped moving since either.

One of the things that galled me about criticism of the GPA in its early days was that it was often spouted by people in the GAA who were well looked after themselves when it came to charging expenses to attend meetings and other activities. They tended to get pretty good seats for All-Ireland finals too, yet they felt entitled to lambast players for trying to improve their own conditions.

In fairness to the GAA, the appointment of Paraic Duffy as Player Welfare officer in Croke Park was a progressive development. It not only recognised the need for such a role but also put in a man who understood that the way forward was to work with the players.

Nowadays, there's a good relationship between the GPA, and their team led by Dessie Farrell, and Croke Park but there's always more work to be done.

The issues facing players nowadays are different to some degree than in the past. Unemployment, emigration and the stresses of modern life are all presenting challenges which need to be taken on. Neither the GAA nor the GPA can solve them on their own, but they certainly can combine to support players.

At the core of everything is respect for the role of the player and, unfortunately, it took a long time to get that established. It has nothing whatsoever to do with pay-for-play but rather with an acceptance that if players can benefit from their involvement with hurling and football, let them at it.

If you go to a solicitor or an accountant, you pay the going hourly rate so players have every right to expect that if they attend a launch or whatever, they will be paid. And if a player is offered money to wear a certain type of boot, what's wrong with that? Surely it's better from a GAA viewpoint, that it's going into an amateur player's pocket than to a highly-paid professional from another sport.

Presenting medals is different. That has nothing to do with commercialism – it's about giving back to the game and should be done for free, except for genuine travelling expenses. No one should be out of pocket but no one should make money from it either.

There's no doubt that players are looked after a whole lot better now than they were even ten years ago, most of which is down to the establishment and development of the GPA. I'm no longer directly involved since I retired but I'm happy that I played my part in those early, difficult years when there was so much official opposition to the GPA.

It's a pity that so much energy was devoted to trying to keep it down, especially since it was done for all the wrong reasons. Nowadays, the GPA is part-funded by the GAA and works quite closely with Croke Park across a number of areas, which is in everybody's interest. If only the GAA bosses could have seen the positive benefit of that thirteen or fourteen years ago. It would have avoided a lot of unnecessary angst for both parties.

CHAPTER 16

AMERICA CALLING

The good folks in Wake Forest University, North Carolina probably thought I was mad. They were offering me a fully-paid scholarship to their famous college and I was saying, "thanks for that but I won't be taking it".

Why so? Hurling, of course. I sometimes wonder what direction my life would have taken if I accepted the invitation to go to Wake Forest after doing my Leaving Cert. I was being offered a place on their physical education programme and all that went with it. In ordinary circumstances it would have been tempting, but I never gave it any serious consideration. Wake Forest is a great institution but to the best of my knowledge, hurling is not on their agenda so they couldn't have been on mine.

Going to America would have meant the end – or at least the suspension for four years – of my hurling career. And since playing for Kilkenny was always my ultimate sporting dream, nothing was going to stand in the way of trying to achieve that.

Wake Forest's interest in me arose from my handball career where, by the way, I had more success than in hurling in terms of winning titles. I loved handball ever since I was a kid. I started playing when I was around nine years old, thanks to our neighbour, Richie Bryan, who was a huge enthusiast for the game. He used to bring his son James and my brother Jack to Goresbridge for games and as soon as I could, I started to tag along.

I took to handball right away and enjoyed it even more as I got older. The different sized courts offered a chance to win a whole range of prizes and titles. Between the handball and the hurling, I had some hectic years. Some very successful ones too. In 1988 alone, I won six All-Ireland titles, two minor and two colleges in handball, plus an All-Ireland colleges hurling with St. Kieran's and minor hurling with Kilkenny.

Handball was great for my hurling. It meant I could handpass the ball twenty or thirty yards quite easily. If you can do that accurately, it's a massive advantage because it enables you to open up play in an instant. It's very hard to defend against a long, well-delivered handpass. People tend to think of a handpass as being all about the palm but when you've played handball, you use the fingers as well. That's where the power and the precision come from.

There must have been thousands of times in my hurling career that I got myself out of tight situations with a swift handpass and because I could toss the ball so far, it was very helpful to colleagues in space. The opposition find it hard to figure out anyone who can make a long handpass. It gives them one more thing to worry about. That's why I'd strongly recommend to young hurlers that they take up handball. It will bring another dimension to your game.

I played a bit of squash too and was fairly handy at it, thanks mainly to handball which showed me how to read the angles of the court. Still I never took to squash in the same way as I did to handball. If you think about it, handball is one of the few sports where you need to be two-handed. Hurling, tennis and squash are all essentially one-handed sports and while both hands are on a golf club when a shot is being made, one of them is dominant. In handball, the left and right hands have to be equally good as either side of your body must operate independently of the other, depending on where the ball is coming from.

I was lucky in that I was equally comfortable with both hands. In fact, I can write with both hands, although I would be naturally right-handed. Being able to write with both hands meant that I wasn't put out to any great extent when I injured one or the other which, as you can imagine, was quite often.

Coaching was minimal in handball back in my early days. Playing very regularly and finding out things about yourself and the game was the real coaching. You can take several time-outs nowadays, even at juvenile level, which I think is all wrong. You have lads banging on the glass, calling players out to tell them what they should be doing, instead of letting them figure it out for themselves. Back then, you only took a time-out if you were wrecked tired which, as a kid, was rare enough anyway. Now, as with all sports, everything seems to hinge on coaching.

To be honest, I find a lot of it comical. Take soccer. A goalkeeper might let in a goal and you'll hear the experts say there was nothing he could have done about it because, technically, he had positioned himself properly according to the coaching manual. He's only criticised if he's not technically correct which, to me, is a bit of a joke. It doesn't matter a damn how the ball is saved, once it's saved.

It's the same with so many aspects of sport. It's all about technique and what the computer or coaching manual says when, in fact, instinct and spontaneity are far more important. That's how I learned hurling. Sure, I was shown how to do things, but most of the learning came in actual games. The more often you play, the better you become. Nowadays, you'll see young lads being taught how to lift the ball and how to hit it. Everything is so coached when, in fact, the really important lessons are acquired in match situations.

It's the same in all sports, including handball, which should be all about instinct and judgement anyway. You're on your own so you have to get on with the game, figuring things out as you go along. What's your opponent's good and bad side? Which area of the court is he least comfortable? Half the fun is in working that out.

After my minor days in handball, I skipped U-21 and went on to junior where I did quite well. From that it was on to senior level where the standard was very high. Because of my hurling commitments, I couldn't give handball as much time as I would have liked, but was still happy enough to compete against the big names.

Then, Duxie Walsh asked me to be his doubles partner. Duxie is, of course, one of the sport's great legends. Mention handball to anyone and the first name they will think of is Duxie Walsh. We won three All-Ireland senior doubles titles together in 1994-95-98 (40 by 20). I respected him hugely as a handballer and he respected me as a hurler so we worked very well as a combination.

I gave up handball at the age of 29 because I was finding it increasingly hard to combine it with hurling. Anyway, I'm not so sure Brian Cody liked to see me involved in the game at the highest level. I remember one occasion partnering Duxie in an All-Ireland semi-final in Belfast and because he was carrying some injury or other, I was trying to play both sides of the court, which I wasn't particularly good at. I was on the floor quite a lot and, the next day, my two elbows were badly swollen. They were actually huge but I couldn't rest them as we had a National hurling League game with Waterford in Walsh Park. I remember Brian eyeing me curiously in the dressing-room and while he didn't say anything, I knew well he was thinking to himself: 'I wish to God Carey would pack in that handball lark.' I did, eventually!

I loved playing doubles, especially with Duxie, who was such a genius. Doubles play is fiercely intense altogether because there's so much going on in a confined space. The ball is whizzing around at high speed, you have four fellas on the court, each trying to mark out his own territory. It's a pretty hectic place to be but is hugely enjoyable when you're in a good set-up as I was with Duxie.

Apart from improving my hurling, handball opened up a whole range of doors to me. I saw the world, thanks to handball, places like San Francisco, Los Angeles, Chicago, Miami, New York, New Mexico, Phoenix, Orlando, Tuscon, Vancouver and Saskatchewan in Canada. I was due to go to Australia one year but missed out with a broken finger.

Playing in all those world handball championships was a brilliant experience. It meant that in my teenage years I got to see places in America – in particular – that your average country lad might never get a chance to visit at any time in his life, let alone when he was still in his teens.

Since the world championships were played immediately after Christmas, it meant I was quite often away for Christmas Day. To be honest, I didn't mind. Christmas was no big deal, certainly not in the way it is now.

Because handball is a minority sport here, people have no idea how big it is in America. It's the biggest participant sport in New York City with over 100,000 people playing one-wall handball. It's a game for the masses, inexpensive and easy to play. All you need is a ball, a wall, and off you go.

I'd love to see handball get more coverage here. The likes of Paul Brady, who has been such a huge success, has done more than his bit to popularise it in recent times and, in general, the game is going pretty well in Ireland but because it not a great sport for TV, many people know very little about it. Still, it's an ideal sport for male and female and can be played by all ages.

I won two world handball titles at U-23 level but might have done a lot better in earlier years only for a cock-up over ages. I was born in November and since January 1 is the normal cut-off point for deciding on eligibility for various grades in Irish sport, I regularly missed out by a year, whereas someone who was born in January was eligible, although they were only two months younger than me.

However, in world handball the eligibility date was decided by your age at the time of the tournament. So while we were using the January 1 cut-off in Ireland, it should have been the date of the tournament. It meant that for quite a few years I wasn't playing in events for which I was eligible age-wise. I was nearly 23 years old by the time that mistake was discovered.

Being born in November meant I missed out narrowly on an extra year at minor and U-21 level in hurling too but there was nothing I could do about that. Still, it would have been nice to get another year in both grades, especially since I was only six weeks too old.

My handball exploits brought me to the attention of Wake Forest University – hence the offer of a scholarship – but as I've said, nothing was ever going to come between me and my hurling

Playing so much hurling and handball left me with little time for others sports but I suppose it was inevitable that I would eventually try my hand at golf, which I did at the age of 26. I didn't really like it all that much early on, but gradually the bug began to bite harder and I bought into the game. I got my handicap down to 3.5 at one stage but it later drifted out to six. I haven't played a whole lot in the last few years for various reasons.

When I was playing regularly, I could hit the ball a long way but the direction wasn't always what it might have been. I'd be fairly even-tempered by nature but when golf decides to frustrate you, it knows how to yank every chain. I reached breaking point one day but thankfully there was no one around to see it.

I was playing by myself in Mount Juliet and hit a few balls off the tee, one worse than the other. Left and right they went, as if deliberately trying to annoy me. After one particularly wayward hit, I flung the driver away in disgust, before retrieving it and slamming it into my bag. At the next hole,

I whipped it out, let fly with another tee-shot, only for the head of the driver to whizz half way down the fairway. I had obviously damaged it with my petulant throw and it wasn't going to take any more of that behaviour. It was a very expensive driver so that particular experience taught me a valuable lesson.

Because of my profile in hurling, I was lucky enough to be invited to Pro-Am and charity golf outings fairly regularly, which I enjoyed immensely. I got to meet some very famous names, including Tiger Woods, whom I had dinner with on one occasions and found him very friendly. I didn't have the pleasure of playing with him but I did get to play with, among others, Colin Montgomery, Seve Ballesteros, Ian Woosnam, plus, of course, the Irish lads, Padraig Harrington, Paul McGinley and Graham McDowell.

It's only when you play with the professionals that you realise just how far ahead they are. I still laugh when I think of the nonsense that went around when I announced my retirement in early 1998. Because I was playing a fair amount of golf at the time, I was supposed to be lining up for an attempt to make it as a professional.

It never even crossed my mind and if it had, I would have knocked it straight away for the very simple reason that my game wasn't remotely good enough to take me within a million miles of that exclusive world. Nor was it ever likely to be.

Apart from hurling, handball and golf, I also tried my hand at Gaelic football and even had the distinction of wearing the black-and-amber of Kilkenny in an O'Byrne Cup game. It was my one and only outing for the footballers and came at the age of 29 in January 2000. Current County Board chairman, Ned Quinn was on a drive to raise football's profile in Kilkenny and asked me would I play in the first round of the O'Byrne Cup. I had played football for the club just before that so Ned grabbed the chance to get me onboard for the county.

I lined out in the familiar No. 12 jersey against Wexford in Horeswood and while we lost by 2-15 to 1-8 I thoroughly enjoyed the experience. I even scored a point but the bulk of our tally came from John Maher while Matty Forde did enormous damage for Wexford at the other end. Paddy and Richie Mullally were on the Kilkenny team that day but then, like a lot of well-known hurlers, they were fine footballers too.

I would have liked to play more football but the chance didn't arise. Besides, at the age of 29, it wasn't really on to become a dual player. I have to say I'm disappointed with the way things have gone for Kilkenny football. There's a decent standard in the county and I have no doubt that if a group came together and gave it the necessary commitment, they could hold their own in Division Four. The difficulty with football in Kilkenny has always been that many of the best footballers are top hurlers too. The Mullallys, Eddie O'Connor, Michael Phelan, Pat O'Neill, Adrian Ronan and Liam Simpson were, among others, fine footballers, lads who could hold their own on a lot of county teams if circumstances were different.

I would love to see a group brought up from U-14 level and nurtured up through the ranks. That way, a base might be put down which would draw others in. The trouble at present is that everyone wants to play hurling and even lads who are good at football aren't all that interested in giving it a shot at county level. That's a pity.

It doesn't look good for Kilkenny that we're no longer fielding a team in the National football League. Now I know the argument will be made that hurling is going so well that nothing should be allowed to interfere with it but I don't see it as an either/or situation. Hurling will always be No. 1 in Kilkenny but there's no reason why football couldn't slot in as a comfortable No. 2. Okay, so Sam Maguire might not be coming to Nowlan Park anytime soon but we would at least be represented on the inter-county scene. It's the least you expect from any county, whether in hurling or football.

CHAPTER 17

THE STATE OF PLAY

I can still remember the reaction of the Down team and the band of loyal supporters who made the journey south to Nowlan Park for a National League game in March 1993. We were All-Ireland champions at the time but Down not only matched us all over the field, they out-scored us too, winning by a point.

The Down contingent celebrated as if they had won the All-Ireland final, which was perfectly understandable since their team had pulled off a rare treble, having beaten the All-Ireland champions, earned themselves a place in the League quarter-final and sent us hurtling through the relegation chute. We had most of our All-Ireland winning team on duty but, on the day, Down were worthy winners.

Two seasons earlier, Kilkenny were very lucky to beat Antrim in the All-Ireland semi-final and, two years prior to that, Antrim beat Leinster champions, Offaly in the semi-final. That shows the level Antrim were at in that period. I know that 'Sambo' McNaughton, a great warrior figure in Antrim hurling for so long, has always regarded the 1991 semi-final as one their best ever performances in Croke Park. He would know more about that than me but I can certainly vouch for the quality of their performance that day. Antrim were every bit as good as us but the breaks went our way.

I mention all that by way of regret with what's happening in counties like Antrim and Down nowadays. They are no longer competitive at the high end of the scale, which is a great pity. It's also something that should be examined by the GAA. The hurling heartlands of Antrim and Down are special places, populated by dedicated enthusiasts who are doing all they can to promote the game. I visited them dozens of times over the years and always came away feeling inspired by the devotion and passion they have for hurling.

They would love to have successful county teams but it's not happening nowadays. That's surprising in Antrim's case, in particular, since their county champions often do very well in the All-Ireland club championship. Indeed, Loughgiel Shamrocks won the title in 1983 and 2012 while Dunloy reached several finals over the years. Clearly, the standard of club hurling is high in Antrim but, for some reason, it is not reflected on the county scene these days.

The move into the Leinster championship in 2009 hasn't worked out as well for Antrim as everyone hoped for and, sadly, things look stagnant at present. Down no longer compete for the Liam MacCarthy Cup and while it was encouraging for them to win the Christy Ring Cup this year, it would be even better if they were good enough for the Liam MacCarthy Cup tier.

Unfortunately, even the most devoted Down fan would agree that the standard of the county team is a long way from the days when they could beat Kilkenny in Nowlan Park as they did twenty years ago. A year earlier they won their first – and only – All Star hurling award when Gerard McGrattan was chosen at right half-forward. He scored five points from open play in the 1992 All-Ireland semi-final against Cork, underlining just how good he was, even against top line defenders. There were plenty of other fine talents around too who could compete with the very best anywhere.

Antrim always had players in contention for All Star awards around then too while Derry were also quite competitive. 'Sambo' McNaughton in 1991, Dessie Donnelly and Olcan McFetridge in 1989 and Ciaran Barr in 1988 all won All Star awards while several others were nominated and later travelled as All Star replacements. Those were good times for Ulster hurling and we all thought that the improvement would continue but it hasn't. Instead, their fortunes have plummeted.

For a long time, John O'Shea used to run a fund-raiser for third world charity GOAL in the week after the All-Ireland final when the new champions played a Rest of Ireland team. The 'Rest' selection usually included some Antrim and Down lads, who would happily make the long trip south for the midweek game. They loved being part of the occasion and, quite often, gave some of the best performances.

So what has happened over the years? Why has Ulster hurling slipped so much?

Ultimately, it's up to every county to examine its own situation but the GAA as an organisation should play a role too. If more funding is needed to support hurling in places like Antrim, Down, Derry and Armagh, it should be provided immediately. Cost should not be an issue when it comes to preserving and developing the great game in any part of the country where there are enough people willing and able to promote it.

People who live south of a line between Galway and Dublin have no idea what it's really like to be a hurler from an Ulster county. Even something as routine as organising a challenge game involves a lot of hard work for the likes of Antrim and Down because they have to travel a long way south if they want to play one of the stronger teams. It takes so much time and effort that it's very often not worth the trouble but, of course, the downside is that they are not getting the games that would help them improve.

The many changes which the National hurling League has undergone over the last decade hasn't benefitted the likes of Antrim. I don't think it has done anything for the game overall but it has certainly been bad for counties below the top flight.

The six-team 1A and 1B system was very restrictive. Take Antrim, for example. They weren't strong enough to get into the top six, which meant that they didn't get a chance to play the likes of Kilkenny, Tipperary and Galway, who were in 1A. The argument could be made that if Antrim – or any other county who found themselves in a similar situation – weren't good enough to get into the top six, then they could have no complaints about not playing some of the top counties but it's not that simple.

Hurling needs all the nourishment it can get and that definitely involves top teams playing in Casement Park and other venues that don't see big action very often. I played my first game as a Kilkenny forward in Casement Park (I had a few runs in goal earlier on) in 1989 before a big crowd. The atmosphere was great and you could sense the general sense of excitement around the ground, which had to be good for the promotion of Antrim hurling.

A League system which greatly reduced Antrim's chances of playing Kilkenny (or some other top teams) in Casement Park should never have been introduced. The aim should always be to give hurling people everywhere the best possible chance of seeing the leading counties at local venues.

It's astonishing that the National League set-up has been changed so often without having the need to boost counties just outside the top band as a priority. I know it's not easy to have a structure that suits everybody (look at all the unrest over the last decade and especially in 2013) but it can't be that hard to settle on a format that ticks most of the boxes, both in terms of fairness and promotional impact.

It has usually been the case that weaker counties have a better chance of beating the top sides in the League rather than the championship – hence the need to have an inclusive system that gives them a chance of doing that as often as possible.

The League format that applied in recent years failed on that score. Having six teams in a group meant that some counties only had two home games every second year which made no sense. It was bad from a promotional viewpoint at a time when hurling needs all the exposure it can get. Hopefully, the League will better fulfil counties' needs in the future but the last few years have been a real mess which did the game no favours.

I also find it hard to fathom why the interprovincials (Railway Cups as we used to know them) aren't more successful. I loved playing with Leinster, even if I never recall a big crowd at any of the games. It was nice to work with players from the other Leinster counties in what was one of the few opportunities we got to mix with lads who would normally be your enemies, in a sporting sense of course.

I won Railway Cup medals in 1993 and 1998 and lost a few finals too but, for me, the important thing was to make myself available for selection. It didn't matter how well I was going for Kilkenny or how many All-Irelands I had won, I still regarded it as a huge honour to be selected for Leinster.

Most players I have met thought the same but, for some reason, the public switched off a long time ago and are showing no signs of returning.

I cannot understand why that is the case. It's strange that rugby people identify with the province, yet GAA supporters don't. Oddly enough many GAA fans will follow their province – or maybe even an adopted province – in rugby, but not in hurling or football.

Of course, the interprovincials have not been helped by being thrown all over the fixtures' calendar over the years. They should be given a fixed spot on the schedule, actively promoted and treated like something the GAA is proud of rather than something to be tolerated, as seems to be the case. Several top GAA officials have called for their abolition in recent years which isn't exactly the best way to encourage the public to turn out.

The whole area of promotion is still well behind where it should be, not just for the interprovincials, but right across the board. Hurling isn't sold nearly as vigorously as it should be. For instance, we still insist on playing the Leinster hurling final in Croke Park, knowing that it's going to be more than half-empty, which creates a hollow atmosphere.

Compare that with the atmosphere in Nowlan Park for the two Kilkenny-Tipperary games in the League final and All-Ireland qualifiers this year. The ground was packed, there was a special buzz in the town for hours before and after the games and everyone who experienced the two days felt uplifted. Why not play more games at provincial venues?

Playing in a half-empty Croke Park makes no sense for a lot of games, including most Leinster hurling finals. Still, while that remains the policy, greater effort should be made to get more people through the gates. The Leinster final is played in early July at the height of the tourist season so surely it should be possible to sell the game as a major sporting event in the Capital city.

Lots of tourists come to Ireland to enjoy the special atmosphere and culture of the country, yet you will probably find that many of them are wandering around Dublin on Leinster hurling final Sunday without having any idea of the unique sporting event that's going on fifteen minutes from the city centre.

It's the same in August when Croke Park is rarely full for All-Ireland semi-finals, yet I bet you that most of the tourists have no idea the games are on.

The Americans are able to turn the Super Bowl into a major international event so why can't we sell hurling and football as a unique part of our heritage and culture?

Does the GAA even have an international division? Every time you turn on your television you will see various minority sports being shown from all over the world, even if some of them are mind-numbingly boring. Hurling and Gaelic football are easy sports to understand and are also a whole lot more exciting than much of what we see on TV, yet they remain a secret as far as the rest of the world is concerned. This year's hurling championship provided fabulous entertainment week after week, yet apart for Irish people at home and abroad who knew about them?

It's long past time to be much more aggressive on the marketing front. The changing face of media world-wide should make it easier to bring Gaelic Games to a much wider audience. The scene has changed from the time when the only GAA games shown 'live' on TV were All-Ireland semi-finals and finals and Railway Cup finals. There's an urgent need to exploit that for the good of the games we love and cherish.

If it's important to sell hurling abroad, it's even more crucial that it's promoted here. The more youngsters you see with hurleys in their hands the better for the game which, unlike some other sports, has to be taken up at a young age. I did my bit over the years with the DJ Carey School of Hurling, a Leinster Council initiative which was a great success.

Nickey Brennan, who was Leinster Council chairman at the time, asked me if I would be prepared to lend my name to the idea and back it up by working with young lads from all over the province. The plan was to bring groups of selected 14 year-olds from Leinster counties together in St. Kieran's College for a residential school of hurling for two weeks each summer.

It was an excellent idea and it ran very successfully for seven years. I was there as often as I could and several other inter-county players and managers came in to give coaching sessions too in what was a very player-friendly set-up. Apart from improving their hurling skills, young lads got to mix with their peers from other counties in an enjoyable atmosphere.

It's not run anymore, which is I think is a pity. Obviously my name in the title would have to come to an end at some stage once I was no longer playing with Kilkenny but there was no reason why it couldn't have moved on to being called the Henry Shefflin or the Tommy Walsh School of Hurling.

It was great fun working with young lads from all over the province, even if there were times when I learned from them rather than the other way around. And it wasn't always good either!

At one particular session, I was showing a group the importance of being in close to your opponent when you pulled on the ball. I would run alongside the young lads shoulder-to-shoulder practising pulling on the ball on the ground and then stop and talk to them about it. I always emphasised the importance of listening carefully to their coaches and doing exactly what they told them.

Having stressed that, we set off again. I was running alongside this young fella and we went to pull on the ball (at least I did) when he whacked me across the ankles. I thought at first it was a mistake but as I started to show him how he should have hit the ball he said: "but you told me to do exactly what my coach tells me."

"Yea, every time."

"But that's what he tells me to do," he said with an innocent look.

I could tell it was time to go back to basics with that lad! As for his coach, the less said the better.

CHAPTER 18

TOP CATS (KILKENNY 1990-2013)

Selecting the best team from any era in Kilkenny is an extremely tough challenge, all the more so in the period covered here (1990 to the present). My senior championship career ran from 1990 to 2005 but I decided to extend the selection to the present team because many of the players I played with towards the end of my days with Kilkenny were at their best afterwards so I couldn't ignore that.

One of the criteria I applied for selection would not be immediately apparent to people outside Kilkenny or, indeed, to some inside the county either but I think it's very important.

I always felt that the effort a player made for his club should be considered as part of the overall package. I know it's a huge thing for Brian Cody and I would fully agree with him. The club gives you the chance to become a county player but once you get there, it adds to the responsibility to be a leader with the parish team and the lads you grew up with, who helped make you what you are.

Apart from that, all were – or are – brilliant hurlers whose contribution to the enrichment of the lives of Kilkenny people can never be fully quantified. They have done hurling in general a huge service too.

Goalkeeper: James McGarry

If James didn't have such a good defence in front of him he would probably have won a string of All Star awards. Instead, he finished his career without winning even one, which was a pity. He was nominated most years but always lost out to someone else. In fairness, he was up against some incredible talent in lads like Davy Fitzgerald, Brendan Cummins, Damien Fitzhenry and Donal Óg Cusack, who shared most of the awards between them during James' time with Kilkenny.

He might not have won an All Star but it in no way takes away from his reputation as a brilliant goalkeeper. James always made the difficult look easy, which is a real sign of talent in any sportsperson. That may have been bad for his All Star chances since he wasn't seen to be making spectacular saves all the time but he was still getting the job done most effectively in his own quiet way. Much of that was down to his natural ability to judge the angles with total precision so that he was always in the right position. He was superb under the high ball too.

I know James likes to remind Brian Cody how he left him off the panel when he took over as manager in late 1998, opting instead for Joe Dermody and my brother, Martin as the two first choice goalkeepers. James got his chance when Martin went on honeymoon and Joe picked up an injury. Brian called James back in and the rest is history. It goes to show that a player never knows when, or how, his big chance will come. James took his opportunity when it bounced his way and went on to become a massive figure for Kilkenny.

Michael Walsh is my second choice. He won two All Star awards in 1991 and 1993, both richly deserved too, it must be said. He had brilliant reflexes and could produce the most unlikely saves. Indeed, we would probably not have reached the 1991 All-Ireland final only for the brilliant save he made against Dublin right at the end of the Leinster final when we were two points in front. That save not only ensured we won the Leinster title but also helped us to get into the All-Ireland final. And while we lost to Tipperary, the experience stood to us in 1992.

It wasn't, as they say, from the wind Michael took his goalkeeping talent! His father, Ollie is regarded as one of the greatest goalkeepers in hurling history so Michael certainly wasn't short of smart advice when he started out, or indeed throughout his career, during which he won both his All-Ireland senior medals with his Dad as manager, which was lovely for both of them.

Kevin Fennelly was first choice goalkeeper when I came into the Kilkenny panel but was coming to the end of a career where, of course, he played as a forward a lot of the time. To be able to play inter-county hurling as a goalkeeper and a forward says it all about how gifted he was.

Right corner-back: Michael Kavanagh

It's close between Michael and Eddie O'Connor but I'm siding with Kavanagh. It would be hard to leave out a man who won eight All-Ireland medals, seven as member of the starting team. Michael began his Kilkenny career as a wing-back before slotting in at No. 2 in 2000, where he stayed for the rest of his days.

Eddie and Michael were different types. Eddie played from the front all the time. He would shoot out ahead of the forward whereas Michael minded his patch and took on whoever ventured into it. He was rarely beaten to a ball played in over the top for a forward to run onto. He would judge it spot on every time but then he was a brilliant reader of the game. For instance, in the 2009 All-Ireland final, Michael got across the pitch to cut off a Tipperary attack on their right hand side just after Henry Shefflin had goaled the penalty late on. Although Michael's feet crossed the sideline as he slid down to fetch the ball, he kept the upper part of his body in play, got up and sent a long clearance downfield which led to Martin Comerford scoring another goal. It was typical of Michael's instinctive ability to anticipate play and to get to the point of the action as required.

I never played on him at club level because St. Lachtain's were in a different grade to Gowran whereas I had plenty of battles with Eddie and Glenmore. He would eat you without salt! He wasn't in any way a dirty player but was fiercely determined and go-go all the time. He would begrudge an opponent getting the ball – hence playing from the front all the time – whereas Michael concentrated on minding his patch and making sure that anyone who entered left without the ball. Eddie wasn't as tall as Michael but it was still very hard to beat him the air. He operated on the basis that a taller opponent had to get his hand up for the ball so he had his ways and means of stopping that. He'd do it fairly, I must add, but I can also guarantee you it was not easy to get your hand up for a ball when Eddie was marking you. John Henderson was the right corner-back when I first came on the scene but was nearing the end of a great career, having been a regular since the late 1970s. Nobody lasts that long in such a demanding position without knowing the art of corner-back play inside out which John did. Kilkenny are lucky to have a very good No. 2 in Paul Murphy at present. If he avoids injury, he will be around for a long time.

Full-back: Noel Hickey

Was it Mick Lyons of Meath who once said that playing at full-back is like being a member of the mafia – a case of kill or be killed?

Full-backs have a high 'kill' count but then they have to. Noel is my choice at No. 3, with Pat Dwyer as the alternative. JJ Delaney has been converted into a full-back because circumstances demanded it after Noel's departure. JJ is so talented that he transferred easily but he is a better half-back, although we are unlikely to see him there anymore.

Noel and Pat were completely different types. Pat was an out-and-out hurling full-back whereas Noel would use his physical presence a whole lot more. You would come off the field after being marked by Pat and think you had been out for a casual run whereas you could be black and blue after a clash with Noel. He was by no means a dirty player but his style was such that you would find yourself in a lot of close-up battles, most of which you lost. Pat based his game on making sure you didn't get the ball and was very good at doing it. He had great wrist skills, which made him a wizard at dispossessing an opponent. As I say, you wouldn't feel sore after being on him but you might not have hurled a whole lot of ball either. He was fierce frustrating to play against because his skill level was so high.

He wasn't there as long as Noel but would certainly go down in my book as a really great full-back. Noel battled back to his very best after illness in 2005 but had some injury problems later on which curtailed him. Would we have beaten Galway in 2005 if Noel were playing? Who knows but I'll say this: we lost by three points and there were days when he was worth a lot more than that to Kilkenny.

Left full-back: Jackie Tyrrell

Jackie, Willie O'Connor and Liam Simpson are the contenders. Willie has to be on the team but I'm moving him to the half-backs because he played a lot of his hurling there. It shows how versatile he was, which also helped to make him an automatic selection in my eyes.

Liam was a brilliant athlete, one of the fastest men on the squad in the sprints, but not all that fond of the laps! He was a very reliable corner-back but I would put Jackie ahead of him. You could tell from the day Jackie came into the squad that he was going to make No. 4 his own and remain there for a long time, which is exactly what happened.

Has anyone ever seen Jackie taken to the cleaners? Most corner-backs have a day when they're well beaten but not Jackie. His consistency is unbelievable. You will hear people saying that the way to trouble him is to despatch a speed merchant in his direction. It has been tried but it hasn't worked. That's down to his innate grasp of what defending is all about, in terms of reading the play, getting his positioning right and correctly predicting what the opponent will do next. Also, he is very quick, despite what some would have you believe. Jackie is a feared figure among opposition which is quite an advantage for any defender to take into a game.

Right half-back: Willie O'Connor (Captain)

At half-time in the 2000 All-Ireland final against Offaly, Willie was lying on the bench in the middle of the dressing-room in severe pain, having taken a blow to the ribs in the first half. Dr. Bill (Cuddihy) was working on him but it wasn't looking good. Willie was in agony. Brian Cody and the selectors knew the situation and were planning to bring Sean Meally on in a re-organised defence.

Once Willie spotted what was going on, he made it clear in no uncertain terms that he had no intention of leaving the action. "Take me off if I'm not playing well, otherwise leave me alone," summed up his uncompromising attitude. He was Kilkenny captain and would continue to lead the team, which he did, despite being in awful pain. It was typical of Willie. He was a phenomenal performer, a man with an unbelievably competitive spirit. He still has it – he'd kill you in an indoor soccer game to this very day!

Right half-back wasn't his natural position, but he was so comfortable moving between the half-backs and full-backs that you could slot him in anywhere. Quite simply, he has to be on my team and what's more I would make him captain. There are several lads on this selection who captained Kilkenny but if I had to select one to lead a team into war, it would be Willie.

Anyone who trained with Willie was the better for it. From the moment he went out, he was full on. If you were unlucky enough to be paired with Willie hitting the ball across the field, you would be worn out. And if you mis-controlled the ball or were off line with a delivery, Willie would let you know very quickly. That was his nature. It was a central part of what made him such a powerful presence for so long.

Centre half-back: Pat O'Neill

As well as being the best centre back I have ever seen, Ger Henderson was my all-time hero and I was lucky enough to get to play with him a few times in 1989 when I started out as a goalkeeper. However, he was retired by the time I made my senior championship debut in 1990.

Of the centre-backs I played with over much longer periods, my Gowran clubmate, Pat O'Neill was the best. Brian Hogan has been a powerful figure for several years and Peter Barry did well before him, while Eamonn Kennedy was brilliant in 2000, but Pat would still be my first choice. He was man-of-the-match in the 1992 All-Ireland final against Cork and was as good in the 1993 final against Galway.

A big man with huge strength and great hands, he had all the necessary attributes for centre-back. There was nothing as inspiring for his colleagues as the sight of big Pat soaring into the air, grabbing the ball, driving opponents out of his way and firing the ball downfield. He moved to full-back later in his career but I never thought it suited him as well as No. 6. He was unfortunate with injuries in his later years which probably cost him another season or two more.

Left half-back: JJ Delaney

He's one of those players that you wouldn't consider putting anyone up against him. He has, out of necessity, been at full-back for a number of years but No. 7 is his best position. You could play him at No. 4 either.

He has every quality you want in a defender, whether in the air or on the ground. I've always believed that he was helped by being a left hander. Most hurlers are right-handed and are used to playing against other right handers so it's different when you encounter a left hander. Right handers catch the ball with their left hand so when you come up against someone like JJ who is catching it with his right, it can be hard to get used to it. They are coming in from a different angle which makes it confusing, especially under a high ball. Not that JJ needs anything extra to be good under the dropping ball – he always seems to be able to clear a path for himself. It's as if his hurley acts like a lightning conductor for the ball, guiding it safely into a secure hand.

Midfield: Tommy Walsh & Michael Fennelly

Tommy has to be on the team and while he is largely recognised as a right half-back, he also won All Star awards at left full-back, midfield and left half-forward. That's some tribute to his versatility. I would love to see a situation where Tommy was given the freedom to do what he wanted, rather than be tied down to a particular position. I suppose hurling can't be played like that, but it would be very interesting to see how Tommy would fare in a game where he was allowed to go wherever he chose at any time. I could see him scoring at one end, blocking at the other end and picking up a lot of ball around midfield too – that's the type of player he is.

Wing-back is his best position in the game as it's played now because he likes to be facing the ball. It took a few years to settle on him as the No. 5 but once he established himself there, he was always going to have the jersey for a very long time.

I have been very disappointed with some of the comments about Tommy in recent years. People try to portray him as a dirty hurler, which he is not. As for claims that he is living on the edge, that's precisely where he should be. Indeed, it's where every player should be if he's going to get the best out of himself. It can be done while remaining within the rules which, as far as I'm concerned, is how Tommy plays. If he fouls, he's penalised, which is as it should be but depicting him as a guy who gets away with nasty stuff is plain wrong.

Yes, you'll see Tommy tangling with opponents quite a lot, either at the start of a game or after a sub comes on. The cameras will zoom in and there's Tommy in the middle of it. However, the wrong impression is often given. Opponents target Tommy in an effort to get him booked, which leaves him in a weakened position as he has to be very careful from there on. They deliberately barge into him, trying to cause a flashpoint. I have seen subs come onto the field and run straight into Tommy. What's he supposed to do? Back off or stand his ground? He's doing nothing wrong, yet he finds himself in trouble for standing up for himself after someone runs at him.

I've played on guys who were dirty, who would get in the sneaky hit or make something look accidental when you knew damn well it was deliberate. Tommy is not like that and never has been.

We all knew right from the start when he came onto the panel that he was going to be something special and he didn't disappoint. Derek Lyng, Andy Comerford, Michael 'Titch' Phelan and 'Cha' Fitzpatrick were all excellent midfielders, but my choice as Tommy's partner is Michael Fennelly. He is a powerful man and a real driving force when he pounds through from midfield, pumping his legs in long strides. He has been unlucky with injuries, as was the case this year, but when he is at peak fitness and his game is right, he's unstoppable. Derek Lyng would be my third choice. For a man who blossomed quite late, he had a fantastic career, driven on by an incredible sense of determination. He would graft all day, every day, but there was a lot more to him than that. If you look back on his record, you will find that he scored in most championship games. He had the happy knack of popping up at exactly the right time to score crucial points.

Right half-forward: Martin Comerford

The 2003 All-Ireland final was Martin's greatest day in a career where he probably didn't get the widespread acclaim he deserved. We beat Cork by 1-14 to 1-11 in the 2003 final, with Martin scoring 1-4, all from open play. It was an unbelievable performance but then he had a knack of delivering in All-Ireland finals. Indeed, his goal in the 2009 final, after coming on as a sub, ensured a Kilkenny win and must have been very satisfying for him. He had started in all the games up to then, but was left out for the final, which would have been very disappointing. Yet, when he was brought in as a sub, he switched on to the high-tempo game straight away and made a huge impact. He was comfortable at wing-forward or full-forward, but I always thought that No. 10 suited him best.

Centre half-forward: John Power

I would not have had anything like the career I enjoyed if it weren't for John. He was the most unselfish player you would ever come across. I don't mean that solely because he brought other lads into the game with his passing. He did that all the time but the real unselfishness came in how he took belts for other lads and put hand, head and every other part of his body on the line in order to help the cause.

As well as that, John liked to mind his colleagues. If I took an unfair blow, I knew well that John would be in to deal with the perpetrator the next time the ball came his way. Everything about John's game was for the team. He couldn't care less if he never scored. Once he was keeping the ball moving, breaking up play and opening up the gate towards the opposition goal, he was happy. Lads like that are invaluable on a team. They don't always get the credit they deserve but then they don't seek it either. It's all about hard work and a selfless attitude, which puts the team above everything else. When it came to that, John was a ten out of ten man every day he played.

Having been on the panel since the late 1980s, he was left out in 1998 but Brian Cody brought him back when he took over and it turned out to be a very wise move. I was certainly delighted to see John return because I knew what he would bring to the squad.

Left half-forward: Henry Shefflin

I can still recall in early 1999 when a tall, gangly young lad arrived into training. Henry had just turned twenty years of age at the time and while we knew him to be a good hurler, we had no idea of the phenomenon he would turn out to be. He didn't have a particularly big reputation from underage hurling but you could see straight away that he had so much scope for development that it was only a matter of time before he made a real impact. In fact, it happened quite quickly and we know the rest.

I have selected him at No. 12, not because it's necessarily his best position but because he is so versatile that he could be named anywhere from No. 10 to No. 15, whereas some of the other lads I have chosen were most comfortable in specific posts.

Henry took over most of the free-taking duties from me in his first championship season and as I have explained elsewhere in the book, I was perfectly happy with that. In his early days, Henry was often put on the opposition's smallest defender so that he could exploit his height and while opponents tried to get around that by sending someone else to mark him, it meant that he got a lot of experience all over the forward line quite quickly.

To me, the biggest assets Henry had, right from the start, were his willingness to learn, his appetite for work and his general can-do attitude. Obviously, he had lots of talent too, but not everyone with technical skills makes the grade, let alone rises to the extraordinary heights he has achieved. He improved every single facet of his game and, even then, he always kept striving for more.

He has given so many outstanding performances that it's difficult to remember many of them but his contribution to last year's drawn All-Ireland final summed up his true greatness. His leadership, his organisational skills and the sheer effect of his personality – both on his colleagues and on Galway – were immense and played a massive role in saving the day for Kilkenny.

I played with Henry from 1999 to 2005 but would have loved another five or six years with him. A player can't pick his era, but I would have really enjoyed the years after 2005 when Kilkenny had an unbelievably strong panel and were the dominant force for so long.

Everyone has their time, I suppose, whether you're Christy Ring, Eddie Keher, Brian Whelahan or Henry Shefflin. Is Henry better than Christy or

Eddie? I have no idea because I never saw Christy play and only saw Eddie at the very end of his career as a club player.

People like to compare players from different eras but while it might be fun, it can be no more than that because it's all down to opinion. For instance, take the Team of the Millennium. I was supposed to be disappointed (we're back to rumours again) over not being selected, but how could I be upset by something like that? Every player wants to be chosen on any team for which he is eligible, but when it comes to selecting players from over a one hundred year period, how could anyone be disappointed at missing out?

I'm sure Lory Meagher and my grand-uncle, Paddy Phelan, both of whom got on the Millennium team, were great players but how many people who were alive in 2000 saw them play? Did they deserve to be on the team? I'm sure they did. Did others who weren't selected deserve a place? I'm sure they did, but then there were only fifteen positions so everyone couldn't be accommodated. Nicky Rackard was chosen at full-forward on the GAA Centenary's Year in 1984 but Ray Cummins got the slot on the Millennium Team. Ray's career finished before 1984, yet he wasn't chosen on the Centenary Team, but 16 years later he replaced Nicky on the Millennium Team. It's all about opinion, so people should not take these things too seriously. I certainly didn't when I wasn't selected on the Millennium team.

I mention all this in the context of Henry Shefflin because when the next big all-time selection comes about, I'm sure there will be a place for him. There should be.

Right full-forward: Eddie Brennan

My club mate Charlie Carter had many great days in the No. 13 jersey but I would have to go for Eddie Brennan who came into his own after Charlie's premature departure in 2003. Up to then, Eddie had been in and out of the team but once he settled down as a regular starter, he was brilliant. As someone who always liked to have a go for a goal if the half-chance presented itself, I admired the way Eddie was always sniffing for the big one too.

He had a tremendous goal-scoring record over many years, often hitting the jackpot in the really big games. Charlie was a great corner-forward too and could really turn it on when he hit form but he wasn't there for as long as Eddie, having decided to quit the panel in 2003. I still say he should have stayed on and taken his chances.

Full-forward: Liam Fennelly

Any forward who played on the same team as Liam was the better for it. He was as cute an operator as you would ever come across, knew every angle and approach route to goal in detail and always had the happy knack of popping up in the right place. He did it so often that it was no accident. He had an instinct as to how and where the ball would break that made him a nightmare for defenders.

There was another side to his game that should be remembered too. Nowadays, forwards are expected to tackle like backs but it was, to some degree, different in Liam's era. Many forwards saw themselves essentially as scorers who had no responsibility to mark anybody. In fact, some of them saw such basic graft as beneath them. Not Liam. He was always in there, tackling, blocking, hooking and generally making a nuisance of himself among defenders.

As I've said, if you didn't learn from playing alongside Liam, then you had to be pretty slow on the uptake.

Left full-forward: Eamonn Morrissey

Wexford supporters must have had a horror of him because he always seemed to reserve his best performances for wars with the purple and gold. He had some very good days against Dublin too before leaving Kilkenny to play for them in 1996. He had a very high skill level, was a beautiful striker of the ball even in the tightest of corners.

His ability to turn and shoot in an instant gave him a big advantage against corner-backs, who might think they had him cornered only to find that he had not only found an escape route but also got his shot away in one slick movement.

Richie Hogan can do much the same and, like Charlie Carter on the other side, would be a worthy choice except for being up against such quality opposition. The same goes for Richie Power at centre-forward and Eoin Larkin at No. 12 but, of course, the two Richies and Eoin are still playing so there's more to come from them.

CHAPTER 19

A SPECIAL BREED REST OF IRELAND (1990-2013)

If selecting the Kilkenny team of this era is difficult, choosing a Rest of Ireland XV from the same period is all but impossible, since there are so many contenders for each position that the permutations are virtually endless.

As with the Kilkenny team, I covered 1990-2013, as it's a time-frame with which I am very familiar. There might be some surprise that Clare and Offaly lead the way with three representatives each but this team is based purely on individual talents, not on any broader issues or how various counties did in the period involved. Basically, I considered all the available options as if selecting a team to play for the Rest of Ireland against Kilkenny in a final trial for a full Irish team.

It didn't matter whether or not players had won All-Ireland medals (four of my selections haven't). Would the Rest XV beat the Kilkenny team that I have selected? I'll leave the public to adjudicate on that!

Goalkeeper: Davy Fitzgerald (Clare)

Apart from Davy Fitz, there's Brendan Cummins, Damien Fitzhenry, Ger Cunningham and Donal Óg Cusack to consider. It has been a golden era for goalkeepers and that's before you even consider my fellow-Kilkenny men, James McGarry and Michael Walsh.

Overall, I would give the nod to Davy. Apart from his shot-stopping talent, he was an inspiring figure behind his defence, always organising them, keeping them on their toes and generally being the boss. His save from John Leahy in the closing minute of the 1997 All-Ireland final against Tipperary was as good as you will ever see. It won the All-Ireland for Clare. People talk about forwards taking scores under pressure but this was a case of making a save under enormous pressure. After all, you can't get a more demanding time to be facing one of the top forwards in the business one-on-one than in the last minute of an All-Ireland final when your team is a point ahead. Davy rose to the challenge, just as he did so often throughout a very long career. I had my own experience of Davy's brilliance in the 1997 All-Ireland semi-final, when he saved a penalty which I had hit as well I was capable of. I was sure it would fly into the net, but Davy saved it. He's up against unbelievably high-quality opposition but he still gets my vote. As well as having been a superb goalkeeper, he always brought huge personality to the game, something he has continued to do as a very astute manager.

Right full-back: Brian Corcoran (Cork)

When a 19 year-old corner-back in his debut season wins the Hurler of the Year award, he must be something special. Brian Corcoran achieved that in 1992 and went on to become one of the best players of his generation, moving from corner-back to centre-back before switching to the attack, where he was equally effective. He was a class act wherever he played, invariably concentrating on being first to the ball and always playing without the tiniest hint of negativity. He had to wait a long time to win his first All-Ireland senior medal in 1999 as a centre-back and added two more as a full-forward in 2004-2005. All three were richly deserved. Rather unluckily, Limerick's Stephen McDonogh never won an All-Ireland medal but that in no way takes away from what was an excellent career as a very tight and tidy No. 2.

Full-back: Brian Lohan (Clare)

Davy Fitz in goal; Brian Lohan at full-back; Seanie McMahon at centre-back. Any wonder it was so hard to make progress through the heart of the Clare defence during the Ger Loughnane years and indeed beyond? Lohan guarded the square as if it were his own personal property and once he put up the 'do not enter' sign, you ventured into his space at your own risk. He was fiercely strong under the dropping ball and once he got it in his hand he was virtually impossible to stop as he burst out. The sight of Lohan's red helmet driving forward before getting in a lengthy clearance was a real rallying call for his colleagues and indeed the Clare supporters. It didn't do much for opposition confidence, mind you.

Martin Hanamy (Offaly)

Ollie Canning and Frank Lohan were excellent corner-backs, albeit with different styles, but Hanamy would be my No. 1 choice. He was incredibly strong and forceful but could hurl too, so you needed to be at the top of your game to get anything off him. He was the All Star No. 4 in the 1988-94-98, which shows how consistent he was for a full decade. That's no mean feat in a position where even the smallest mistake can prove costly. He typified the Offaly spirit in every way during a period when they inflicted a fair share of misery on us Kilkenny men and, indeed, on many others too.

Right half-back: Brian Whelahan (Offaly)

I'm inclined to name him and leave it at that, since no explanation is necessary as to why he makes the team. Still, I want to pay tribute to him as one of the finest players hurling has ever seen and one of the nicest gentlemen the game has produced. My battles with Brian go back to when we were young lads, him with St. Brendan's Community School, Birr and me with St. Kieran's College. We knew nothing about each other at the time (college lads just hurl and don't think very much about who they are up against) but our careers would later become very much entwined at underage level with Offaly and Kilkenny and, of course, over fifteen year as seniors.

Brian made his senior championship debut before me, coming on as a sub in Offaly's shock defeat by Antrim in the 1989 All-Ireland semi-final, but when I got my big chance as a senior in the following year's Leinster championship, he returned me to the subs' bench inside half an hour. I've written about that elsewhere but, suffice to say, it wasn't the best of starts for me.

I'd like to think it evened out after that; he had his good days on me; I had my good days on him. After the first few years, we didn't come up directly against each other all that often, due to the positioning we both took up. Still, I encountered him often enough to know just how good he was in every facet of the game. I'll say this for him – he was as fair a player as I ever met. From our juvenile days, right to the end of our senior clashes, I never took a single dirty stroke from Brian. It was all about the ball with him and since it was the same for me, we had some very enjoyable tussles. I was delighted to see him selected on the Team of the Millennium in 2000. And if there was ever any doubt he was going to get the honour, it ended in 1998 when he became a one-man demolition squad against us after moving up to full-forward in the All-Ireland final. Any man who is selected on the best team of all time must be a special talent. Brian was exactly that. He wore it well in a fabulous career.

Centre half-back: Seanie McMahon (Clare)

No. 6 is a position that attracts inspiring characters, men who control the keys to the first set of defensive doors. It's very difficult for a team to function efficiently if their centre-back is not a dominating figure, a problem that never arose for Clare during Seanie's time. He had every quality required in a centre-back and, in addition to that, he brought the added bonus of being a magnificent long range free-taker. He rarely finished a game without scoring a minimum of three or four points from long distances. He was so good at it that the opposition had to be very conscious of the risks of conceding frees even well inside their own half. He holds the distinction of being the first Clare man to win the Hurler of the Year award (1995), an honour he fully deserved. It was Clare's breakthrough time and the remarkable thing about Seanie was that the standards he set for himself that season were retained throughout the rest of his career, which went on for another eleven years.

Left half-back: Ciaran Carey (Limerick) (Captain)

When Limerick needed someone to do something special, Ciaran was the man. More often than not, it involved putting the ball on the hurley and driving upfield from the half-back line, a skill which he perfected. Everyone remembers his stunning point against Clare in 1996 when he ran the length of the Gaelic Grounds before firing over the winner in the Munster semi-final but there were lots of other times too when he became an extra forward, including a memorable performance in the 1992 League final when Limerick hauled back an eight-point lead to beat Tipperary.

Ciaran's style of play lifted those around him – that's why I have chosen him as captain of my side. All fifteen are leaders – indeed most of them captained their county teams at some stage – but there was that little something extra about Ciaran's inspirational qualities that stood out for me.

Midfield: Ken McGrath (Waterford) & John Leahy (Tipperary)

It can be argued that midfield might not have been either's best position but it doesn't really matter. These lads were so versatile they had to be on the team. Ken played in every line except goalkeeper but would be best recognised as a centre-back. He played for Waterford for more than 15 years without winning an All-Ireland medal but so what? It's a pity that the big prize eluded him but the imprint he left on the game was in no way diminished because of that.

John won two All-Ireland medals, both as a wing-forward, but spent a lot of time around midfield too. He was a very forceful performer, hard to knock off the ball as he took on opposing defences with real menace. When he played well, so did Tipperary.

Right half-forward: Johnny Dooley (Offaly)

Remember his goal from a free that began the Offaly fightback against Limerick late in the 1994 All-Ireland final? People who criticise the Limerick defence are missing the point. Offaly needed a goal to get back into the game so Johnny had to hit the ball well enough to give himself a chance of getting it through the wall of defenders. After that, it was in the lap of the gods but the first essential was to hit it sweetly, which he did.

Mind you, it was no surprise as he was a lovely ball striker from frees and open play. Game after game, he returned a high score. He always looked so calm and laid back in everything he did but then he had the innate skill to make difficult things look easy, which is always the mark of a great player in any sport.

Centre half-forward: Joe Cooney (Galway)

Joe and Nicky English were two of my favourite players from long before I got anywhere near the Kilkenny senior team. They were different types but had so many natural skills that anyone with the remotest interest in hurling could see they were special talents. One of the aspects of Joe's play that fascinated me was the amount of time he always seemed to have on the ball. He wasn't one of the quickest guys in the game, yet he had the knack of eluding opponents and creating space to get either a shot or a pass away. I often wondered how he did it, but then that's how it is with top-quality players who always seem to have more time on the ball that their opponents. Nobody ever quite knows how they manage it but they do.

Left half-forward: Martin Storey (Wexford)

Martin was go-go-go all the time. He didn't back away from anything and loved taking on opponents with his strong-running, direct style. Martin was part of a generation of Wexford men who had to wait an awful long time for their rewards but they never lost heart. It didn't matter how often they were beaten, they came back for more the following season. The important thing was that their spirit always remained intact. It was a mark of true character and deserved to be rewarded, which it was in 1996.

Naturally, I wanted to win the All-Ireland every year, but when Wexford knocked us out in 1996, I was hoping, as a Leinster man, that they would go on and win the title. Besides, they had endured so much disappointment over the years that they deserved a break. They couldn't have had a better captain than Martin Storey to lead them through the big adventure.

Right full-forward: John Mullane (Waterford)

John is one of four players without All-Ireland medals on my team, although Joe Canning still has plenty of time to rectify his situation. I would never judge a player on whether or not he won an All-Ireland medal, which is why I have two Waterford men on my team. John was more than just an outstanding forward. He brought character and swashbuckling style to the game at a time when it appeared to be losing that spark of individuality which brightens up the scene. There was no more inspiring sight in hurling than John darting out to collect the ball, heading off on a run and firing over a point, followed by a clinch of the fist as he urged on his colleagues. It lifted the Waterford crowd on many a big occasion. Hurling needs more John Mullanes.

Full-forward: Joe Canning (Galway)

You look at Joe and Galway and you think they will win a load of All-Irelands and then you look again and wonder: will they win any? It would be a terrible shame if Joe never won a senior All-Ireland at county level (he has won a few with his club, Portumna) but every year that goes by makes you wonder all the more about what's happening in Galway.

They keep producing excellent underage talent but what happens when they move on to senior level is a mystery. Not in Joe's case, as he is one of the best you will ever see. I love watching him because you never know what he's going to do next, or what magic trick he'll pull out of the hat. One thing I cannot understand is why he spends so much time out in the half-forward line or sometimes even further away from the opposition goal.

Joe is a natural goal-scorer, a rare enough breed in the modern game, but not even he can score goals from out the field. If I were in charge of Galway,

I would base everything on having Joe close to the opposition goal. It's up to others to get the ball into him and if he's in there all the time, the goal chances will come. Being Joe, he will take a higher percentage of them than most others. He will also attract the attentions of two defenders in a lot of cases, which should leave room for his attacking colleagues.

The opposition like to see Joe drifting outfield because that removes his goal-scoring threat. I love the art of goal-scoring and when you have someone like Joe who is so good at it, he should always be close enough to the whites of the opposition goalkeeper's eyes to torment him. I just cannot figure out why he spends so much time out the field. Better to have him inside, even living off limited possession, than fifty or sixty metres out where his goal-scoring threat is removed. He is one of the genuine stars of the game, often worth the admission money on his own, but I don't think Galway have been getting the most out of him by playing him so far out.

Left full-forward: Nicky English (Tipperary)

Any man who scores 2-12 in an All-Ireland final, as Nicky did in 1989, deserves special recognition. Some people will say "sure it was only against Antrim" but that's deeply insulting to Antrim and to Nicky. Antrim were there on merit, having beaten Leinster champions Offaly by three goals so no one should question their right to be in the final. Nicky gave a superb display that day, but then he had been doing it for years. Like Joe Cooney, he was one of my all-time heroes when I was growing up and, of course, we eventually got to play against each other in the 1991 All-Ireland final.

Quite simply, he had it all: pace, poise, touch, instinct and intelligence. One of the true greats.

DJ – THE OUTSIDE VIEW

It started out in O'Connor Park, Tullamore on a bitterly cold February day in 1989 when Kilkenny beat Offaly in an Allianz hurling League game and ended on a pleasant August afternoon in Croke Park in 2005 when Kilkenny lost an All-Ireland semi-final to Galway.

DJ Carey's inter-county story was launched in goal before he moved to the attack where he played from the end of 1989. His senior inter-county career took him into orbits which made him a genuine contender to be regarded as the greatest hurler of all-time. That's a very exclusive club, reserved for those with a talent and temperament which marks them apart, players who crossed the class lines taking them from good to better to best.

DJ was very much in that category in a career where he played 57 senior championship games with Kilkenny, scoring 34-195 while winning every honour in the game. His highest individual match total was scored against Galway in the 1997 All-Ireland quarter-final in Thurles when he landed 2-8 in a game which Kilkenny won by two points after trailing by ten in the first half. It was possibly his greatest day in the black-and-amber jersey during a 16-season championship career which yielded five All-Ireland, ten Leinster and four NHL titles, as well as nine All Star and two Hurler of the Year awards.

The following pages provide a real insight into what made DJ such a special performer, as seen through opposition eyes. Nine of his peers, Brian Corcoran (Cork), Tom Dempsey (Wexford), Davy Fitzgerald (Clare), Fergal Hartley (Waterford), Steve McDonogh (Limerick), Terence 'Sambo' McNaughton (Antrim), Niall Rigney (Laois), John Twomey (Dublin) and Brian Whelahan (Offaly) share memories from their encounters, each providing his own personal recollection of games involving DJ and what made him such a brilliant performer.

The managers' view is represented by Babs Keating (Tipperary) and Cyril Farrell (Galway) who reflect on what it was like for those in charge of teams to be confronted by DJ's talents while Dickie Murphy (Wexford) provides the referee's angle.

All share a common theme. The respect and admiration for a man who often made life so difficult for them and their teams shine through in every word. It is heart-felt and sincere, reflecting a broader view, which made DJ one of the most popular players in hurling history.

Martin Breheny

BABS KEATING (TIPPERARY)

It must have been a comical sight but then it was almost dark so there was no one except ourselves on the course. Johnny Murray and myself were playing golf with DJ in Carlow one day and by the time we were finished, it was getting dark.

Then, DJ discovered that he had lost his watch. He reckoned it happened in the rough somewhere and since he had been hitting the ball fairly straight all day, there weren't that many places the watch could have been. We got permission from the club, jumped into the car and headed out to have a look for his timepiece. I had a fair idea of where he had been in the rough and, sure enough, we found the watch after a short search. There it was, shining in the headlights off a par five.

When it came to golf, DJ was rarely off track and, when he was, you knew exactly where he had been which is how we were able to find the watch. I played a lot of golf with DJ over the years and will say this: anytime I asked him to play in a charity outing or to support some cause, he never let me down. There are hundreds of people who would say exactly the same but that's his nature – as genuine as they come.

As a hurler, where do you start? Probably the only real difference between DJ and the great Christy Ring was in size. Ring would have been a stone or more heavier and a bit more powerful as a result. But when it came to skill, DJ was on a par with anyone who ever played the game. There was no area of his game where you could say: "he's a bit weak there".

If speed, stamina, style and skill are crucial to score-making and score-taking, the player who adds killer instinct to the mix is the one that becomes really great. DJ did that, which is why he was so special.

On top of that, he was as brave as they came. Also, his sense of positioning and timing was incredible. It came from pure instinct, that special ability to be in the right place all the time. It can't be coached, certainly nowhere near the level DJ reached. Basically, he had every quality you would ever want in a hurler.

DJ

TERENCE 'SAMBO' McNAUGHTON (ANTRIM)

DJ Carey was – and always will be – a genuine friend of Ulster hurling. There was never a time when I asked him to come to Antrim to coach youngsters, present medals or talk to a team that he said no. If it was at all possible, DJ travelled and brought every bit of his natural friendliness, enthusiasm and genuine passion for hurling with him.

What's more, he never took a single penny in expenses. DJ is a modest man but he knew he was a huge name in hurling during his great playing career and felt that it carried a responsibility to promote the game in whatever way he could. When that involved coming to the Glens of Antrim, he did it with a smile and a warmth that made him such a popular figure among everyone up here. Top players can often be so wrapped up in their own game that they don't look beyond it. However, DJ saw himself as having an obligation to do whatever he could to promote hurling, even when it involved long journeys.

I remember seeing 200 juveniles lining up for a presentation and he had time for every one of them. They brought a lot more than autograph books for him to sign but he didn't mind. He stood there signing everything that was put in front of him until the last kid was satisfied.

All ages loved his coaching sessions where he was patient with everyone and never in any way acted like the superstar that he undoubtedly was. DJ will always be remembered as one of the greatest players hurling has ever known but he was so humble about his talents that he would make the person he was talking to feel like the star.

I'm proud to regard DJ as my friend even if he may have cost me an All-Ireland medal! Antrim's performance against Kilkenny in the 1991 All-Ireland semi-final was possibly our best ever, but we came up two points short, due in no small way to the damage DJ inflicted on us. We were like lambs to the slaughter when we reached the 1989 final, but two years later we would have been much more street-wise if we got past Kilkenny. We weren't the only ones to suffer at DJ's hands over many years!

Still, he was – and is – a true gentleman, who will always be welcome in Antrim.

CYRIL FARRELL (GALWAY)

There's never a good cowboy around when you want him! If only I could have found one in Thurles on the day of the 1997 All-Ireland quarter-final, I would have paid him anything to saddle up his horse, head out onto Semple Stadium and lasso DJ.

It was either that or fire a tranquilising dart because the usual means of stopping him pepper our goal sure as hell weren't working. We turned over for the second-half leading Kilkenny by nine points and while the exchanges had been a lot closer than the scoreline suggested at half-time, it was still a handsome lead.

Well, it would have been if DJ hadn't decided to turn in one of his best-ever performances. John Power, who came on at half-time played a blinder too, but DJ was unstoppable. Left or right, high or low, he was in the action all the time. He ended up scoring 2-8, created a goal for Ken O'Shea and set up some points for others too, as Kilkenny fought back to win by two points.

It's easy to be critical of defenders but there was nothing anyone could do about DJ that day – he was unmarkable. It wasn't that he hadn't warned us. In a League game in Ballinasloe four months earlier he took us for 2-9. It was Galway's bad luck to find him in such an explosive mood twice in the same year but then most counties had similarly painful experiences at some stage.

People talk about great players from different eras, Teams of the Century and Millennium but I have no doubt that DJ was right up there with the very best who ever played the game. There were times during his career when he carried most of the scoring responsibility in the Kilkenny attack – both from frees and open play – but he always thrived on the challenge.

His inter-county career ended in 2005, just before Kilkenny went on to win six of the next seven All-Ireland titles with probably the best team of all time. Imagine what it would have been like if DJ was still around.

As for the 1997 All-Ireland quarter-final, I picked up the *Irish Independent* on the following morning and saw that DJ had been rated ten out of ten in the match ratings. I couldn't disagree. It said it all about his performance.

DJ

DAVY FITZGERALD (CLARE)

First impressions last. That certainly applied for me when it came to DJ Carey. I played in goal for St. Flannan's against St. Kieran's in the 1989 All-Ireland colleges' final in Nenagh when we came up against a certain DJ. We had conceded no goals for a few games prior to that but it all changed in the final.

DJ stuck three in the net and scored 3-3 of St. Kieran's 3-5 in their two point win. It was the first time I came across such ferocious spin on a ball. I thought I would stop one particular rocket when I got my hurley to it but there was so much spin on the ball that it flew off the stick and into the top of the net. The spin he could put on the ball was unreal, something I was always conscious of every time I came up against him over the years.

In the 1997 All-Ireland semi-final, Kilkenny got a penalty at a crucial stage and, of course, up stepped DJ. I would always have done a lot of visualisation before games so I'd know in my own mind what was coming in any given situation. I saved DJ's penalty that day and I could say it was all down to visualisation but it wasn't. DJ said to me afterwards that he had hit the penalty as well as he possibly could. So how did I save it? Pure reflexes! When it came to stopping DJ's shots, they were usually all a goalkeeper had.

He was a genius, the best hurler I have ever come across. He could do just about anything with the ball. Remember the point he scored against us from out on the right late in the 2002 All-Ireland final? Unbelievable skill.

He had so much natural ability which also came with great vision. A defence might think they had all routes closed down but with one flick of the wrist, he would fire out a thirty yard pass to a colleague and open things up.

On a personal level, DJ has always been a gentleman. I remember being on holidays in the early 1990s – well before Clare made the big breakthrough – and meeting DJ who was there with the All Stars. He was as warm and friendly as could be, but then he always treated everyone the same whenever or wherever he met them.

FERGAL HARTLEY (WATERFORD)

DJ. The name was, is and always will be a brand. Very few people enjoy the sort of name recognition that DJ has. Everyone knows who DJ is – there's never a need to mention his surname. He had that special aura about him from the start and it kept growing right throughout his career.

I remember my father coming home from a Leinster championship game in Croke Park in the early 1990s and talking about the great tussle he had witnessed between DJ and Brian Whelahan. When I got onto the Waterford team I came to experience DJ's greatness at first hand, even if I rarely marked him directly.

DJ was one of those players that opposition planned for in advance and then hoped it would work out. Waterford's planning did not include assigning me to mark him (something to do with pace, I think!) but even if you weren't on him directly, he could spook you. I remember a League game in Walsh Park early in my career and at one stage the ball spun out near the corner flag in our half.

As I was running out to collect it, I knew DJ was coming after me at lightning speed. I kept thinking to myself: 'get this ball up cleanly first time or else he'll pick your pocket and be heading in on goal in a flash'. If it was anyone else, I wouldn't have thought anything about it, but DJ had that effect on opposition – he got inside their heads just by being around.

The upside was that when you beat DJ to a ball or got in a block on him, it gave you – and the rest of the team – a huge lift. He was the most tightly-marked man in hurling, but seemed to revel in it. Everything for him was about playing the game in the right spirit and while he took the odd belt from time to time, he never complained.

Off the pitch, he is a real gentleman too. I remember playing golf with him one day, when he had to spend a lot of time in bushes and rough looking for the ball. Not his, I hasten to add! He patiently searched for my wayward drives, usually while his ball was sitting happily on the fairway. It was a familiar story in whatever sport you took on DJ.

DJ

JOHN TWOMEY (DUBLIN)

When the late, great Lar Foley was Dublin manager he would go to various lads from time to time and say: "I have a job for you."

When Lar ear-marked a player for a special job, the chances were that it was particularly tough so you needed to have all your wits about you.

When that job was marking DJ Carey, you knew you needed all that and a bit more too. Having got the "I have a job for you" instruction from Lar on a few occasions, I know all about how demanding it was to be assigned to DJ.

No question about it, he was the hardest player to mark that I ever came across. But then he had every skill in the book and some that weren't even in the book, so you were always trying to second-guess him. There was so much to think about when you were marking DJ because he brought such a wide range of dimensions to his game.

I would regard his vision as the finishing ingredient that made him so outstanding. He knew instinctively which way to turn, could see things ahead of everyone else and was usually on to the ball before opponents realised what was happening. His handpassing skills also gave him an extra edge. He always did it with great purpose and accuracy, bringing colleagues into the game from various angles.

He possessed every skill required to make him the complete player on and off the ball and, on top of that, he was deadly on frees so he had you every way. Defenders knew that giving away a free was the same as handing a point to Kilkenny because he rarely missed.

He valued sportsmanship very highly and while he might make his marker's life hell with his wizardry, you knew that it was all about the ball with DJ.

Off the pitch, DJ was always one of the most popular players in the game and has remained so since his retirement. I lived fairly close to him in Dublin for a time and also met him at various golf outings so I got to know him fairly well.

He is universally liked and respected but then that's not surprising, given the way he deals with people. As for those of us who marked him over the years, we all have our own memories of how tough that was.

NIALL RIGNEY (LAOIS)

"Carey or Shefflin?" It was the night of the 2011 draw Kilkenny county final between 'The Village' and Ballyhale and I was sitting with Brian Cody and 'Fan' Larkin.

I was managing 'The Village' at the time and while I was in the company of two of the club's finest, we weren't talking about the game. Enough had been said about that and anyway there was a replay to come. Instead Cody throws in a mischievous one. "Carey or Shefflin?" he said, glancing at me.

What a question! Now, Henry Shefflin's brilliance is well-documented (as it should be) but DJ had something different. Quite simply, he was the greatest goal-scorer of all time.

I had the honour of playing with him for Leinster where I enjoyed watching him terrorise defences but also played against him with Laois when he put the fear of God into us. You could mark him for 68 minutes and think you were doing well, only to be buried in two minutes.

All great players have vision, balance, speed, touch, good hands and good feet. DJ had them all in bucket-fulls but they were topped off by huge bravery. The combination made him special.

He had so many magic moments but one stands out for me. We were a point behind Kilkenny (who had won the League a few weeks earlier) with seven minutes remaining in the 1995 Leinster quarter-final in Dr. Cullen Park. Our full-back, Bill Maher, had done a fine job on DJ all day.

Then a long clearance dropped in our square, DJ was on to it in a flash and as we all closed in on him, he dropped-kicked the ball. Talk about brilliant touch, vision and split second timing! The ball flew past our goalkeeper, Ricky Cashin, just under the crossbar. However, it squeezed between the net fitting and the crossbar and the umpire waved for a point. We all knew, including DJ, that it was a goal but his moment of magic only yielded a point. A lucky escape for us but we still lost by two points!

Players everywhere admired him, not just for the exceptional talent he was,but also for the person he was and continues to be.

As for Brian Cody, I didn't give him an answer that night in 2011. Mind you, neither did he nor 'Fan'.

I'll say this now – for me, DJ was THE KING.

STEVE McDONOGH (LIMERICK)

The only way to stop DJ Carey doing damage was to prevent him getting the ball in the first place. Easier said than done! When you were marking him, you hoped your colleagues were doing well enough out the field to keep the supply fairly scarce.

It's quite simple really – DJ was one of the greatest hurlers the game ever produced. There was nothing he couldn't do. He had lightning pace, great touch, incredible vision and when he put them all together he was a nightmare for defenders.

He could hit the ball left or right while going at full pace so you can imagine how hard that made life for his marker. He also had the knack of grabbing the ball high in the air and turning, all in one movement, which gave him that extra second to get away. On top of all that, he could handpass the ball further than anyone else. That was probably down to his handball experience, but wherever it came from, it added another string to his bow.

If anyone needs reminding of just how good he was, all they have to do is look at a collection of his goals. Some players won't go for a goal unless the odds are very much in their favour, but DJ was different. If he thought there was any chance of a goal, he'd go for it. What's more, he usually got it.

I never played against DJ in the championship but came across him often enough in the National League and Railway Cup to know exactly how hard it was to mark him. Even when you thought you had a particular situation covered, he would often come up with something new and different but then, that's the mark of a truly great player.

He had an amazing career during which he won every honour but remained very modest. He was always very respectful of opponents.

Off the pitch, he is a real gentleman too. My mother and my late father, John met him on holiday in Barbados some years ago and they couldn't speak highly enough of him. He even gave them a signed hurley, which my mother still has. I had seen enough of DJ's hurley on the pitch to last me a lifetime during my career but I'm still looking at one!

Still it was a lovely touch by a decent man.

TOM DEMPSEY (WEXFORD)

It's one thing to influence a game in the course of the seventy minutes, but DJ had the rare ability to make an imprint even before the throw-in. Before the 1996 Leinster quarter-final, there was a doubt over whether he would play against us because of a hamstring injury, so when Kilkenny came onto Croke Park, thousands of anxious Wexford eyes turned towards him.

He was there alright, but one leg was heavily strapped. Wexford lads glanced at each other with a knowing look and while we didn't say anything, it improved our mindset, realising that even if he did play, DJ would not be at full power, which turned out to be the case.

We won by three points in what went on to be our All-Ireland season. Wexford weren't the only county to experience what might be termed 'DJ-itis'. If he wasn't playing or went into a game carrying a knock, it raised opposition spirits; if he was buzzing, it drained confidence.

As a player, DJ had everything: skill, speed, aerial strength, anticipation, balance, discipline and courage. He also had a great temperament. Whatever happened, he just got on with the game. In the 1997 Leinster final, he took a fierce hit from Rod Guiney. It was perfectly legal but it jolted DJ onto the flat of his back. When Rod hit you, you knew you were hit!

Did DJ stay down and look for a free or sympathy? No. Did he moan to the referee? No. Instead, he bounced back up, played the ball away and then went down on his hunkers to get his breath back. It was typical of how he played.

You won't find an opponent who will say a bad word against him. He would break your heart with his skills, but he was as honest as the day is long and he never, ever looked for the soft free.

Off the pitch, he was fierce obliging. I remember he came down to my club, Buffers Alley, at a time when the sheep shearing championships were being held there. There was a long queue of autograph hunters and DJ stood there signing for ages until the last one was satisfied. Even some of the sheep were back at home by the time he was finished but that's DJ – obliging to the last.

A gentleman all the way.

BRIAN CORCORAN (CORK)

I first came across DJ Carey in the 1988 All-Ireland colleges' final, while lining out for Midleton CBS against St Kieran's and again later that year in the All-Ireland minor final while playing for Cork against Kilkenny. Our paths would cross numerous times during the next 16 years, right up to the 2004 All Ireland final. The two games in 1988 resulted in victories for the Kilkenny sides and it was obvious even then that DJ was a special player and destined to be a star.

Cork entered the 1992 All-Ireland senior final as favourites but, on a wet day, a very well-taken DJ penalty just before half-time turned the game in Kilkenny's favour. DJ had his first All-Ireland senior medal, which was followed by his second a year later. Not counting league and challenge games, it would be seven years later before we met in championship again. Cork won the 1999 final when the final whistle sounded, DJ was the first man to shake my hand. He was devastated after losing two finals in a row but showed his character that day by staying on the field and congratulating the Cork players. He would make up for that disappointing day with a five-star performance against Offaly in the following year's final.

He added two more All-Irelands with victories over Clare in 2002 and Cork in 2003 before our final career encounter in the 2004 final. It would be DJ's last All Ireland and, unfortunately for him, it resulted in defeat, but again he was around the players' lounge congratulating the Cork team. That is a sign of a great sportsman since a person's character is more evident in defeat than in victory.

DJ was not a big man physically, but his skill, speed, grace, balance, bravery and hurling brain made him stand out from his peers. His ability to catch a high ball under severe pressure, land, turn quickly and take off like a bullet led to many fantastic goals and points throughout his career. He played the game honestly and fairly and was a brilliant role model for every up-and-coming hurler anywhere in the country. When people talk about the greats of the game, DJ's name will always be mentioned. Different players had different attributes over the years, but I have never seen a more skilful hurler than DJ Carey. It was an honour to have played against him.

BRIAN WHELAHAN (OFFALY)

Oh no, not DJ Carey. Of all people to see racing onto the ball in the early minutes of an All-Ireland final, the last one the opposition would want was DJ Carey. It happened to us in the 2000 final and sure enough, he made it count. We were a goal down and heading for trouble. He got another goal shortly afterwards and Kilkenny were on their way to the title.

So much for DJ supposedly not playing well in All-Ireland finals! I never believed that anyway and we certainly felt the brunt of his talents in that particular final. The thing about DJ was that whether Kilkenny were going well or poorly, he never let up. I'll give you an example. We led Kilkenny by fifteen points with around ten minutes to go in the 1995 Leinster final, but DJ got two goals in the closing minutes. To him, there was no such thing as a lost cause. Just as well we had a big lead that day because if he had another ten minutes, you'd never know what he would have done.

DJ was the supreme entertainer of his generation. People were happy to pay the admission fee just to see him alone. There aren't many players in that category but he was definitely one of them. Our careers ran pretty much parallel through colleges, underage and senior so we had some great tussles over many years. I came on as a sub in the 1989 All-Ireland semi-final against Antrim but my first championship start was in 1990 on the day DJ made his championship debut for Kilkenny.

Marking DJ was the ultimate challenge because you knew that if you weren't on your game all the time, he could destroy you in a few minutes. That was one of the keys to his greatness. You never knew what he was going to do with the next ball so even if he was relatively quiet for an hour he could explode over the closing minutes and leave you wondering: 'how did that happen?' Every opponent he ever played against will tell you the same.

We always had a huge respect for each other as players, but while you're still playing you tend to leave it at that. However, since we retired we have become a lot more friendly. DJ was always a gentleman on the field and is the same off it.

DICKIE MURPHY (REFEREE)

Being a referee had one advantage when it came to dealing with DJ. It gave me a chance to be on the pitch with him, watching his amazing skills from close up, without worrying about how to stop him. There were times you'd feel sorry for his opponents because when DJ was on song there was little anyone could do to hold him.

He played in the first All-Ireland senior final that I refereed in 1992 and made a big impact. It was a wet, windy day but that didn't bother DJ. I awarded Kilkenny a penalty in the first half (Cork's Denis Walsh still keeps telling me the foul took place outside the square!) and while the wind and rain were straight in DJ's face, he fired the ball to the Cork net. It was one of the key moments.

Wexford people know plenty about DJ and all those steps he took before scoring the winning goal against us one year and, probably because of that, referees were always listening to opposition complaining that he over-carried. But then, he was so quick that he could cover a lot of ground in a split second, making it look as if he was over-carrying.

He was a joy to referee because whether you went for or against him on a decision, he took it the same.

I would love to see DJ in the modern game, where defences are more crowded. It would present him with a different challenge but I have no doubt he would cope with it. He had unbelievable pace, was strong in the air, could turn on a sixpence but, most of all, he could put it all together in a flash of brilliance which would mesmerise everyone. He would have been a genius in any era.

I hold the distinction of being mistaken for DJ on one occasion, which I'm quite proud of! I was at a Players' Player of the Year (the now defunct *Sunday Press* ran it) awards dinner in Dublin in 1993, a year DJ won every accolade. I sat down at a table and a woman who was already there welcomed me warmly: "nice to see, you DJ". I had to politely explain that much as I'd like to be as good as DJ, it wasn't going to happen. But then it was the same for just about everyone else too!

DJ – MAJOR CAREER LANDMARKS

1988-89 (2): All-Ireland SH Colleges' Titles (St. Kieran's, Kilkenny)

1988: All-Ireland Minor Hurling Title

1989: Kilkenny Senior Debut (v Offaly NHL)

1990: All-Ireland U-21 Title; SH Championship Debut (v Offaly)

Leinster Senior Hurling titles (10):
1991-92-93-98-99-2000-01-02-03-05

All-Ireland SH titles (5): 1992-93-2000-02-03

NHL titles (4): 1990-95-2003-05

Interprovincial Titles with Leinster (2): 1993 and 98

Kilkenny SHC Titles with Young Irelands (2): 1996 and 2002

All Star Awards (9): 1991-92-93-94-95-97-99-2000-02.

Hurler of the Year Awards (2): 1993 and 2000

Senior Championship Games: 57

Total SHC scores: 34-195

Last game (Kilkenny): 2005 All-Ireland semi-final v Galway.